TOWARDS GENDER HISTORY

Images, Identities and Roles of North Indian Women

Towards Gender History

Images, Identities and Roles of North Indian Women

with special reference to Panjab

Kamlesh Mohan

Towards Gender History
Kamlesh Mohan

First Published 2007
Reprinted 2022

ISBN 978-81-87879-65-7 (HB)

Published by
AAKAR BOOKS
28 E Pocket IV, Mayur Vihar Phase I
Delhi 110 091, India
www.aakarbooks.com

Printed at
D.K. Fine Art Press, Delhi

To

My father Janab Kashmiri Lal Zakir

&

Professor Bipan Chandra

who nourished my creativity

in unexpected ways

Preface

Writing a book is a long process spreading over several years. While doing this challenging yet enjoyable work, I have piled a variety of debts. Some of these must be acknowledged. My heart-felt thanks go to a number of men and women who patiently answered my probing questions about their lives and experiences as activists or witnesses to social and political struggles during the past seven or eight decades. Initially, it was problematic for them to retrieve factual details about the significant phases or events from their ancient memories. Gradually, their enthusiasm became infectious. I remember Dr. Sushila Nayar, a close associate of Mahatama Gandhi, with tremendous regard and affection. She took me along on the long journey to Sevagram in order to enable me to understand the life and mission of Gandhi's women disciples who had been inspired to leave their homes and families for the national freedom struggle and related services. Many lesser-known personalities also contributed to my research.

Those whom I managed to coax to define and elucidate their self-image, world-view, identity and roles with the help of popular sayings, proverbs, jokes, myths and folktales regarded me as an eccentric person wasting time over familiar things. Nonetheless, they showed indulgence and empathy for my task. I am extremely grateful to them for their hitherto unrecorded insights about their shared cultural memories. My grandparents and other senior members of my extended family let me do my detective's work graciously.

In the course of my research and writing, a number of scholars, students and veteran teachers, who regularly participated in the Weekly Seminar of Department of Sociology, Panjab University (Chandigarh) helped me to sharpen my arguments. Dr. Amrik Singh, Ex-Vice-Chancellor, Punjabi University (Patiala) made my task of selecting essays and preparing the final draft easy through his valuable suggestions and comments. Dr. Pushpinder Syal has also helped me in tightening the narrative where required.

I am especially grateful to Professor David Washbrook, Director Centre for South Asian Studies, for offering me a fellowship in St. Antony's College (Oxford), which enabled me to finalize three essays in this book. Dr. Pritam Singh, Professor Ian Talbot, Dr. Shinder Thandi and a number of participants in the Weekly South Asia Seminar in Oxford and special lectures in Coventry University contributed to the making of this book in several ways. I made insistent claims upon time and generosity of Dr. Bipan Chandra, Professor Emeritus, Jawaharlal Nehru University, and Dr. V.N.Datta, Professor Emeritus, University of Kuruskhetra.

I can never thank my father, Shri K.L. Zakir, adequately for sharing my burden of proof-reading and removing ambiguities in expression. By overlooking my lapses in fulfilling social obligations, he enabled me to concentrate on my research and writing.

I acknowledge gratefully the unstinting service of the staff of Bodleian Library (Oxford), British Library (London), National Archives of India and Nehru Memorial Museum and Library (New Delhi) in locating records, books and other source-materials in the course of my research.

As these essays had been written in different contexts, a bit of repetition was bound to occur for the sake of clarity. I seek the indulgence of readers of this book on this issue.

Finally, I thank Shri K.K. Saxena, of Aakar Books, Delhi for showing endless patience and concern for meticulous printing and impressive get-up of the book.

I own responsibility for any lapses or mistakes in the book.

Chandigarh
10 September 2005

Kamlesh Mohan

Acknowledgements

I wish to thank editors of books and journals wherein the following articles had been published:

1. 'Clamping Shutters and Valorizing Women: Tensions in Sculpting Gender Identities in the Colonial Punjab', appeared in Pritam Singh and Shinder Thandi eds., *Globalization and the Region: Explorations in Punjabi Identity (London, 1996).* It was reprinted by Oxford University Press (1999) under the title *Pubjabi Identity in Global Context.*
2. A preliminary version of 'Conceptualizing Women in the Sikh Tradition and Beyond' has been printed in Irfan Habib ed., *Religion and Material Life (2004)* under the title *'Women in the Sikh Tradition: A Discourse of Liberation or Ambivalence.'*
3. 'Jallianwala Bagh Tragedy: A Catalyst of Indian Women's Consciousness' was first published under a different title in the *International Journal of Pubjab Studies (London),* July-December 1996. Its modified version appeared in V.N. Datta and S. Settar eds., *Jallianwala Bagh Tragedy: Its Impact on the Indian National Movement (2000).*
4. 'Fashioning Minds and Images: A Case Study of *Stree Darpan'* appeared in a shorter form in the *Proceedings* Volume, Indian History Congress 52nd session (1992) and a modified version in Kiran Pawar ed., *Women in Indian History: Social, Economic, Political and Cultural Perspectives (1996).* Its enlarged version was printed in Aparna Basu and Anup Taneja eds., *Breaking Out of*

Invisibility (2003).

5. 'Jawaharlal Nehru on Democracy and Women', was published as a monograph by the Department of Public Relations, Government of Punjab (1990).
6. 'Globalization and Cultural Invasion: Its Implications for Indian Men and Women' was printed in its earlier version in Raj Mohini Sethi ed., *Globalization, Culture and Women's Development (1999).* Its modified version was published in S.Settar and P.K.V. Kaimal, *We Lived Together (2000).*

Contents

Introduction

The present book on gender history is a product of my passionate engagement for over two decades with the formidable task of understanding the socio-cultural, political and economic processes in colonial India, especially the Punjab in view of their crucial role in determining the character of a variety of human relationships. My growing interest in women's past is rooted in the belief that "women have history, women are in history".[1] Linked with this is my conviction that the study of a fragment of human past, i.e. doings of men in power alone, does not yield a balanced picture of society, polity and economy whether at local, regional or national level. My exploration into the images of women in religious scriptures, folk literature and writings of Gandhi and Nehru, processes of recasting of gender identities and their roles in the colonial times is motivated by a broader concern—its implications for their status and empowerment in the contemporary and future India. It is, indeed, a tall claim. However, I have tried to contribute my little share to the ambitious feminist project, designated as 'gender studies'. It has engaged the attention of a many veteran scholars from various disciplines during the past two decades. As a result, a sizeable number of trend-setting research-based studies have been published.

Writing the history of women in a colonial setting presents other challenges than faced by the Western scholars who have experimented with writing additive history, genderized history or contributory history. As students of Indian history, we have to take cognizance of two dominant approaches: colonial and nationalist discourse. Colonial histories have focused upon the civilizing mission of the British which professed to rescue Indian women from their own culture and society. Similar claims are now being made by the Euro–American nations. Their project of globalization of trade and commerce is underpinned by their long-term objectives of acquiring a decisive role in the formulation of politico-economic and social policies as well as control over the daily lives of the people, their choices of food, dress as well as accessories, behaviour patterns and such other matters. As women have always played a central role in organizing family life and its material needs, they have once again become the site of contest between the capitalist countries and the Third World countries.

The nationalist discourse (which subsumed reformers' socio-religious agenda), according to Partha Chatterjee, resolved the 'women's question' by the end of the nineteenth century.[2] The Nationalist historians have argued that Gandhi had retrieved 'woman's question'. By bringing politics to the home space, Gandhi had facilitated the entry and active participation of women in public life. He had enabled them to use his tested tools to fight their battles for securing their social dignity as well as rights and contribute to the national struggle for freedom. This is rather a simplistic view which ignores the story of women's resistance in private and public space before Gandhi assumed leadership. What I mean to say is that Indian women have not been as silent as generally portrayed.

The subaltern school of historians,[3] who published the first volume of *Subaltern Studies* in 1982, have opened a new research area. They have utilized the rich potential of the hitherto neglected lives and struggles of the ordinary people such as labourers, workers and peasants. Women have received scant attention in their writings which have been largely concerned with the 'history from below'. This approach can be used as one of the heuristic devices for uncovering Indian women's self-images, world views, their unspoken hopes, fears, frustrations, longings and aspirations which cry for articulation and space while performing their nurturing and other services for men, community, society and nation in the past and present times. Nothing more needs to be said about this much discussed approach. However, it is useful for us to remember Gayatri Spivaak's sharp warning about the limitations of valorizing 'the concrete experience of the oppressed'.[4] The subaltern project of giving independent identity to the underprivileged and inarticulate social groups must give due weightage to their triple burden of oppression by colonialism, patriarchy and Western scholarship.[5] Spivaak's advice is likely to help those who write women's history, in producing a rigorous analysis of the evolution of patriarchy.

Feminist intellectuals need to shift the focus from collective protest to other varieties of contest such as everyday forms of resistance, which are non-confrontationist in character. This approach, originally pioneered by James Scott,[6] has been effectively used by Douglas Haynes and Gyan Prakash.[7] Its application for the analysis of gender relations is likely to be more effective as women have traditionally used both resistance and accommodation as tactics in order to get some kind of power and space in the domestic affairs. In other words, women's role as subjects,[8] who continue to live and act in patriarchal society, must be examined in order to capture the complexities of their responses to the social pressures to modernize their nurturing as well as household management skills, their behaviour patterns and personality without giving up their traditional feminine virtues and qualities.

It also implicates an exploration into their individual dilemmas and tensions caused by the clashes between the expectations of the urban-educated husbands, orthodox parents and aspirations of the 'new' woman. Such an enterprise is really problematic because women do not form a single and homogeneous category. If that is conceded then the problem is how to reconcile and relate the images and identities of women (whose deprivation and subordination varied with race, caste and class) in the course of the national struggle against colonialism and capitalism. I have confined myself to women who belonged to the numerically dominant Hindu and Sikh middle classes, interspersed by references to Muslim women in the colonial north India particularly the Punjab excluding the Princely States. It must be emphasized that the overwhelmingly agrarian character of economy of this region had reinforced the persuasive dominance of peasant culture. It had permeated social thinking on the issue of gender identities and role of the bulk of the middle classes who remained firmly anchored to their moorings in their native villages. The small number of urban mercantile families, apart from participating in social and intellectual fermentation, was obliged to reckon with the peasant ethos, oral tradition and popular culture brought by the sons (rarely daughters) of the ambitious village literati and rich peasants to the cities of Lahore, Amritsar, Rawalpindi and Multan. This formulation is, perhaps, valid for similarly situated cities in some parts of north India.[9]

Besides, the British land revenue policy coupled with the self-interested actions of urban money lenders facilitated the transfer and eventual internalization of the values of an agrarian society regarding institutions of marriage, family and property relations. From the angle of the students of social, particularly, gender history, its significance lay in forging links between the social ethos of urban and rural areas.

In my view, exclusion of other religious communities and marginalized people including Dalit, agricultural and bonded labour as well as peasant and working class groups is a serious limitation. The geographical scope of the book in view of the regionally differentiated intervention of colonialism is also limited. Despite its limitation in terms of its representativeness, the book is glued together by my overarching concern for the changing images, identities and roles of Indian women. It does not offer a chronological account and analysis of gender history. However, the essays taken together show the variety of relationships which patriarchies contract with class, social reform, nationalism and colonialism and globalization from the 1880s to the 1980s. My tentative conclusion is that there is an interactive relationship between feminism of all shades and patriarchies as articulated through the 'invented tradition' by the colonial state and by the nationalist leadership in the course of political and social movements.

Let us turn to the contents of the book which show three distinct yet overlapping strands: *(i)* male-led reform projects in the nineteenth century; *(ii)* women as active agents in recasting their images, identities and roles; *(iii)* their gains and predicaments as they live through the democratic experiment and make sense of the Euro-American agenda of globalization and its implications for their status and empowerment. In the first strand, the important point is that the project of reforming women was guided by the male perception of the rationale and timing for modernizing women and not by the wishes or desires of women themselves. Similarly, the British policy for social legislation to rescue Indian women from their 'barbarous' men and religion was also not geared to the deeply felt needs of society. Motivated by concern for the loyalties of their orthodox but powerful allies, the British were selective in enacting laws for upper-class women and matrilineal social groups.[10] In fact, as Romila Thapar suggests, women's freedoms were no more an issue for British men than they were for Indians.[11] Despite J.S. Mill's influential election address on women's suffrage in 1865, even liberal governments remained hostile to the idea of equal suffrage rights in Britain until 1928.[12]

In the second strand, wherein women figure as subjects, their social and political activism testifies to their growing awareness of discrimination, subordination, social tyranny, economic dependence owing to their biological identity. Emboldened to cross from domestic to public space as a result of the traumatic personal experience of imperial oppression and racial vendetta against their male relatives in the course of the Jallianwala Bagh episode and the Martial Law atrocities, the Indian especially Punjabi women learnt to perceive a vital link among the individual, family and national fortunes. Having become aware of their creative potential in the form of songs and poems on 'Dyerism', these budding intellectuals used print media in a variety of ways. A number of women's magazines, particularly *Stree Darpan,* had enabled the Hindi educated women to 'seize speech' in Herman's phrase for expressing their anger, silence or new consciousness about male domination and possibilities of new social and political roles and of self-definition. It must be pointed out that the influence of the Western feminist discourse was marginal in Bihar, Uttar Pradesh, Madhya Pradesh and Punjab owing to the dominance of either feudal values or peasant culture coupled with widespread illiteracy.

The third strand in the book focuses on Nehru's fight for women's rights which ended in legislating a truncated Hindu Code Bill. The crucial question is whether radical women had withdrawn from their struggle for gender equality and justice. Or there were other social forces and economic interventions and challenges to Independent India from the capitalist countries which have diverted their attention from their objective of breaking the patriarchal hegemony. I have tried to find partial answers to these questions in the last essay on globalization and its implications for Indian women.

My choice of the source material has been guided by my objective of writing contributory history. As gender history does not exclusively belong to the realm of cultural history, I have used historical sources, including official and non-official, published and unpublished in combination with oral tradition and its other sources. It has enabled me to understand the varied cultural formulations and their interaction with each other especially interplay between formulations and their interaction with each other especially interplay of economic processes,

Indian culture and British culture on 'women's question' despite their inherent contradictions. Another very important source is women's writings including diaries, pamphlets and feminist magazines which has helped me to map out differences between genderized perceptions of 'masculinity' and 'femininity' and pinpoint persistent tensions on this terrain.

REFERENCES

1. Gerda Lerner's pithy observation has given a new direction to thinking about gender. An American pioneer in gender studies, she was the first person to hold a Chair in women's history.
2. Partha Chatterjee, 'The Nationalist Resolution of the Women's Question', in Kumkum Sangari and Sudesh Vaid, eds., *Recasting Women: Essays in Colonial History* (Delhi: Kali for Women, 1989).
3. These historians have borrowed the term 'subaltern' from Antonio Gramsci. Through their writings they have sought to explicate the interplay of coercion and consent during 200 years of British rule. In the course of their analysis of hegemonic processes, the subaltern historians have brought to light the stories of the suppressed segments and social groups.
4. Gayatri Chakravorty Spivaak, 'Can the Subaltern Speak?' in Cary Nelson and Lawrence Grossberg, eds., *Marxism and the Interpretation of Culture* (Urbana and Chicago: University of Illinois Press, 1988), p. 275.
5. *Ibid.,* p. 295.
6. James Scott, *Weapons of the Weak: Everyday Forms of Peasant Resistance* (New Haven: Yale University Press, 1985).
7. Douglas Haynes and Gyan Prakash, *Contesting Power* (New Delhi: Oxford University Press, 1991), pp. 1–2.
8. Nita Kumar, *Women as Subjects: South Asian Histories* (Charlottesville and London: University Press of Virginia, 1994), p. 4.
9. Kamlesh Mohan, 'Ruchi Ram Sahni and the Pursuit of Science in a Colonial Society', in N.K. Sehgal, Satpal Sangwan and Subodh Mohanti, eds., *Uncharted Terrains* (Delhi: Vigyan Prasar, 2000), p. 108.
10. Joana Liddle and Rama Joshi, *Daughters of Independence: Gender, Caste and Class in India* (Delhi: Kali for Women, 1986), pp. 30–31.
11. Romila Thapar, 'History of Female Emancipation in Southern Asia', in Barbara Ward, ed., *Women in the New Asia* (Paris: UNESCO, 1963), p. 485.
12. Midge Mackenzi, *Shoulder to Shoulder* (Harmandsworth: Penguin, 1975), p. x.

Reforming Women

1

Conceptualizing Women in the Sikh Religious Tradition and Beyond

What shall we do with religion? This question has assumed great significance as its power to divide human beings rather than unite them is on the increase in the Third World countries. It is also being used to manipulate political power and subjugate women. It influences women to a greater extent as their lives have been interwoven with religious traditions, rituals and practices throughout history. It tugs at women and it hurts them through scriptural absolutism. Owing to its crucial role in shaping our social–cultural values, processes and institutions as well as the location of men and women in various religious traditions, we need to analyze their scriptures. Here, I have focused my attention upon the Sikh religion whose founder and successors sought to fight against social injustice, inequality and oppression of the weak, especially women and the lower castes through their teachings and practice.

In this essay my objective is two-fold. Firstly, I shall try to map out the radical shift in the conceptualization of women in the Sikh religious tradition, and its rootedness in Brahminical patriarchy while making some departures from the Hindu religious tradition. Its eventual freezing, in fact, a distinct retrogression was visible in the stereotyping of roles as religious boundaries and identities became sealed from the late nineteenth century onwards. Secondly, I wish to underline the negative role of the patriarchal mindset and attitudes of the Sikh community having the numerical majority of the high status Jats, in inhibiting and blocking the process of achieving gender equality not only in demographic terms but also in terms of their social and economic empowerment and their dignity as human beings. Of course, I shall examine the implications and the increasing priority given to the conscious development of martial culture rather than its initial commitment to socio-religious reform in the course of the evolution of the Sikh Panth.

I shall divide this discussion into four sections. In the first section, the role of socio-historical environment and its interaction with material factors in shaping new religious protest movements such as the Sikh movement and its agenda will be briefly discussed. In order to delineate it, I have analyzed Guru Nanak's perception and observations upon contemporary society and polity as he had founded the Sikh religion. The second section will pinpoint essential components in the images and roles of women as envisaged in the hymns of *Adi Granth* whether showing a radical shift or rootedness in Brahminical patriarchy. The third section highlights the gap between precept and practice. In the fourth section, I shall try to deal with the broad question: What can women do with religion and how can they use religious tradition and values to their advantage and for changing society?

I
SOCIO-HISTORICAL ENVIRONMENT

Generally speaking, nearly all the new religious protest movements arise in a situation of socio-economic dislocation and conflict caused by changes in political authority and masters. In other words, these are protests against the changes and socio-economic injustices accompanying them. These movements, however, embody attempts to come to terms with these changes, to create new value-systems in which they can be accommodated and their negative oppressive impact made bearable. In each movement, the relative strength and specific characteristics of the elements of social protest and accommodation will be different. They also tend to change as the movements progress[1] as is evident from the shift in emphasis from peaceful change to the use of arms in the case of the evolution of Sikh religion.

In order to understand the birth and growth of Sikhism as a protest movement, and its valiant drive to remove prejudice against women, we must locate its founder Guru Nanak in his socio-historical environment.[2] We must realize that the process of the establishment and consolidation of Muslim Turks' political authority from the eighth to the twelveth centuries was associated with bloody wars and conquests, indiscriminate plunder and killings of countless innocent people, as well as desecration of places of worship and conversion of thousands of Hindus, either by persuasion or by force or by the lure of patronage of the ruling authorities. The process continued throughout the period of the Delhi Sultanate and later during the rule of the imperial Mughals. It may be conceded that periodic respite came depending on the nature and policy of a particular Sultan or emperor or their governors and on the exigencies of political or economic patronage or support expected or received from the relevant sections or areas inhabited by the Hindus. It may be pointed out that the Punjab bore the brunt of this great socio-political upheaval. The situation became piquant owing to the inability of the already degenerate Hinduism to cope with the fierce proselytizing zeal of the conquerors and the egalitarian message of Islam. Amidst this confusion and conflict, the people watched helplessly the desecration of the temples and shrines of popular Hinduism and their social world with terrific rapidity. They were forced to redefine reality, political loyalties, economic relationships and their religious beliefs and protect identities by prostration or compromise.

Unlike the ordinary people and the pragmatic social as well as economic elites, the non-conformist creative thinkers and visionaries articulated their anger, protest and critique of the existing socio-cultural institutions and practices, ritualist and scholastic Hinduism, Islam and Buddhism as well as unjust and oppressive policies of new political masters. For example, Kabir's hymns represent the agony of an individual who tried to make some sense of the delegitimized Hindu world with his inward resources. With his highly-developed socio-political consciousness, Guru Nanak chose to go beyond expressing individual dissatisfaction and discontent with the existing political and socio-religious authoritarianism and hierarchization. Transformation of a conventional householder, belonging to a fairly well-off *Khatri* caste, into a social visionary and non-conformist religious leader was facilitated by his 'first-hand knowledge'[3] of the politico-administrative arrangements as an employee of the Nawab Daulat Khan Lodhi and also of their discriminatory policies and harsh behaviour towards their subjects. His observations on contemporary polity and socio-religious conditions shall be discussed a little later.

In the process of discovery of his life's mission, Guru Nanak developed a broad protestant movement based on his three-fold critique: One concerns the several forms of human folly and ignorance; the second is directed against the cruel, unjust and discriminatory policies of the contemporary Muslim rulers; the third is focused upon God's seeming indifference to the human predicament.[4] Whether called a critique or response to the contemporary reality, it must be pointed out that the Sikh Gurus especially Guru Nanak, Guru Arjun and Guru Gobind Singh perceived a close relationship between political abuses, social degradation, cultural anomie and consequent miseries of the people. That is why *Gurbani* protrays human beings, especially man in a variety of social situations, contexts and roles : householder, thinker, devotee, pedant, preacher, ruler and leader, *Gurmukh* and Brahm-gyani.[5] The synoptic vision of the *bhaktas,* sages and Gurus, whose hymns have been included in the *Guru Granth,* touches all aspects of human life: individual, familial, social, moral, religious and humanistic. On a close analysis from this perspective, the *Guru Granth* can very well be called a social document and political critique. It is also a record of dynamics of a vibrant protestant movement which had been initiated, nursed and carried forward by a number of creative individuals.

How far are these responses, critiques and protests relevant for mapping out the distinct if not radical shifts in the conceptualization of woman and her roles? In this context, Guru Nanak's response to the existing political situation has a two-fold significance. The first lies in his conception of an ideal king, his duties and the primacy of spiritual over temporal power. While elaborating his conception of an ideal king and his duties, he has underlined the inherent greatness of woman as a mother, usually dubbed as evil in Hindu and Christian religious traditions. For illustration, let us read this line:

> *So Kio Manda Akhiyai Jit Jammeh Rajan*[6]? (Why should we call woman 'evil' who gives birth to kings?)

It may be pointed out that his stipulations that a king should be valiant, righteous, just and solicitous of his subjects' welfare underline his anguish over the prevalent political chaos, oppression and corruption. Guru Nanak's anguish is compounded by his awareness of the use and exploitation of women for sexual gratification through abduction, prostitution and polygamy. Thus, the second significance of his response to political reality lies in his extreme sensitivity to the vulnerability of women (irrespective of their affiliation to any caste, religion or economic group) under immoral and licentious rulers and in the volatile situations of war, social and economic dislocation. Despite her apparent handicap, a moral woman, according to Nanak could play a crucial role in resolving the spiritual dilemma of those times and thus bring about a positive change in political and social order. It may be said that his moral fervour had moulded his perception, message and practice.

In order to buttress my argument, I shall refer to Nanak's poetic observations and denunciation of the moral damage caused by foreign invasions and war. In *Babarvani,* for instance, these hymns are striking:

> Babur has descended upon India with the wedding-party of lust and forcibly demands surrender of the bride.
> Decency and law have hidden themselves. The evil is strutting about in triumph. Mohammedan and Hindu priests are discarded; And Satan is solemnising the marriages.[7]

Guru Nanak's observations, apart from being a commentary upon the prevailing chaos, loss of social values and misappropriation of traditional roles by the new political masters and their functionaries draw our attention not only to the total demoralization of the dispossessed ruling elite but also its unsettling effect upon the Brahmins and the *Qazis*. Their stupefaction led them to adopt *Kumravriti,* i.e. withdrawal into their own shells like a tortoise. The Brahmins, in particular, could no longer perform their function as socio-religious leaders partly owing to the loss of royal patronage and partly to their gradual deviation from their spiritual mission for the sake of material gains.

The struggle for political power had serious implications for families, especially women who lived in the areas falling on the route of the Mughal invaders. Guru Nanak's references to the miseries and degradation of women, sometimes direct and sometimes indirect, are suggestive of their helplessness arising from threats of physical violation and dependent position in the family system; subjected to indiscriminate rapes by the Mughal soldiers, the Muslim women invoked God in despair and the Hindu women of all castes found themselves in a similar plight. In *Rag Asa,* these women-sufferers have been described as *hinduani, turkani, bhattiani* and *thakurani.*[8]

War also caused numerous deaths and murders of ordinary people, soldiers, nobles, princes and kings in the battlefield. It left behind countless wailing windows. This aspect of women's predicament and misery has been brought out by Guru Nanak. It must be pointed out that his anguish has a moral dimension to it. A firm belief in God's omnipotence, immanence and superintendence restrains him from an outright condemnation either of the conqueror or of the conquered, the victimizer or the victim.

However, his moral judgment extends to the luxurious lives of men and women, their glittering marriage ceremonies and wreckless indulgence in conjugal as well as extra-marital sex without any thought of God.[9] The senseless pursuit of pleasure by the rulers and nobles alike is contrasted with their helplessness after Babur's ascendancy to power. It is evident from the following verse:

> They had never remembered Ram,
> now they cannot invoke *khuda.*[10]

Underlying his scathing criticism of the debauchery of the Muslim ruling elite and their discriminatory policies is Guru Nanak's keen awareness of their growing political authority and its disturbing effect on the socio-economic life of the people and their public conduct. It is in this context that the hypocritical behaviour of the Brahmins, who had enjoyed the highest position in the varna hierarchy,[11] has to be viewed. With the destruction of the Rajput sovereignty (as a consequence of Turkish invasions and later establishment of Mughal power), they had lost not only the political patronage but also their formal legal and economic power.[12] However, as a priestly class, their informal authority and subtle but pervasive influence over the humbler and more numerous class of patrons expanded.[13] Despite the numerical dominance and high economic status of Jats in this region,[14] the crucial role of Brahmins in fixing gender roles, norms of feminine behaviour as daughter, wife and mother through religious prescriptions and *vrata kathas* should not be underestimated in the medieval society in the Punjab.

Let us make a brief reference to the social position of a Hindu woman and the customs enforcing her subordination from the eleventh to the fifteenth century in order to understand the significance of Guru

Nanak's call for social, especially, gender equality. For example, Alberuni noticed that a Hindu woman was inferior and subordinate to man[15] notwithstanding the respect given to her as a daughter, wife and mother among the Brahmins, the Rajputs and the Khatris.[16] A respectable Hindu wife was expected to be completely devoted to her husband and prove her fidelity at the cost of her life.[17] The rite of *jauhar* lost its relevance in the Punjab owing to the dissolution of the Rajput kingdoms. The wide prevalence of the custom of sati, i.e. self-immolation by the widow on her husband's funeral pyre among the high castes such as Brahmins, Khatris, and Rajputs was noticed by Alberuni.[18] While Ibn Battuta recorded a case of sati in Pakpatan,[19] in the Punjab, the other travellers noticed several such cases at other places. Amir Khusrau, too, had great appreciation for the sacrificial act of a Hindu woman. The custom of sati continued to be practised in Punjab as late as the nineteenth century, as Ganesh Das recorded.[20] The construction of *sati-chauras*[21], i.e. spots of worship in honour of those who immolated themselves, showed that young widows were socially discarded, humiliated and treated as domestic drudges in case they chose to live.

Similarly, prohibition on the remarriage of widows has been sanctified through several centuries. Child-marriage, which was a common practice before 1200 A.D., required the girls to be married before the age of puberty; infanticide was also widely practised by the Brahmins, Khatris and Rajputs in this region.[22]

As for as the religious milieu in the Punjab was concerned, it was characterized by a variety of religious beliefs and practices relating especially to Islam, Hinduism and Buddhism. It is relevant to point out that the vicious grip of ritualism, scholasticism and superstitious beliefs had submerged the original message and vitality of all the three religions. In north India, the growth of several esoteric cults and sects, tantric practices and gimmicks of sadhus, jogis and fakirs had facilitated the exploitation of the gullible masses and oppression of women, irrespective of their religious affiliation.

In the contemporary Punjab, for example, *Nath-yogis,* particularly Gorakhanath and Puran Bhagat represent 'what is left of Buddhism'.[23] As staunch *Nath-yogis,* they advocate renunciation of all worldly ties and pleasures as a prerequisite to *sadhna.* Their opposition to association with women is based on the belief that they are a great temptress in the path of a yogi who aims at suppressing and sublimating all sexual desires. While Kabir shares their antipathy against women, Guru Nanak denounces them for their denigration of women and favours the achievement of salvation by his disciples without neglecting their duties as householders. Obviously, the *bhaktas'* perceptions of women, which varied depending upon their socio-cultural background, was crucial to their positioning as seekers of spiritual goals. For example, Guru Nanak's thought is in many ways consistent with the Bhakti trend, which opposed the traditional monopoly of Hindu priests and the caste system. With regard to women and the Bhakti movement, Katherine Young has rightly conceded that "popularity of Bhakti resulted in no small measure for its inclusion of such marginal groups as women and Shudras... . Being female was generally no bar to Bhakti."[24]

It may be pointed out that the gender dichotomy and tension appears in a glaring form in the community of *bhaktas*. The break is to be seen between a tradition transmitted by word of mouth among women and elaborate search and evaluative legacy transmitted through written texts among men.[25] In other words, it is the dichotomy between the oral and the written, hidden behind the dichotomy of the feminine and the masculine. It is evident in the compilation of Bhakti hymns of *Adi Granth*. Exclusion of the hymns of women *bhaktas* such as Mirabai,[26] Lal Ded[27] and Akkamahadevi[28] shows the gender bias despite the proclaimed spiritual egalitarianism by the Sikh Gurus. Obviously, gender dichotomies complement already existing socio-cultural rifts especially the entrenched hold of multiple patriarchies: Brahmin and Jat patriarchies in the case of the Punjabi society.

II
IMAGES AND ROLES OF WOMEN IN *ADI GRANTH*

How do the multiple patriarchies articulate themselves? Images and symbols are the most often used means of projecting realities of women's life and position within a particular socio-cultural milieu. Traditional Sikh approaches to the question of gender, which have presented Sikhism as radically different from other religions on this issue, claim gender equality, primarily on the basis of selected scriptural passages. By pointing out a variety of feminine images such as maternal and bridal in the scriptures especially *Adi Granth* and

Dasam Granth as well as grammatically feminine theological concepts, a recent scholarly study has argued that the feminine principle is predominant over the male.[29]

Guru Nanak's philosophy and style has provided a model for the successive Gurus. In view of his keen awareness of a woman's degraded position in the late fifteenth century, his idealization of her image and roles and advocacy of social dignity for her, though a radical proposition for the contemporary society, was accepted and elaborated by Guru Amar Das and Guru Gobind Singh especially. I endorse McLeod's observation that for the *Tat Khalsa,* in fact, for the majority of Sikhs, every explanation begins by Guru Nanak. Almost always they will cite the following sloka from *Asa di Var*:

> From women born, shaped in the womb, to women betrothed and wed we are bound to women by ties of affection; on woman man's future depends. If one woman dies he seeks another; with a woman he orders his life.
>
> Why should one speak evil of women, they who give birth to kings? Women also are born of women; none takes birth except from a woman.
>
> Only the true one, Nanak, needs no help from a woman. Blessed are they, both men and women.[30]

This sloka is regarded as representative of the total attitude of all Sikhs to the ideal place of women including conventional view of his times. Guru Nanak repudiated the prevalent notions about *stri swabhava,* i.e. women's inherent nature as 'evil', 'unclean', temptation-incarnate, fickle, mean, impure, treacherous, indiscriminate, avaricious, etc.[31] Keen to associate women with the religious reform process, he protested against their ill-treatment and social victimization through the inhuman customs of infanticide, purdah, child-marriage, sati and many other male practices such as polygamy, adultery and sex crimes.

Guru Nanak's positive views about women's character, role and position nucleate around maternal images. In the Sikh sacred scriptures, motherhood is indeed celebrated. It is replete with images of gestation, giving birth and nurturing. As the woman is valued as an individual and a human being, (instead of being worshipped as a goddess in a hidden sanctuary), the structure of her body is prized. Thus, the *Adi Granth* is not reticent about the natural process of female body such as menstrual bleeding. Nikky-Guninder Singh regards these scriptural statements about mother's physical acts of creation, nurturance and sustenance "as the bold affirmation of the glory of motherhood which is at the heart of contemporary feminist thinking in religion".[32]

The other recurrent images of mother in the *Adi Granth* are based on their grammatical usage. For example, *joti* (light), *kudrati* (cosmos) or nature and *mati* (wisdom) have been projected as an evidence of the acceptance of not only the concept of harmony among man, woman and cosmos in the Sikh tradition but also of the unity and equality of human kind irrespective of sex, caste or creed. Believing that *joti* is all-pervasive and transcendent, a popular couplet from the *Adi Granth* is often cited for its positive social implications:

> Allah first created its Light; and from that all were made.
> From that one light came the whole cosmos.
> Whom shall we then declare good, who bad.
> *(Aval allah nuru upaia kudrat ke sab bande.*
> *Ek nur te sabhu jagu upjia kaun bhale kaun mande.*[33]*)*

Whereas *joti,* in the Sikh view is the Divine spirit, *kudrati* is creation itself. Grammatically feminine, *kudrati* is regarded as manifestation of the Transcendent. A Sikh scholar, while analyzing the varied connotations of *kudrati,* has argued that it is also vital for the modern feminist conception of society as the offspring of the 'Mother'.[34] Creativity is the common quality of God and mother; thus, there is no conflict but harmony.

Further on, the equation between mother and wisdom has been underlined in the *bani* (also cited as an evidence of the dominance of the feminine principle in the Sikh vision as the Gurus used the grammatically feminine word '*bani*' for their message). The following line from a couplet has been cited for support:

> Mother is wisdom; father, contentment. (*Mata mati, pita santokh.*)[35]

Let us turn to the argument of abundance of bridal imagery in Guru Nanak's hymns as an evidence of gender equality in the spiritual and mundane life of the followers of Sikhism.[36] It has been suggested that the bridal symbol develops the "nuances of intimacy and passion in the human relationship with the Divine".[37] It has also been argued that it (the bride symbol) further confirms the feminine principle which pervades the Sikh vision of the Transcendent because the individual's quest for union with God has been presented in terms of bride–groom relationship throughout the *Guru Granth Sahib*. The soul-bride is longing day and night to see him with her own eyes[38] (*Darshan piasi dinsu rati*).

The bride has also been lauded as a 'paradigmatic person' because she enables the devotees to do away with traditional anti-thesis and dualism by interconnecting family, society, cosmos, nature and the Transcendent.[39] Without going into a detailed discussion about variety of meanings and values of the bridal finery and ritual embellishments as a preparation for her nuptial union with God, two points must be stressed. Firstly, these signify the bride's good deeds and secondly, physical beauty and intellectual qualities play a complementary role in the spiritual quest. For example, a few slokas in the *Guru Granth Sahib* which describe the very powerful and positive effect of cosmetics on her eyes, show the interactive relationship between physical eye and mental eye, sight and insight in the pursuit of unity with God, as pointed out by Nikky-Guninder Singh also.

The imagery of the soul-bride in the scripture has been projected as an evidence of "a more egalitarian and open-minded social structure"[40] among the Sikhs in general. It may be conceded that Guru Nanak's description of mystical experience gained through senses and his emphasis upon the centrality of household in an individual's religious life has raised the concept of conjugal relations to a sacrosanct spiritual level. By dubbing the escapist *siddhas* as runaways from social responsibilities,[41] he had rejected the prevalent belief in the value of celibacy and asceticism as facilitators to salvation.

The succeeding Gurus have contributed to the clarity and enrichment of Guru Nanak's unconventional ideas about women's roles, images and healthy marital relationship. For illustration, let us read Guru Amar Das's hymn:

> The bride and groom are not those who, though together in body, are in spirit alone. It is when the two bodies have a single soul that they become one.[42]

Guru Nanak, too, had laid a high moral code for husband and wife. His exhortation to the virtuous wife reads as follows:

> Make truth, contentment, kindness,

All noble qualities thy make-up
Says Nanak, only then art thou
A truly faithful wife and dear to thy God.[43]

And to the virtuous husband, he advises

True, husband thou art,
If touchest not a plant belonging to others
In this blossoming Garden
That world is.[44]

Nanak's message inspired his successor to make an effort to reduce the quantum of social oppression of women by condemning the widely current customs and practices such as female infanticide, seclusion, sati, polygamy and prostitution. While taking a clear stand against widow-burning, he gave it a new meaning but did not call for the abolition of the inhumane practice:

Do not call her a suttee who burns herself with (her husband's) corpse.
Know her as a suttee, Nanak, who dies in the agony of separation.[45]

This couplet condemns callous violation of her right as a widow who was (is) compelled to commit sati in times of extreme emotional vulnerability. Another couplet defined sati from an unconventional angle:

Know her as a suttee who dwells in purity and peace,
Who serves her husband and calls upon him when she awakens.[46]

Undoubtedly, the Sikh Gurus' messages seem radical in the existing patriarchal set-up which saw nothing wrong in the desertion of wives, polygamy, adultery and prositution. Apart from creating awareness about the social victimization of women, the Sikh Gurus had given legitimacy to the their right to initiation into (Sikh) religion and participation in religious gatherings without being veiled. Their views were upheld by the Sikh *Rahit Maryada*.

The few Sikh scholars, who have dealt with the gender perspective in the sacred writings of their religion, laud it as an emancipatory tool without taking into account the problems either with the idealistic view or its misogynistic tendencies. For example,

Harbans Singh,[47] Nikky-Guninder Singh[48] and J.S. Grewal[49] have focused upon the positive aspects of maternal and bridal images whose negative implications influence male behaviour in private especially domestic and public life. It may be pointed that these traits and images have been used for essentializing notions of ideal womanhood and gender roles in society. These stereotypes have also been manipulated as tools of social control of women—their dress code, behaviour patterns, self-images and world view.

I wish to argue that the existing social ethics and ideological dominance of Brahminical patriarchy continued to influence the Sikh Gurus' formulation of ideal womanhood despite their critical temper. Abundance of feminine images within the Sikh scriptures as well as the use of grammatical feminine form in theological concepts is not a sure evidence of the dilution of gender bias or the myriad forms of patriarchy. Nikky-Guninder Singh has contended that the "Sikh word is not a masculine logos, it is the beautiful and formless *bani*".[50] The feminine form reiterates the Vedic belief wherein the notion of sacred speech is defined as the goddess.[51] It is not definite whether their articulation of sacred speech is simply indicative of the influence of the surrounding milieu or of the actual intent of the Gurus to honour women.

As opposed to the general conclusion of the Sikh scholars regarding the domination of the feminine over the male in their scriptures, Harjot Oberoi has pointed out:

> ... in the early Sikh traditions God was almost exclusively conceived in masculine terms (*Akal Purukh, Karta Purukh*) and metaphors. The devotee was a bride yearning for God in bride-groom.[52]

Even the epithets used for God in the verses in the female devotional voice are masculine, such as *Prabh, Ram, Rangila, Manohar, Parmesar, Pritam, Sajan, Mit, Sahib, Lara, Kant* or *Khasm*. The 'relationship' of the soul-bride, i.e. woman with God is that of *prem* or *preet*. It is in this context that the woman is depicted in several states metaphorically including her girlhood (*balari*), wifehood (*sohagan*), bad woman (*dohagan*) and lovelorn (*birhan*).

In the Sikh scriptures, the two dominant images of mother and bride contain elements of misogyny. Despite the celebration of motherhood, there are indications of ambivalence. For illustration, let us read the following verse:

> As does the mother cherish her pregnancy in her son pinning her hope;
> That grown up, would he give her wherewithal,
> And bring joy and pleasure.
> Even such is the love of God's devotee to the Lord.[53]

This verse reflects the son-preference in the patriarchal value system of the contemporary Punjabi society through the nature of dependency between God and the devotee.

A similar kind of ambivalence runs through the images of 'bride', and 'wife'. On the one hand, feminine traits are glorified; on the other, woman is projected in the contemptuous manner. Her qualities of submissiveness, self-abnegation, obedience to the male-master have been glorified. Although the language of *Adī Granth* is allegorical, it reflects the popular social perception about the ideal woman:

> Possessed of thirty-two merits, holy truth is her progeny
> Obedient, of noble mien
> To her husband's wishes compliant.[54]

> The Lord is my husband, I His wife
> The Lord is immensely great, I so small.[55]

and

> A wife faithful to Lord must devote herself body and soul to him.
> And must behave in all respects as the faithful wedded wife.[56]

It is not merely ambiguity but contempt for femaleness is reflected in the following verse which upbraids men but praises women for obedience and subservience:

> Men obedient to their women-folk
> Are impure, filthy, stupid
> Men lustful, impure, follow their
> women-folk counsel.[57]

There are numerous passages which show that duality of body and mind, opposition between sensual and spiritual and stereotyped image of woman as evil have not been negated. It is evident from the couplets cited below that all bad qualities and *maya* have been associated with woman:

> The egoist is like a loose woman,
> A bad woman, given to casting spells.[58]
>
> *Maya* attachment is like a loose woman. A bad woman given to casting spells.[59]

and

> *Maya* afflicts one who by egoistic
> thinking is intoxicated;
> It afflicts one involved with progeny and wife;
> It afflicts too one attached to elephants, horses and material objects.[60]

The bridal imagery also reflects not only ambivalence but also feudal mentality. In the *Adi Granth,* the relationship between God and the soul-bride has been valorized in terms of the relationship between man and woman in a feudal society. The relationship is not of equality but of inequality where husband is treated as the Lord and wife exists merely to serve him and yearn for his grace. The following couplets illustrate this point:

> Blessed is the Bride who knows her True Lord,
> And submits to the Command of her Master and sheds her Ego;
> And imbued with her Lord revels in his love.
> O! my loved Mate, know thou the signs of the union with the Lord;
> That, she alone is united, who dedicates her
> Body and soul to her Lord, and cares not for what the world says.

and

> I, the Lord's Bride, have now assumed
> full control of my (Mind's) Household, by the
> Guru's Grace;
> And, through my Lord's Mercy, my ten
> sense-organs slave for me.[61]

It may also be pointed out that the principle of gender equality, upheld by Sikhism through its advocacy of monogamy, was violated by the sixth and tenth Gurus. Later on, Banda Bahadur, Maharaja Ranjit

Singh and other Sikh rulers also had many wives. Why was polygamy not rejected and discouraged by the Sikh Gurus and their followers?

Now, let us examine the issue of the persistent rootedness of the Sikh tradition in the Brahminical patriarchy in some respects. The Sikh religion, which was surrounded by an androcentric society, could not shake off the overwhelming Brahminic influence. Despite Guru Nanak's endeavour to break free from the existing socio-cultural ethos, his teachings and exhortations to his followers to practise gender equality and justice failed to change the negative attitude of his followers towards women. It is reflected in two essential points: a normative model for women and social practices and customs.

Firstly, the normative model and roles prescribed for women in the Sikh sacred literature are very much in line with the Brahminical conceptualization. Not only is the Sikh history of five hundred years a record of the activities of men, but the Sikh society and institutions too have been overwhelmingly male-centred. As the Sikh Gurus, scribes and historical writers were invariably male, their symbols and images reveal their perceptions about woman's ideal behaviour. Obviously, images utilized in the Sikh sacred writings focus upon women's important functions in the domestic arena and not in the public arena. Thus, the *Adi Granth* is replete with images of mother, bride and feminine roles as discussed earlier.

The influence of Brahminical culture is also evident in Guru Gobind Singh's writings. His incorporation of the powerful Hindu goddess Durga as a literary figure into the *Dasam Granth,* which has been projected as a tribute to the positive Sikh attitude towards the feminine power,[62] needs to be evaluated in a socio-historical context. Considering the fact that Gobind Singh's formative years were spent in the Shivalik Hills, which was the stronghold of the Shakti cult and Durga cult, his choice of the latter goddess out of the large pantheon is understandable. Instead of being proof of the 'feminine affirming mentality', it was a spontaneous assimilation of the contemporary hill-culture and its later penetration into Jat Sikh culture of the plains. Its real significance is to be read in the growing complexity of patriarchal patterns wherein ambivalence may often be mistaken for positive intent.[63]

However, valorization of these very images has been instrumental in the essentialization of notions of womanhood and feminine roles in society. For example, the theological concept of service (*seva*) makes no distinction between 'male' and 'female' tasks but experiential reality shows the gap between the ideal and the practice.[64] First, the deep-rooted prejudices regarding sexual division of labour are accepted as a norm in Sikh as well as Hindu households. The majority of the Sikh men who cook, clean and serve food happily in the *gurdwara,* look upon domestic chores as low and mechanical requiring little intelligence. Thus, Brahminical patriarchy has been resurrected in a more liberal form with its inherent contradictions.

Second, the Brahminical influence is also reflected in the sociological patterns of Sikhs and their practice of gender discrimination. Despite their condemnation of the evils of caste systems, the Sikh Gurus neither rejected it nor tried to organize their followers into a casteless order. Converts to Sikhism from lower castes, who were attracted by its egalitarian message, have failed to get rid of their inferior status in ritual hierarchy even after the baptism ceremony. Disabilities for women get compounded as they are subject to prejudices and stereotypes associated with caste and gender. This is evident from the exclusively male gender and high caste status of the Guru lineage. The Gurus certainly conferred equal opportunity on both men and women of all castes but it was "equal opportunity of access" to spiritual liberation. It was not equality in the sense that "women might do everything that might be open to men".[65] While elaborating upon this point, W.H. McLeod has further argued that it is "misleading to see in his (Guru Nanak's) teachings or those of his successors a reordering of society ... wherein organization and control of vital and long-term decisions were exclusively in male hands". Despite many emancipatory elements in their teachings, the Gurus indirectly upheld the existing order which was shorn of its authoritarian aspect to some extent without dismantling the core structures.

However, the current stereotypes and prejudices against women have remained strong because the socialization process in the family could not be reoriented by the radical beliefs of the Sikh Gurus alone. The institution of family continued to legitimate the low value of daughters through the inhuman practice of female infanticide by a number of social groups, namely Bedis[66] and Mohyal Brahmins in the nineteenth-century Punjab. The widespread social custom of dowry payment (as a maintenance fee for the daughter) to the groom's parents and transfer of property to male heirs among the followers of Sikhism especially the land-owning castes further reinforces son-preference mentality. Ironically, the patriarchal society in north India, particularly Punjab devalues women but valorizes them as the guardians of family honour, purity of lineage and cultural traditions, particularly religious values and practices, exclusively formulated by men.

The Singh Sabha movement, described as the 'greatest social reform movement of the Sikhs',[67] became retrogressive in the process of formulating public morality with dominant patriarchal content. Its vigorous drive to construct a 'separatist' Sikh history and distinct identity for the followers of the *panth* (whose cultural ties with the other social groups had been denied and cut off) was matched by its persistent efforts to establish distinct rites de passage through well-planned propaganda and widely circulated printed literature.[68] The spirit of the entire reform agenda, especially the life-cycle ceremonies, which nucleated around the universal patriarchal precept that 'society must be ordered and controlled by men', is best illustrated by the Anand Karaj ceremony. Codified on 22 October 1909 after over three hundred mass meetings and a number of petitions,[69] the Sikh marriage ritual enjoins the bridegroom to be 'the protector of the (bride's) person and her honour'. Then the officiant (*granthi*) counsels the bride to accept her husband as 'master of all love and respect'. Its real implication was that women needed protection which patriarchy provided if the former complied with the modernized forms of competent domesticity in the late nineteenth-century Punjab.

The ritual changes introduced by the new cultural elite among the Sikhs called *Tat Khalsa* were ultimately inserted in the manuals of conduct, whose latest version has been published under the title *Sikh Rahit Maryada* in 1950. Exemplifying the modus operandi of the 'invention of tradition', to use Hobsbawm's eloquent description, these *rites de passage* continue to have special bearing on the reconstitution of the personality of Sikh men and women and their perceptions of identity, communal solidarity and a particular vision of history. It had far-reaching implications in the crucial positioning of women in the process of transmission and conservation of the new cultural tradition. Entrusted with the responsibility of socializing the girl-child to internalize the male-constructed symbols, images, codes of behaviour and dress and other values conducive to the patriarchal control of social and economic structures, institutions and resources, women had to be co-opted to defend religious tradition and their roles as nurturers of family, community and nation. While 'inventing' the Sikh tradition, the Singh Sabha reformers made little departure from the essentials of Hindu patriarchy. For example, a rigid division of feminine and masculine functions, roles and spaces was integrated into their ideology. It is not surprising that the reproductive potential of women rather than their productive capacity in economic terms and intellectual capabilities was and continues to be prized by the majority of Sikhs.

The leading ideologues of the Singh Sabha movement, namely, Bhai Takht Singh, Bhai Mohan Singh Vaid and Bhai Vir Singh perceived the crucial role of ideal women in the moral uplift of the Sikh people who had to get rid of their defeatist mentality. That was why they had focused upon writing, publishing and circulating a wide variety of didactic literature including tracts, short stories and novels as well as school magazines for students in Sikh Kanya Mahavidyalaya, Ferozepur,[70] for potential wives and mothers. For example, Bhai Vir Singh crafted super-women in his novels *Sundari* (1898), *Baba Naudh Singh* (1921), *Satwant Kaur* and other literary writings.[71] Sensitive to the inspirational value of historical novels in mobilizing support for socio-religious reform, Bhai Vir Singh permitted his fictional heroines to cross over from the domestic to the neutral territory of jungles which symbolized public space. Portrayal of his model women as incharge of community meals (*langar*), serving and nursing the sick as well as the wounded soldiers reinforced the legitimacy of their traditional functions. Their rare appearance in a skirmish and subsequent capture by the enemy indirectly emphasized a woman's inherent vulnerability rather than social acceptance of her engagement with unconventional activities and roles.

III
GAPS BETWEEN SIKH PRECEPTS AND PRACTICE

In the second section, I have already underlined the misogynistic tendencies in the broadly emancipatory and egalitarian content of the teachings of the Sikh Gurus particularly of Nanak and in the Singh Sabha reform agenda. These scriptural messages, when translated into an operative value system in the context of women, show many deviations. The gap between precept and practice is fairly visible in the lives of Sikh women whom male-dominated society, polity and economy have forced to accept double standards on crucial matters: variation in their status and roles as women, education, health, marriage, access to economic resources including property rights, codes of behaviour and dress. It has led to gender inequalities and injustices which assume a complex form owing to the interpenetration of Brahminical and *Jat* patriarchies and the variables of religion, caste, tribe and class.

As we have already discussed, the rootedness of the Sikh tradition in Brahminical patriarchy, the influence of *Jat* attitudes on the crucial aspects of gender relations needs to be analysed in order to understand the linkages among the dominant caste, gender and religion through past and present times. It is a well-known fact that *Jats* who constitute the bulk of the followers of the Sikh *panth*[72] form the most powerful social group in the peasant society of this region. As high status and honour are attached to the possession and ownership of agricultural land, its loss or transfer to another clan is equated with devaluation of personal and social position as well as prestige. It has been argued that a daughter's claim is well-recognized in the transfer of dowry including cash, ornaments, household goods but not landed property. It may be pointed out that the inheritance of property was patrilineal. Hence, the responsibility of providing dowry was shared by paternal uncles. To guard further against the transfer of property to the widow of a deceased *Jat*, the custom of *Karewa* has continued to force her remarriage with one of the surviving brothers. At any cost, landed property must be retained in the male line.[73] To sum up, it may be said that a definite equation exists between the possession of land and power—social, economic and political. In the Punjab, the majority of Sikhs are *Jats*, who own large areas of agricultural land. As they are unwilling to let land pass through inheritance to daughters or sisters, the issue of landownership has a substantial effect on the authority and position of Sikh women in the family.

Again, a wide divergence between the doctrine and practice is visible when we examine the average Sikh perception of marital relations and motherhood. The Sikh society strongly upholds the patriarchal social set-up in which marriage, motherhood and service to the husband form the essential values for a woman. Ironically, the traditional feminine qualities and functions in the domestic arena are valorized. But a woman is generally placed in a subordinate position to a man. Burdened with the societal expectations of keeping the marriage in place, a wife is obliged to negate or downplay her own personality, intellectual abilities and talent other than domestic skills. Accordingly, a Sikh woman like a Hindu woman has no say relating to number and spacing of children. The prevalent social norms in the Punjabi families whether Hindu or Sikh favour high fertility but these are changing at a painfully slow pace. A sterile woman, apart from daily humiliation, constantly lives with the threat of the second marriage of her husband. While sons raise the status of a woman, daughters bring her ridicule. Sons are eagerly desired for the continuance of the family line, for the performance of the last rites of parents and for their care in old age. In a society where no public security system exists, sons are expected to offer a safeguard. Thus, all these considerations neutralize the positive value of family planning schemes and population-control policies. Table-I,[74] which gives a comparative view of the marital fertility of different religious groups in India, testifies to the relationship between obsession with sons and the fertility in the Indian families.

TABLE 1 : Marital Fertility by Religion, 1971

Religion	*Number of Births per Hundred to Currently Married Women*			*Total Marital Fertility Rate per Hundred*
	Total	*Urban*	*Rural*	
Hindus	150.46	139.37	152.64	5.19
Sikhs	143.76	135.22	145.66	5.39
Muslims	169.93	167.05	170.97	5.77
Buddhists	185.37	195.33	182.39	6.17
Christians	160.94	156.42	164.04	5.97

It is clear from the figures in Table I that Sikhs showed a higher total marital fertility rate than Hindus but the number of births per hundred currently married women was lower in the case of Sikhs. The positive role of the teachings of the Sikh Gurus, which commends married life while advising sexual continence, is negated by the son-preference social norm in the Punjab whether Hindu or Sikh; a newly married girl is greeted by the blessing 'Bear seven sons and live a long married life' *(Sat putri te budh sohagan ho)*. Both the 1971 and 1981 census data (given in Table 2) reveal that Sikhism and Hinduism seem to have exercised similar influence, if at all, on the fertility patterns in the state.[75]

TABLE 2: Fertility Indices, Punjab 1981

Religion	*General Fertility Rate*	*General Marital Fertility Rate*	*Total Fertility Rate*	*Total Marital Fertility Rate*
Christians	137	193	4.7	5.9
Hindus	102	140	3.3	4.1
Sikhs	100	142	3.3	4.5

Evidently, the position of Sikh women is no better than that of the Hindu women in the Punjabi society.

In order to get a realistic picture of the status of women in the present times, let us take into account the other variables such as sex ratio, literacy and employment. Table 3 is useful for getting a rough idea of their growth in numbers over a span of nine decades[76]:

TABLE 3: Sex Ratio (females per 1000 males 1901–1991)

Year	*Rural*	*Urban*	*Sex Ratio in Punjab*	*Sex Ratio in India*
1901	836	804	832	972
1911	785	740	780	964
1921	808	735	799	955
1931	832	721	815	950
1941	855	750	836	945
1951	854	807	844	946
1961	865	817	854	941
1971	868	856	865	930
1981	896	861	879	927
1991	888	868	882	927

A close scrutiny of data in Table 3 shows that the sex ratio in the state has been persistently adverse to women. However, an improvement is visible during the period 1901–1991: from 832 to 882. Women, who constituted 45.41 per cent of the total population in 1901, rose to 46.96 in 1981. Female population increased by 24.58 per cent as compared to 16.18. Despite the decrease in the imbalance between female and male population in this region, the Punjab is still one of those few states (including the Union Territories) which comes at the tail end.[77] However, a favourable trend in favour of women in the rural as well as the urban areas is visible from Table 3 under reference. It can be attributed to growing gender awareness rather than the positive effect of Sikh religion. So far as the second indicator, i.e. the female literacy is concerned, a definite upward trend has been noticed in this region during the decade 1971–81. The female literacy rate was 25.9 per cent in 1971 and 34.14 per cent in 1980,[78] while it was 18.69 and 24.88 per cent in 1971 and 1981 respectively in the case of India.[79] Happily, the female literacy in the Punjab increased at a higher rate than in the rest of the country.

The third crucial indicator regarding improvement in the status of women is their participation in economic activities. Punjabi women do take part in economic activities but that is primarily in the household or in the family farms. The majority of them constitute an invisible labour force. The Indian Census data for 1971 and 1981 show that the total workforce is composed of main workers and marginal workers. During these two decades, the proportion of male main workers to their total population in the Punjab was 53.14 per cent and that of female main workers to the total female population 2.27 per cent.[80] The overall female participation rate of 6.16 per cent in 1981 was not only lower than the total male participation rate of 53.75 per cent in the state but also considerably lower than the national average for females, i.e. 20.8 per cent.[81] The data of 1981 also reveals that out of the total female workforce of 6.16 per cent, 3.89 were marginally occupied. As against this, out of the total male workforce of 53.75 per cent, 0.61 per cent males were marginal workers. Marginality, thus, is a problem for female workers.

It may be pointed out that the female participation rate in the Punjab is the lowest as compared with the other states of India. This (ground reality) is intriguing in view of the female literacy rate 34.14 per cent, which is higher than the national average 4.88 and its tenth ranking among the other states and the Union Territories as recorded in the Census 1981. It is even more difficult to explain the lower participation of the Punjabi women in gainful employment in a state where the majority of its inhabitants are the followers of Sikh religion enjoining upon them *Kirt Kar, Vand Chhak, Namu Jap* (labour for bread, share it and recite God's name). The most plausible explanation for the marginality of women in the labour force is the patriarchal fixation with the sexual division of labour and unwillingness to share employment opportunities. Linked with it is the male perception of correlation between female invisibility in public, her virtue, male honour and economic dependence of women, especially among the high castes whether Hindus, Sikhs or Muslims. In the Punjab, men regard it as undignified to let their women work for wages. As a consequence, majority of Punjabi women work within their homes or in their farms. Their work remains invisible and hence is not computed in terms of economic gain. Obviously, the Sikh religion has not been used as an emancipatory tool as far as Punjabi women are concerned.

The foregoing analysis on the basis of relevant historical sources and limited empirical data underlines the glaring gap between scriptural teachings and the factual situation. Sikh women, like their Hindu and Muslim sisters, too suffer from socio-economic disabilities as they live in a male-dominated society. Subjected to a curious mix of Brahminical and Jat patriarchal norms and practices, a Sikh woman (in fact all Punjabi women) has no real identity. The authority and autonomy that she enjoys are determined entirely by the socialization for gender roles, material and spiritual ambitions of the male members of her family. Thus, the value system as practised by Sikhs in relation to women is sharply at variance with the code of conduct laid down in the Sikh scriptures.

IV
WHAT CAN WOMEN DO WITH RELIGION?

In the preceding analysis of the conceptualization of women in the Sikh religious tradition from the early sixteenth century onwards, I have tried to show that its misogynistic tendencies rather than its emancipatory potential have influenced male perceptions and images of women, their attitude towards sex, gender relations and their postulations for a code of conduct for women in the domestic as well as public space. In the nineteenth century, the Singh Sabha leadership, while defining a separate identity for the Sikh community through the demarcation of religious boundaries and life-cycle ceremonies from the Hindus, had endorsed the ideal of 'competent domesticity' floated by the Arya reformers. Factually, a selective bonding of components of Brahminical, bourgeois and tribal cultures in relation to women was sealed without their consent and perhaps some unrecorded resistance. In the reformed Sikh and Hindu traditions, women have been subordinated to the husband, family, kinship networks and religious community. Since Jats have continued to form the dominant constituency of the *panth,* women are thoroughly subjected to tribal patriarchy, sometimes enforced through polygamy and sometimes through polygyny with a view to retaining power and property in the male line—fathers, uncles, brothers. Inevitability of the transfer of a girl from parental to husband's home has continued to deprive her of authority and individual autonomy in exercising her choice on a number of crucial issues, namely, education, marriage, spacing of children, residence, employment, claim to share in parental and husband's property. It is supported by the broad demographic data (cited in the previous section) which shows a decline in sex ratio, higher female infant mortality, continuing incidence of child marriage, rising rate of reported dowry deaths and bride-burning, low level of female literacy and work force participation in Punjab.

Despite emancipatory directions from Guru Nanak and his successors, their followers continue to subject Sikh women to multiple patriarchies of caste, tribe, family and religion. The persistent demand for a separate personal law for Sikhs is a blatant example of their obsession with the patriarchal agenda, i.e. perpetuation of women's disabilities with regard to marriage, maintenance, inheritance and guardianship. Its legislation has been linked with their autonomy as a religious community. In fact, regulation of women's lives and bodies has been the central concern for men, despite their willingness to modernize their homes, sacred places and agricultural economy through the use of latest technologies. It is evident from the fact that Punjab was the first state to commercialize amniocentsis as early as 1979, a development that has favoured the birth of male babies and elimination of female foetuses.[82] Despite protests by press and women activists against the 1982 newspaper advertisements featuring the New Bhandari Anti-natal Sex-determination Clinic at Amritsar, the State government refrained from ordering any prohibition against amniocentsis.[83] It was indicative of the entrenched male bias against women and their determination to perpetuate concentration of social and economic power in their own hands. It is difficult to say whether the growing popularity of these practices in the Punjab (having the highest number of abortion of female foetuses) shall strengthen the feminist movement and its active intervention in preventing the abuse of medical technologies.

However, it is relevant to identify the factors which have frozen the process of social change specifically relating to women. Firstly, for the Sikh Gurus, who contributed to a positive change in the socio-religious milieu from the sixteenth century onwards, religious reforms was the major issue. The condemnation of the oppressive social customs such as infanticide, sati and polygamy and their injunctions to their followers to treat women honourably had underlined their humanistic perspective. Guru Nanak's teachings had moulded his disciples' attitude towards gender relations and perception of women as essentially virtuous and great rather than evil. However, transformation of the very character of the *panth* from a socio-religious movement into a religio-political movement brought a shift in the priorities of the Gurus.[84] For example, Guru Hargobind's call to arms as a measure of self-defence in the seventeenth century took precedence over their concern for the removal of cruel social customs oppressing women. In fact, their religious commitment for securing and protecting their autonomy against the military might of the Mughal Government in the eighteenth century had diverted attention from women's plight in the Punjabi society. As a result, the positive directions of the earlier Gurus were neither developed at the ideological level nor implemented in daily life. It is likely that some Gurus endorsed the norms of the contemporary male-dominated religious system. It is not surprising that a huge gap exists between the ideals of Sikhs and their sociological patterns, especially their derogatory attitudes towards women.

Nikky-Guninder Singh has noted various reasons for this dichotomy between the 'empowering' messages of the Sikh scripture and actual practice. She has drawn attention to the negative role of the patriarchal exegetes such as translators, commentators and teachers who have been "excising female symbolism and imagery replacing it with a male one. Because the sacred text has not been meaningfully read, Sikh women do not enjoy the status that Guru Nanak wanted them to have".[85] Another explanation for the inability of the comparatively young Sikh tradition to break the stronghold of the existing androcentric culture was the overwhelming presence of the Hindu and Islamic traditions.[86] In its radical task, the developing Sikh religion was severely constrained by the contemporary socio-religious ethos which continues to reinforce the patriarchal values. It may be pointed out that beliefs and attitudes of Jats, who form the dominant constituency of the *panth,* have exercised more influence on the sociological patterns of Punjabi society particularly its Sikh segment than the Brahminical and Islamic religious values.

However, it must be conceded that there is a close relationship between religion and social change. On the one hand, religious traditions have played a seminal role in the transformation of various societies; on the other hand, these have often been used as an instrument for the subjugation and oppression of women in the domestic space. In the hands of the socio-religious reformers, religion has and continues to provide an effective means of standardizing patriarchal agenda, norms and practices for regulating women's sexual behaviour and activities within the four walls of homes and in the expanding public space—schools, colleges, offices, factories, marketplace, etc.

In the present times, many radical-minded women have raised a variety of questions regarding values, norms and code of conduct prescribed for them by Hindu, Sikh and Islamic religious scriptures. One of these questions is: What should women do with religion? Should they reject it or reinterpret it for recasting gender relations of societies in which they live? Devaki Jain has provided answers to this question while discussing Gandhi's effective and creative use of the Hindu religious tradition for mobilizing the Indian masses particularly women for social and political struggles.[87] Through his imaginative approach Gandhi was able to elucidate linkages between the feminine qualities of compassion, caring and tolerance (valued by Hindu, Sikh and Christian and Islamic religious traditions), and strategies for social change.

Punjabi women, having the advantage of being exposed to the composite culture of this region, are in the happy position to identify the positive messages and directions in their religious traditions. These can be used for formulating a gender-sensitive broad-based ethics. For example, two essential teachings of the Sikh Gurus, *Kirat Kar, Vand Chhak* may be used effectively for legitimizing women's right to work and access to economic resources. Similarly, Guru Nanak's emphasis on the desirability of marriage and family life for procreation may be positively interpreted to project the cruciality of joint contribution of men and women in ensuring regular and continuous supply of labour and expertise required for sustaining and enhancing the pace of economic production according to the needs and environmental concerns of this region and of the country at large. Recognition of women's contribution to productivity and intellectual growth can be facilitated through the creative mediation of religion which continues to mould the thinking, values and behaviour of a large number of Indians.

The common value of individual autonomy and self-reliance in Hindu and Sikh thought can be utilized by Punjabi women, who have vital links with family and society, for bringing about social change. Finally, non-violent techniques may be used for organizing social and political movements against crimes, inequality and injustice at the local, regional and national level.

REFERENCES

1. David N. Lorenzen, 'Kabir Panth and Social Protest', in Karin Schomer and W.H.McLeod, eds., *The Sants: Studies in a Devotional Tradition of India* (Delhi: Motilal Banarsidass, 1987), p.293.
2. I have based my observations regarding socio-historical environment on a number of research works. See for example, K.M. Ashraf, *Life and Conditions of the People of Hindustan* (Delhi: Munshiram Manoharlal Publishers Pvt. Ltd., 1959, 1969); Aziz Ahmed, *Studies in Islamic Culture in the Indian Environment* (Delhi: Oxford University Press, 1964); V. Upadhyay, *Socio-Religious Conditions of North India, 700–1200 A.D.,* (Varanasi, 1964); Tapan Ray Chaudhari and Irfan Habib, eds., *The Cambridge Economic History of India,* Vol. I (2 Vols.), C. 1200-C. 1750, (Delhi: Orient Longman in association with Cambridge University Press, 1982, 1984).
3. Ganda Singh, 'Presidential Address', in *Proceedings of the Punjab History Conference,* 1969 (Patiala: Punjabi University, 1970), p. 77.
4. For an interesting discussion of this aspect see Wazir Singh, 'Social Protest in Sikh Gurbani', in the *Journal of Medieval Indian Literature,* Vol. II, No. 1 & 2, March–September, 1978, pp. 34–36.
5. *Ibid.,* p. 31.
6. Gopal Singh, trans., *Sri Guru Granth Sahib,* 4 Vols. (Delhi: World Sikh University Press, 1978), p. 467. Hereafter, the English version of

quotations cited from the *Adi Granth,* unless otherwise noted, shall be excerpted from Gopal Singh, trans.

7. *Ibid.,* Guru Nanak, p. 722.
8. *Ibid.,* pp. 1382–84.
9. *Ibid.,* p. 4.
10. For translation of this couplet see Manmohan Singh, trans., *Sri Guru Granth Sahib,* 6 Vols., (Amritsar: S.G.P.C., 1964, 1965), pp. 382–84; Gopal Singh, trans., pp. 414-15.
11. Edward C. Sachau, trans., Alberuni: India, An Account of the Religion, Philosophy, Literature, Geography, Chronology, Astronomy, Customs, Laws, Astrology of India about A.D. 1030. 2 Volumes in 1. *Alberuni's India* (London, 1960), p. 100. For social change with respect to castes see V. Upadhyaya, *Socio-Religious Conditions of in North India,* 700–1200 A.D., p. 365.
12. K.M. Ashraf, *Life and Conditions of the People of Hindustan,* p. 79.
13. *Ibid.,* S.M. Ikram, *Muslim Civilization in India,* (New York: Columbia University Press, 1964), p. 92.
14. Denzil Ibbetson, *Punjab Castes* (First Published in 1881; reprinted, Patiala: Languages Department Punjab, 1970), pp. 118–19. For a statistical statement on the distribution of *Jats* in the Sikh tract see pp. 120-21-Abstract 5.
15. K.M. Ashraf, *Life and Conditions of the People of Hindustan,* pp. 166-67; A.B. Pandey, *Society and Government in Medieval India* (Allahabad: Central Book Depot, 1965), pp. 203–04.
16. *Alberuni's India, n.* 11, pp. 179–81.
17. *Ibid.*
18. *Ibid.,* p. 155. Romila Thapar, *A History of India* (London: Penguin Books, 1967), p. 152. She has pointed out that *sati* was literally equated with a 'virtuous' woman.
19. H.A.R. Gibb, trans. and ed., Ibn Battuta: *Travels in Asia and Africa,* (London: Oxford University Press, 1953), p. 191.
20. Ganesh Das, *Char-Bagh-i-Panjab,* Kirpal Singh, ed., (Amritsar: Khalsa College, 1965), pp. 188–200.
21. *Ibid.,* p. 252, Ganesh Das has given an interesting description of a case of *sati.*
22. V. Upadhayay, *Socio-Religious Conditions of North India,* pp. 153–54; Kiran Davendra, 'Position of Women in Punjabi Society', in Mohinder Singh, ed., *Prof. Harbans Singh Commemoration Volume,* 1988), p. 238; W.H. McLeod, *Sikhism* (London: Penguin Books, 1977), p. 246. McLeod has argued, ".... The *rahit-namas* of the eighteenth and early nineteenth centuries contain implicit prohibitions of female infanticide, thereby testifying to the practice among some members of the Panth. The Bedis were a prominent caste".

23. Bhai Mohan Singh, cited in Charlotte Vaudville, *A Weaver Named Kabir,* (Delhi: Oxford University Press, 1993, 1997), p. 77.
24. Katherina K. Young, 'Hinduism' in Arvind Sharma, ed., *Women in World Religions* (Albany: State University of New York Press, 1987), pp. 76–77.
25. Guy Poitevin and Hem Prabha Rairkar, *Stone-mill and Bhakti: From the Devotion of Peasant Women to the Philosophy of Swamis* (Delhi: D.K. Printworld (P) Ltd., 1996), p. 260.
26. Mirabai, a rebel *bhakta*, is believed to have been born towards the end of the fifteenth century, within the Rathor Rajput family who held control over the land of Merta (in present-day Rajasthan). Married to the heir-apparent to the throne of Chittor (ruled by the Sisodiyas), she refused to consummate the relationship and declared her love and allegiance for Krishna, god and king of Dwarka. Her bhajans are sung with great fervour by the masses in Rajasthan, Gujarat and Saurashtra. For an unconventional scholarly study of this historical *bhakta* see Parita Mukta, *Upholding Common Life: The Community of Mirabai,* (Delhi: Oxford University Press, 1997).
27. Popularly known as Lal Ded, she was born sometime between 1317 and 1320 A.D., (d. 1372) in a Kashmiri Brahmin family. After twelve years of married life, she became a wandering ascetic. Hailed as the maker of modern Kashmiri language, she composed verses in her own genre *Vaakh.* For more details regarding her life and times, see Jaya Lal Kaul, *Lal Ded* (Delhi: Sahitya Akademi, 1973).
28. Akkamahadevi, one of the greatest Kannada poets of the 12th century, began her life as a spiritual seeker and poet after her departure from the palace of her royal husband in Uduthalli. She spent the rest of her life as a naked *sanyasin* until she reached her destination Kadali, a sacred grove in the hills Srisaila which was the home of her *Isht-devta* Lord Chennamalikarjuna. The most dramatic part of her journey was her visit to Kalyana, the great centre of the 12th-century philosophical debates where she interacted with her peers like Basvana, Allama and Chenna Basvana. The most memorable products of her spiritual journey were her poems, popularly called *vachannas.* These lyrical poems have been described as a sacred journey through the profane world.
29. Nikky-Guninder Kaur Singh, *The Feminine Principle in the Sikh Vision of the Transcendent* (Cambridge: Cambridge University Press, 1993), pp. 3, 7.
30. Gurbachan Singh Talib, trans., *Asa di Var.*
31. I.J. Leslie, *Strisvabhava: The Inherent Nature of Women,* Vol. I, p. 11, N.N. Allen, R.F. Gombrich, T. Ray Chaudhary, eds. (Delhi: Oxford University Press, 1986). This paper is a commentary on Tryambakajavan's *Street Dharampadhiti,* an 18th-century document.
32. Nikki-Guninder Singh, p. 56.

33. Gurbachan Singh Talib trans., p. 1349.
34. Nikki-Guninder Singh, p. 67.
35. Cited in *Ibid.*, p. 69.
36. *Ibid.*
37. Nikki-Guninder Singh, p. 90.
38. *Adi Granth,* pp. 703, 705.
39. Nikki-Guninder Singh, p. 91.
40. *Ibid.,* p. 98.
41. *Adi Granth,* p. 1013.
42. *Adi Granth,* pp. 748, 788.
43. *Ibid.*
44. *Ibid.*
45. *Ibid.,* p. 787.
46. *Adi Granth,* p. 788.
47. Harbans Singh, 'Place of Women in Sikhism' in *Journal of Religious Understanding,* Vol. X, No. 3, July–September, 1990.
48. Nikky-Guninder Kaur Singh. *The Feminine Principle in the Sikh Vision of the Transcendent,* p. 104.
49. J.S. Grewal, 'Gender Perspective on Guru Nanak' in Kiran Pawar, ed., *Women in Indian History: Social, Economic, Political and Cultural Perspectives,* (New Delhi, Patiala: Vision & Venture, 1996), pp. 141–157.
50. *Ibid.,* p. 252.
51. Thomas J. Hopkins, *The Hindu Religious Tradition,* (Belmont, CA: Wadsworth Publishing Company, 1971), p. 19–20.
52. Harjot Oberoi, *The Construction of Religious Boundaries: Culture, Identity and Diversity in the Sikh Tradition* (Delhi: Oxford University Press, 1994), p. 97.
53. *Adi Granth,* p. 165.
54. *Ibid.,* p. 371.
55. *Ibid.,* p. 83.
56. *Ibid.,* p. 31.
57. *Adi Granth,* p. 304.
58. *Ibid.,* p. 639.
59. *Ibid.,* p. 182.
60. *Ibid.*
61. *Adi Granth,* p. 737.
62. Nikky-Guninder Singh, p. 121.
63. It must be pointed out that the powerful and autonomous goddess Durga draws her power from the male gods. Thus, her omnipotence has at best an ambiguous status. Turning from mythical to actual perception of danger and awe of divine female figures of Kali and Durga whether by the illiterate villagers or the urban-educated middle classes, the overall attitude towards women can be characterized as ambivalent rather than

positive. This indication is available in the contradictory signals in a number of verses in the *Guru Granth Sahib* which reject the goddess and denigrate 'women':

He who worships Maha-Maya falls from the pedestal of man to be reborn a 'woman'. (*Adi Granth,* p. 874).

64. Kanwaljit Kaur, 'Sikh Women', in Gobind Singh Man Sukhni, Jasbir Singh Mann, eds., *Fundamental Issues in Sikh Studies,* (Chandigarh: Institute of Sikh Studies, 1992), p, 103.
65. W.H. McLeod, *Sikhism* (London: Penguin Books, 1997), pp. 243–44.
66. In his book entitled *Sikhism* (1997), McLeod has treated explicit prohibitions against female infanticide in the *Rahit-namas,* i.e. manuals of conduct of the 18th and early 19th centuries as definite proof of the practice of this custom among some followers of the *panth.* In his view, practice of hypergamy for the marriage of daughters and inheritance patterns in favour of sons were the two major causes of female infanticide in the peasant society of this region.
67. Gurdarshan Singh Dhillon, 'Character and Impact of the Singh Sabha Movement on the History of the Punjab', (Unpublished Ph. D. dissertation, Punjabi University, Patiala, 1973), p. 39.
68. For an incisive discussion of the construction of *rites de passage* see Harjot S. Oberoi, 'From Ritual to Counter-Ritual: Rethinking the Hindu–Sikh Question, 1884–1915', in T.O. Connel, Milton Israel, Willard G.Oxtoby et al., *Sikh History and Religion in the Twentieth Century* (Delhi: Manohar Publications, South Asia edition, 1990), pp. 136–158. Its appendix contains the list of twenty-four manuals on *rites de passage,* written between 1884 and 1915.
69. Details regarding its legislation have been discussed in I.S. Talwar, 'The Anand Marriage Act', *The Punjab Past and Present,* Vol. II, Part 2. October 1968, pp. 400–410; also Ajmer Singh, *Anand Vivah Par Vichar Ka Khandan* (Amritsar: Sardar Ajmer Singh, 1908). It contains a strong defence of the Anand Marriage ritual.
70. For a detailed account of Bhai Takht Singh's struggle for establishing Sikh Kanya Mahavidyalaya, see *Zinda Shaheed Bhai Takht Singh* in Punjabi (Patiala: Punjabi University Publication Bureau, 1980).
71. For a complete list of his works see Harbans Singh, *Bhai Vir Singh* (Delhi: Sahitya Academy, 1972), 1984.
72. W.H. McLeod, *Sikhism,* p. 232. In McLeod's view, two of the principal castes (*Zats*) of Sikhs are Khatri and Jat. While Khatris constitute only 2 or 3 per cent of the *Panth,* more than 60 per cent of Sikhs are Jats, being overwhelmingly a rural community. For an insightful analysis of the circumstances and the process of the conversion of Jats to Sikh panth see his *The Evolution of Sikh Community* (Delhi: Oxford University Press, 1975).
73. For more details of Jat inheritance patterns, see Paul Hershman, *Punjabi*

Kinship and Marriage (Delhi: Hindustan Publishing Corporation, 1981), pp. 72–80, 242.

74. *Census of India,* 1971, Paper 2 of 1977 Fertility Tables, 1971 Series 1 (Delhi: Office of Registrar General and Census Commissioner, India, 1971). Cited in Upinder Jit Kaur, *Sikh Religion and Economic Development* (Delhi: National Book Organisation, 1990), p. 317.
75. *Census of India* 1991, Series 17 Punjab, Part II, Special Report and Tables based on 5 per cent Sample Data, p. 37, Statement 11. Cited in Upinder Jit Kaur, *Sikh Religion and Economic Development,* p. 318.
76. Compiled from *(i) Census of India,* 1971, Series 17-Punjab, Part II-A, General Population Tables.
(ii) Census of India, 1981, Series I-India, Paper 1 of 1981, Provincial Population Tables.
(iii) Census of India, 1991, (Punjab) Series I, Pt. (I), Vol. I, Primary Census Abstract, Statement 5, p. xciv.
77. One possible explanation for this adverse sex ratio of women is the high female infant mortality rate and high maternal mortality rate, caused by the comparative neglect of females, low availability of nutritional foods, inadequate as well as indifferent health care and high frequency of pregnancies. The second explanation for the depressed sex ratio is the large-scale migration of a large number of male labourers from the other states into the Punjab.
78. For a detailed picture of literacy in this region, see *Census of India* 1981, Series 17-Punjab, Part II-Special Report and Tables based on 5 per cent of sample data, p. 66.

Table 4: Literacy Rate (Percentage) in Punjab by Sex and Stratum, 1971 & 1981.

Stratum	*Persons*		*Males*		*Females*	
	1971	*1981*	*1971*	*1981*	*1971*	*1981*
Total	33.67	40.86	40.38	47.16	25.90	33.69
Rural	27.81	35.21	34.69	41.91	19.88	27.63
Urban	52.49	55.63	58.55	60.73	45.41	49.72

79. *Ibid.* For decade-wise details see Table 5:

Table 5: Literacy Rate for Males and Females 1961 to 1981.

Year	*Male Literacy Rate (Per Cent)*	*Female Literacy Rate (Per Cent)*
1961	34.70	17.41
1971	40.38	25.90
1981	47.16	33.69

80. *Ibid.,* p. 84. For a comparative view see Table 6:

Table 6: Work Participation Rates (per cent) for Marginal, Main and Total Workers, 1971 and 1981

Category of Workers	*1971* Persons	Male	Female	*1981* Persons	Male	Female
Marginal Workers	0.02	0.01	0.04	2.15	0.61	3.89
Main Workers	28.87	52.82	1.18	29.35	53.14	2.27
Total Workers	28.89	52.83	1.22	31.50	53.75	6.16
Rural						
Marginal Workers	0.02	0.01	0.04	2.85	0.78	5.18
Main Workers	29.11	53.75	0.72	29.29	53.66	1.72
Total Workers	29.13	53.76	0.76	32.14	54.44	6.90
Urban						
Marginal Workers	0.02	0.01	0.03	0.31	0.17	0.49
Main Workers	28.10	49.88	2.66	29.51	51.80	3.71
Total Workers	28.12	49.88	2.69	29.82	51.97	4.20

81. *ibid.*
82. W.H. McLeod, *Sikhism,* p. 245.
83. Renuka Dagar, 'Women's Rights in Punjab: Interventionists' Perspective', in Kiran Pawar, ed., *Women in Indian History,* pp. 227, 233.
84. J.S. Grewal, 'A Perspective on Early Sikh History' in Mark Juergensmeyer and N. Gerlad Barrier, eds., *Sikh Studies: Comparative Perspectives on a Changing Tradition* (Berkely: Graduate Theological Union, 1970), p. 34. While discussing the changes in the focus of the Sikh community, J.S. Grewal observes, ".... We have to identify and study the shift in the dominant concerns of the community with the passage of time, looking for historical and logical connections between the activity and ideas of various phases".
85. Nikky-Guninder Singh, p. 253.
86. *Ibid.,* p. 255.
87. Devaki Jain, 'Gandhian Contribution Toward a Feminist Ethics', in Dian L. Eck & Devaki Jain, eds., *Speaking of Faith: Cross-Cultural Perspectives on Women.* (New Delhi: Kali for Women, 1986), pp. 256–270.

2

Clamping Shutters and Valorizing Women

Tensions in Sculpting Gender Identities in the Colonial Punjab

In this essay, I propose to explore the process of gender identity formation, specifically, the issue of construction of 'new' woman as it has a significant bearing on the ongoing search for regional and communal identities from the late nineteenth century onwards. This was also the time when the status of women in Indian society became a political issue and the focus of debate and controversy. Colonial rule, with its moral and civilizing claims, is said to have provided the context for a thorough re-evaluation of Indian 'tradition' along lines more consonant with the 'modern' economy and society, which was believed to have been the consequence of India's incorporation into the 'capitalist world system'.[1] The position of women was, in colonial perception, an indicator of the 'modernization' of a country. It also reflected on the ability of its citizens to rule themselves. Lack of 'masculinity' was a cogent argument around which India's unfitness for self-rule and the protongation of the British rule were justified by colonial rulers. It was in this context that the issue of recasting gender identities, involving the definition of femininity' and 'masculinity', images, roles and relations between man and woman became central to the nationalist discourse and ideologies of social reform movements, particularly Arya Samaj and Singh Sabha.

The main argument of this essay is that the process of construction of gender identities especially selfhood, social experience and roles of women among the enterprising middle classes in the colonial Punjab excluding the Princely states, remained segmented and incomplete.

There are two underlying assumptions in my argument. Firstly, the multi-racial and multi-religious character of Punjabi society (as a consequence of its open geographical frontier) had generated socio-cultural tensions and sharpened contradictions in the mindscape of its people despite the broad acceptance of the principle of co-existence in social, political and economic life. Secondly, the overwhelmingly agrarian character of economy of this region had reinforced the persuasive dominance of the patriarchal peasant culture which persisted in the social thinking on the issue of gender identities and role among the urban middle classes, who remained firmly anchored to their moorings in their native village while they were engaged in modernizing themselves.

For the purpose of discussion, the paper shall be divided into five sections: *(i)* Conceptualizing the Problem; *(ii)* Peasant ethos and Socio-economic Conditions: Their Implications for Women: *(iii)* Social Roots of Middle Classes, Colonial View of Indian Culture and Women, and the Native Response; *(iv)* Sculpting New Gender Identities: Myths of Past and Contemporary Reality; *(v)* Conclusion.

I
CONCEPTUALIZING THE PROBLEM

It is important to delineate the meanings of several terms that will be employed in the course of our discussion, specifically 'gender', 'gender identity', 'power', 'authority', 'autonomy' and 'status' as formulated by feminist scholarship. For a clear understanding of 'gender identity', it is crucial to distinguish between 'sex' and 'gender'. While 'sex' generally carries a biological connotation, 'gender' is a term whose psychological and cultural connotations outweigh the biological component. It refers to the social dimensions of one's existence as male and female. 'Gender' usually indicates the degree of conformity of the individual to the standards of femininity and masculinity in various cultures.

The concept of 'gender' cannot be fully explicated without reference to the concepts of 'gender role' and 'gender identity' Gender roles may be described in two ways: established gender roles of a culture or gender roles of an individual.[2] In terms of culture, it may be described as a social norm or standard which summarizes the culturally constructed characteristics for males and females. The characteristics that define 'feminine' and 'masculine' may cover such diverse features as physical attributes, appearances, overt behaviour and covert attributes including feelings, attitudes, motives and beliefs.[3] Gender roles typically include but are not confined to domestic, vocational, reproductive and erotic roles.[4] 'Gender identity', broadly speaking, indicates the degree to which an individual regards herself or himself as feminine or masculine. It includes an individual's sense of belonging to one sex or the other (or neither) but is more complicated in that it may include characteristics that are both masculine and feminine by cultural definitions.[5]

A few writers regard 'gender schema' as crucial to the formation of 'gender identity'. John Money uses the phrase 'gender schema' as basically equivalent to one's sense of gender on the basis of which one's 'gender identity is formulated'.[6] For most individuals, 'gender', 'gender roles' and 'gender identity' are almost synonymous, but they can be at variance.[7] There is an imperfect co-relation between possession of gender-role characteristics and one's own sense of gender identity. Possession of some gender type characteristic is necessary but not sufficient for a firm gender identity. Money is insistent that gender identity and gender roles are "facets of the same entity". He states that "gender identity ... is the private experience of gender role; and gender role is the public manifestation of gender identity".[8] In short, one could not have a gender identity unless there were gender roles and one has some attributes of that role; existence of gender identity ensures the public expression of that identity which in turn ensures the continuance of that role. In order to underscore the integral nature of gender role and gender identity we shall hereafter refer to gender identity as gender identity/role.[9]

Since gender identities are constructed within the structure of family and society, it is important to clarify the meaning of the concepts of 'authority' and 'power'. According to Dahl, these are 'influence terms' which define the relationship in which one actor induces other actors to act in a specific way.[10] Influence derived from 'authority' requires cultural legitimation. Defined in this context 'authority' means the right to make a particular decision and to command obedience. Family relations especially daughter–father and husband–wife equation operate on this assumption. 'Power' deals more directly with the instruments that endow the holder with a particular status. While 'status' is a descriptive and ambiguous term, 'power' is an analytical concept which implies the ability to influence effectively the persons or things, to secure favourable decisions through coercion, persuasion, manipulation of various sorts, bargaining and other forms of influence.

Power mechanism postulates the superiority of one actor and the inferiority or subordination of the other. Women are subordinated because they lack power to resist injustice, imposition of inequality and exploitation of their sexuality, fertility and labour. Who wields power in society? What are the sources of their power? Which are the institutions that legitimize the subjugation of women? Institutions such as the state, religion and family exercise power in a manner inimical to the well-being and all-round growth of women as autonomous individuals. The legal structure is an example of entrenched power which has apportioned and sanctioned unequal rights between man and woman. Within the family both custom, socialization process and tradition assign a second class and subordinate role to woman as daughter, sister, wife and mother. It is reinforced by official laws of various kinds. In other words, state, religion and family being patriarchal institutions glorify the cult of masculinity.

The concept of 'autonomy' also signifies 'power' and is applicable to individual needs. Its basic assumption is that each individual has the right and opportunity to choose his/her lifestyle, educational prospects, profession, marriage partner, mode of expression of sexuality and control over reproductive functions. As men and women exercise their rights in society and political and economic arena, it is obligatory for them not to infringe upon or abrogate the rights and freedom of others. 'Status' is a vague term. It may mean demonstration of respect or feeling of being respected at the subjective level. Ironically, symbolic veneration, courtesy or respect may co-exist with deprivation of various sorts and oppression. In the historical context of contemporary social situation, 'status' may also subsume the prevalent religious rituals, customs and practices that had formalized or institutionalized social control, restrictions, oppressions, denial of access to knowledge and economic resources. Its cumulative result may imply damage to physical and psychological components of a woman's personality. The context of 'status' today comprises a number of development indicators : health level, education, property, opportunities for use of training and skills that open up chances of employment. It may be pointed out that the concepts of 'power', 'authority' and 'autonomy' are interlinked and useful for conceptualizing the 'status' or situation of women in the colonial Punjab as in other regions. These are useful for understanding the issue of gender–relations as these are mediators in the construction of caste, communal, regional and national identities.

II
PEASANT ETHOS AND SOCIO-ECONOMIC CONDITIONS: THEIR IMPLICATIONS FOR WOMEN

Peasant ethos

In this section, I have tried to explicate one strand of my argument—incidence of overlapping between the beliefs, attitudes and values with regard to the placement of women in a peasant society and those of the expanding urban society in the process of recasting socio-economic contours and adjusting with changes brought about by the colonial rule. In the Central and South-east Punjab, where agrarian mode of production formed the basis of economy, the socio-cultural ethos was heavily coloured by the perceptions of the dominant agricultural castes and in particular by the land-owning castes. A few empirical details concerning the demography and economy of the Punjab will help us in clarifying the argument. In the nineteenth century, the Punjab was basically an agrarian society. In 1881, roughly 87.35 per cent of its population lived in the 34,000 villages of the province and only 12.65 per cent in urban centres.[11] In the three largest cities of the state—Lahore, Multan and Amritsar—lived about a quarter of a million people who controlled the bulk of the long-distance trade and a part of the small-scale manufacturing industry. There were the smaller towns like Jalandhar, Batala, Sialkot and Rawalpindi, each having a population between ten to thirty thousand, which had served as centres of manufacturing. A small number of mercantile families had acquired wealth through trade in luxury commodities (chiefly woven-gold, silk fabrics, Kashmiri shawls and ivory goods) with Central and Western Asia and Europe. However, the rulers and their subjects were primarily dependent upon the fruits of the agrarian economy. The economic situation did not change dramatically because of the British policy to retain and reinforce the agrarian character of

Punjab's economy. A contemporary English official had noted this point: "The Punjab can show no vast cities to rival Calcutta and Bombay; no great factories, no varied mineral wealth but the occupations of its people are still not without an interest of their own".[12] In 1901, about 60 per cent of Punjabis were agriculturists by profession, 20.3 per cent in industries and 6.5 per cent in trade. In the decade 1901–11, while those in agriculture decreased by 2.6 per cent, those dependent on trade and industries increased by 4.5 per cent respectively.[13]

The concept of 'dominant caste', first expounded and applied to a specific region by M.N. Srinivas[14], is valid for analyzing the position of those caste-groups, which had the basic resources, tenacity, drive and aspiration for upward mobility and took advantage of new opportunities created by educational and economic changes under the Raj.

In the case of the two subregions: central Punjab and south-east Punjab, Jats provided the best example of a 'dominant caste' group. Economically and numerically dominant, they had overcome their handicap of a low ritual status by virtue of being landowners for possession of land was regarded as the symbol of a high social status. In the central Punjab, racially, the Jats and Rajputs accounted for nearly 28 per cent of population but numerically the *Jat–Rajput* ratio was 3:1.[15] The Jats had inhabited the central part of *Bari Doab, Rechna Doab* and *Chaj Doab.* In the south-east Punjab, particularly Ambala, Gurgaon, Hissar, Karnal and Rohtak, Jats formed nearly one-third of the local population and held the bulk of agricultural land as peasant-proprietors.

The Khatris, who also owned lands but were engaged in shop-keeping like other mercantile classes, constituted about 7 per cent of the total population of the province. *Brahmins,* who enjoyed distinct superiority in social and ritual hierarchy in South India, possessed neither any political authority nor wealth nor learning nor social influence[16] in these two sub regions, and whatever social and political weightage they had enjoyed in the past (hill states being the exception), had been neutralized under the pervasive impact of the new operational values of Sikh religion such as self-respect, dignity of labour, and egalitarianism upon the Punjabi society, particularly the Jats who joined the new brotherhood in large numbers owing to their low standing in the Hindu society. By giving them land-grants and political patronage, Ranjit Singh had further boosted their social and economic status in the Central Punjab in the nineteenth century.[17]

In the south-east Punjab, propagation and acceptance of the Arya Samaj, especially among the land-owning Jats, led to their emergence as the 'dominant caste'. It is evident from the official observation in the *Census of Punjab, 1901* that "there is no caste above a Jat". Such was the dominance of the peasant-model, that majority of the *Brahmins* chose to become cultivators and landowners as priestly castes were not valued. In a turbulent province like Punjab, the *Brahmins* commanded no respect and it was believed that in times of need, "A dom, a Brahman and a goat were of no avail".[18] The British, who regarded the Jats as the best cultivators and excellent soldiers, reinforced their superiority as a social group over other communities and encouraged their customs and norms for women. With official support combined with their advantages, the Jats emerged as a 'dominant caste' in social, economic and numerical terms and they also became a crucial community in the politics of the central and the south-east Punjab. Despite internal economic differentiation and disparities, the Jats as the single 'dominant caste' became a viable model in shaping the attitudes and customs for social control of women, their placement in kinship structure and their exclusion from social, economic and political power. It was so because transmission of oral culture and customs was mediated through the agency of the second generation which initially went to the neighbouring cities for education and settled down there after getting jobs. However, they retained their links with their native villages.[19]

Socio-economic Conditions: Their Implications for Women

Geographically, the British Punjab (including Kashmir lying to its north but excluding Kangra Hills) occupied the extreme north-western corner of India. Its ecology—climate, incidence of rainfall, geographical location of a particular area and the kind of soil—not only determined the patterns of cultivation, labour processes, nature of agrarian relationships and functions but also the position of women. It can be divided into three sub regions: *(i)* the South-eastern Punjab; *(ii)* the Central Punjab; and *(iii)* the South-western Punjab. We shall focus our attention on sub regions *(i)* and *(ii)* as they shared a common land-ownership pattern and dominance of Jats. While the Central Punjab possessed the most fertile and intensively cultivated lands, the south-eastern Punjab comprised dry lands but production of millet and grain did not require additional irrigation despite inadequate rainfall. In both these regions, peasant-proprietorship was the prevailing land-ownership pattern. Small landlords co-existed with the peasant-proprietors in the second half of the nineteenth century.[20] Dependence on family-labour was crucial for producing subsistence crops such as wheat and gram in the central Punjab, millet and gram in the south-east Punjab. Women in the family had to shoulder most of the burden of agricultural work except ploughing. Animal husbandry was their exclusive responsibility.

As the twentieth century began, a new fourth region in the Punjab, known as Canal colonies, was carved. Its distinguishing characteristic was the high productivity of land under canal irrigation, an average of 59 per cent in 1902 and nearly 63 per cent in 1921. Another salient feature was specialization in the production of export crops, primarily wheat but also cotton both indigenous and superior American varieties. This region expanded at a fast pace. In 1901 only one district of the Punjab, i.e. Layallpur, had more than 55 per cent of its land under cultivation but by 1921, there were six. Most of these settlers in the canal colonies were drawn from other parts of the Punjab, specifically, from the central districts. The single largest cultivating caste was comprised of the Sikh Jats, who made up a quarter of the settlers in the Chenab colony; of these 60 per cent were Hindus and 40 per cent were Sikhs.

The Canal region, which soon displaced the central Punjab in the volume of wheat and other crops for export, had grave implications for the migrant women. Without getting any increased access to economic resources of the family, these women were required to work even harder in agricultural operations such as weeding, cotton-picking and sugarcane peeling; their husbands performed back-breaking labour in converting the wild jungles into lush green fields. However, these migrant peasant families could barely earn enough to maintain the family estate and raise the next generation.

Unable to stand the competition from the Canal colonies, the peasant-proprietors in the central Punjab were forced to become share-croppers or to hire out their labour. Hard-pressed by economic necessity, primarily caused by the realization of escalating land revenue in cash, the family head or adult males went to work in the cities or abroad or joined the army thus leaving womenfolk to push themselves to the extreme limit of physical endurance without any change in their status.[21]

In the south-east Punjab, colonial exploitation had added contradictions and tensions in gender relations. It also worsened women's daily life and social status. Possessing poor resources as compared with other parts of the Punjab, this region remained backward and undeveloped in agriculture under the colonial rule. In addition to its geo-economic handicaps, it suffered from the British policy of excessive investment in Canal colonies and almost total neglect of the interests and needs of agrarian economy in this part of the Punjab. As a result of the official premium on the low value food-cum-fodder crops, the south-eastern Punjab was condemned to remain a supplier of draught animals to other parts of this region and provinces of British India.

Notorious for chronic crop failures, famines and deficit production, agriculture in the south-eastern Punjab was totally dependent upon family labour and some hired hands. It was not surprising that such economic conditions in an area of inadequate rainfall and poor irrigation facilities reinforced the obsession for sons. It may be inferred that the attitude to women in general and the norms of behaviour prescribed for a mother in particular are conditioned by the prevailing socio-economic conditions of a particular region. An agriculturally primitive society needs many hands for tilling because it cannot always ensure good harvest because of many natural calamities and the use of primitive tools. It also needs sons and daughters. Thus, huge premium was laid on female fertility, especially, on male lineage. Pride in women's capacity for mothering and ability to get gratification from it are strongly internalized in an agriculture society[22] because no other channels of expression and creativity are available.

The dominant social thinking found expression in popular proverbs and sayings. It was not considered practical to be satisfied with one son as ecological conditions had made agriculture as much dependent on uncertain monsoons as on sturdy and hardworking sons. Thus, the death of an infant daughter was perceived to be a sign of luck for parents and the death of a son as a terrible misfortune. The following proverbs show how economic conditions fed the patriarchal biases against the girl-child in the south-east Punjab:

Chohara mare nirbhag ka,
Chohri mare bhagwan ki.[23]

(The one whose son dies is unlucky
and the one whose daughter dies is lucky).

In the central Punjab, too, these popular sayings reflected the rural psyche:

Rohi bhaun, spoot ghar, aur satwanti naar
Ghorian ute charna, chaar surag sansar.[24]

(A heavy soil, a meritorious son in the household, a faithful and virtuous wife, and the availability of horses for riding are just four heavens on Earth).

The obsession with sons is also illustrated from the blessings often showered by the elderly women upon the young married women.

Budd Suhagin, sat puttari ho![25]

(May you enjoy married status till your old age and be blessed with seven sons).

Keeping in view the vagaries of the monsoon, frequency of famines, chronic crop failures and infertile soil, agriculture was labour intensive. Thus, the birth of a son was as welcome as life-giving rain. It is illustrated by a local saying in Karnal:

Meehin aur bettya to koon dhappya sae.[26]

(Who can be satisfied without rain and son! For cultivation both are indispensable).

A number of population censuses, conducted in the colonial Punjab, recorded satistical evidence of the bad consequences of son-preference value system and adverse female sex ratio. These attributed the favourable male sex ratio to a high rate of mortality caused by frequent pregnancies among physically immature girls and their neglect at an advanced stage.

Owing to poor nutrition, women were also more vulnerable than men to recurring famines, droughts and epidemics. Convergence of all these factors lowered the female sex ratio thus giving the Punjab the notoriety of having the smallest number of females as compared with the other major provinces of India.[27] In his memoirs, Prakash

Tandon described the methods used to kill the infant girls among various social groups in the Punjab. The widespread prevalent custom of hypergamy and dowry system also reinforced social and parental bias against girls. An elderly doctor's observations reflected the continuance of the perception of girls as a liability. While pointing towards his little grand-daughter, he remarked:

> *Choti roti khave, vadi boti khave.*
>
> (While in her childhood, the daughter eats bread, as a marriagable girl, she bites into the flesh of her parents).

Nevertheless, Jat women, whom patriarchal values denied autonomy, freedom, public space and access to economic resources, were harnessed for agricultural and domestic labour. A *Jatti* was regarded the most suitable as wife as the following proverb illustrates:

> *Ran Jatti, haur sub chatti.*[28]
>
> (Only a *jatti* makes the best wife. All others are a drain on one's resources).

In the popular mind, the image of a Punjabi wife especially *jatti* was constructed as a sturdy and hard-working woman. The agricultural sayings and proverbs of the Punjab celebrate her multiple functions: domestic chores of cooking for the joint family (which gradually became nuclear units), cleaning and scrubbing, nursing the children and extensive animal-husbandry work. Animal-husbandry which involved tending, feeding, milking the cattle, churning, preparing ghee (refined butter oil), was the exclusive responsibility of women and their invisible contribution to the hard-subsistence economy whose backbone was the small peasant-proprietor. Besides, she performed various agricultural operations such as picking cotton, weeding and peeling sugarcane. Two proverbs, couched in local dialect, are equally applicable to both the sub regions of the Punjab. She is chided for her laxity and dubbed as *kupatti* (bad and careless woman):

> *Mein koli nahin dupatti*
> *Kya chuggegi kuppati.*[29]
> *Kappah guddina duppatti*
> *Tun chuggan ki ayi kuppati.*[30]

Qualities of passivity, docility, submissiveness, pliability, rigid self-restraint, tolerance and readiness for self-sacrifice, suffering and hard work, valued in a wife by the peasant society, were grafted in the urban milieu, with cosmetic changes. The agricultural proverbs project these norms:

> *Duman bhala jo bolna*
> *Noan Bhali jo chup*
> *Sawan bhala jo barsana*
> *Jeth bhaleri dhup.*[31]

(For the birds, it is good to speak and sing; for the daughter-in-law it is proper to be bashful. Rains during the monsoon month of *sawan* [mid-July to mid-August] are good and normal; and the bright and hot sunshine is necessary during the month of *jeth* (mid-May to mid-June) to mature the *rabi* crops).

> *Paike ne sohrion, vattar na vahian*
> *Sawan ne tarel pai, tenain autar gyian.*

(All these things bear no fruit: the life of a girl who did not cultivate the habit of working in her father's home while unmarried and also not after marriage in her husband's home; the labour spent on a field which was not ploughed when in 'water' [the right state of soil-moisture], and the advent of the monsoon month of *sawan* [mid-July to mid-August], if it passes away rainless.

> *Chhole vadh ke beej de narma*
> *Ae chunan nu main takri.*

(My husband sows American cotton after harvesting gram. I am equal to the task of picking it).

> *Na beej nikhatua cheena*
> *Moongla le ke charan lagi*
> *Chittar ho gaya hina.*[32]

(O my bad and unsuccessful husband! Don't sow the inferior millet [*cheena*]; I began to pound it in the mortar with a large pestle. As a result, my buttocks became sore. So arduous is the job of pounding it).

This proverb expressed her suppressed resentment before her peers instead of chiding her husband openly. Thus, tension simmered in gender relations, but the only escape route for women was the world of fantasy, woven in their songs.

Some other notions about women in peasant culture also coloured the perceptions of the Punjabi urban society while reconstructing gender identities. For example, the customary law prevailing among the agriculturists regarded the wife and anything associated with her such as her ornaments, or her earnings (if she was a wage-earner) as the property of her husband.[33] Her worth was measured in terms of her parents' social and economic statues. It is illustrated by the following two proverbs:

Janani so jo pakion rani
Zamin so jis de ser te pani,

Uh zamin rani
Jis de sar te pani.[34]

In the peasant culture of the central Punjab, widowhood was regarded undesirable and the married state earned social approval, status and respect. To be acceptable in marriage, a girl ought to be beautiful. These find expression in this local proverb:

Dhi kani, naun randani, khu di vingi lath
Raste ute kheti, chare chaur chaupat.[35]

(A half-blind daughter, a widowed daughter-in-law, the curved *lath* (shaft of the Persian wheel) and a crop in a field on the roadside, all these four are not desirable).

However, widow remarriage, known as *Karewa* or *Chaddar Andezi* was practised among the agricultural castes especially Jats and the lower castes. Brahmins of these two sub-regions, who were land-owners and not priests, followed the dominant social custom of *Karewa* or *Chaddar Andezi.* Rajputs were the only exception and looked down upon this custom.[36] The widespread acceptability of widow remarriage underlined the contradictions of purdah culture and *ghunghat* culture, both being distinct from each other. It was not indicative of liberal attitudes but a device for retaining family hold over property through the control and monopoly of a widow's sexuality.

The deep-seated patriarchal urge for the social control of women was rationalized by glorifying chastity and superior worth of a secluded woman. For illustration see two popular proverbs:

Beerbani ghar ki bani.[37]

(A woman who remains at home adorns it.)

The *Multan District Gazetteer* contains another such local saying:

Ander baithi lakh di
Bahr gayi kakh di.[38]

(A woman in her home is worth a lakh, outside she is worth nothing.)

Thus, the peasant ethos of the central and the south-east Punjab furnished the basic essentials for sculpting gender identities by the middle classes in urban areas, who borrowed and tried to inculcate some of the qualities of Victorian women in their wives. Prakash Tandon has emphasized this aspect of change in Punjabi society in his comment: "His (father's) generation founded the new Punjabi middle class and added some modern values to the old Punjabi character, but what they lost in the process was the colour of my grand-uncle and his age".[39] It may be mentioned that the middle class in Punjab in the early stages of its development was largely rural-based. It was comprised of the small number of the already settled urban professional and trading classes as well as of those drawn from landed-classes and small land-holders, i.e. peasant-properietors and village literati who sought jobs in the colonial administration and related professions. The British officials, while touring the villages of the Punjab, recruited a number of promising young men as *patwaris* who had no formal educational qualification or degree. In the course of their interaction with their officers and exposure to town or city life, they became ambitious and sent their sons and brothers for education and later on for employment to Lahore and other cities in the Punjab.[40]

III
SOCIAL ROOTS OF MIDDLE CLASSES, COLONIAL VIEW OF INDIAN CULTURE AND WOMEN AND THE NATIVE RESPONSE

Social Roots of Middle Classes

In this section, it is not my intention to examine the causes or factors responsible for the emergence and growth of the middle classes in the

Punjab but to identify their social roots. I wish to argue that the prevalent social norm of associating land-ownership with high social status in the predominantly agrarian economy of the Punjab had tempted the rich urban caste groups other than the notified 'agricultural tribes' to invest safely in the purchase of profitable land property. For example, merchants and money-lenders, who later formed the bulk of commercial middle class in the Punjab, owned substantial landed property by the beginning of the twentieth century either through purchase of land or through the alienation of land of the heavily indebted peasant. The illiterate peasant, ignorant of law, was compelled to borrow from the village *sahukar* for the payment of land revenue in cash as required by the total monetization of economy under the *Raj*.

According to Fox, "This process of monetization was accomplished by a combination of British revenue policy and the self-interested actions of indigenous money-lenders and merchants."[41] From the angle of the social historian, its significance lay in forging links between the social ethos of urban and rural areas. Even a good number of the recruits in the ranks of the rising professional class was drawn from the rich peasant-proprietors and zamindars (constituting the agrarian middle class) because they prepared their sons to join various professional careers by sending them to new schools and colleges which imparted Western education as is evident from Ved Mehta's perceptive portrayal of the fast changes in the socio-economic life of the Punjabis.[42]

These impressionable boys, conditioned to the values underlying the institutions of marriage, family and property relations, had carried their biases and social experience of gender identity and roles to the cities where they were exposed to the cultural values of the colonial rules. Their interaction with their British officers and their admiration for the frank and confident behaviour of English women urged them to discard some of the customs of peasant culture such as seclusion of women and educate their women for 'competent' domesticity.[43] The new elite made lame attempts to Westernize their wives by asking them to wear English dress and play the harmonium. However, the Punjabi women showed enough attachment to tradition to prevent the change from swamping old values. Commenting upon the complexity of the process of modernization, Ved Mehta remarked, "Our fathers changed rapidly, our mothers slowly and between them my generation managed to learn the new without entirely forgetting the old".

The Western education affected their thinking process in two ways: *(i)* the colonization of their consciousness which aroused their admiration for English education particularly its rationalism and scientific achievements and the democratic institutions leading to imitation of their life style; *(ii)* the second response implied their defence of Indian culture especially 'spiritual domain' wherein they were unwilling to acknowledge subjugation and inferiority. On this terrain, the position and status of Indian women became a crucial issue in the wide-ranging debates between the social reformers and the British functionaries as well as rulers in the late nineteenth and early twentieth-century India, particularly in the Punjab. In order to understand the parameters of this debate and the Indian response, let us turn to a brief review of the colonial view of Indian society and culture.

Colonial View of Indian Culture and Women and the Native Response

The bulk of colonial writing about India focused on demonstrating the peculiarities of its civilization and barbaric practices relating to women among Hindus, Muslims, and Sikhs especially. The circulation of the damaging negative perception was much wider than the romanticized versions of Orientalist scholarship and preceded and survived their descriptions of India's lost glory. Of those who built up a systematic indictment of the 'hideous features of Indian society', James Mill is the most representative of this trend of thinking. James Mill's monumental work, *The History of British India* (1840), has been termed as a national balance-sheet of moral lapses and strengths of Indian and Western civilizations. He regarded the position of women as the major criteria for evaluating the quality of any civilization. His critique underlined the 'state of dependence' and the 'habitual contempt' of Indian men for their women. As an indicator of their extreme degradation, "women were ... excluded from education and of a share in the parental property... . That remarkable barbarity, the wife held unworthy to eat with her husband, is prevalent in Hindustan".[44]

Mill's indictment of the degenerate Indian civilization and the abject position of women, who required 'protection' and 'intervention' on humanitarian grounds, was ingrained in the colonial ideology. These two issues became central in the colonial legislation on social issues and politics too. The third issue was the 'effeminacy' of the Hindu men who were unfit to rule themselves. The entire argument was crystallized into a rational justification of the perpetuation of the British rule in India on grounds of moral superiority.

Almost eight decades later, Mill's line of argument would reappear in *Mother India* (1917) whose author Katherine Mayo had drawn a negative portrait of the Indian male's personality, characterized by "inertia, helplessness, lack of initiative, orginality and sterility of enthusiasm".[45] By raising doubts about his flawed 'masculinity' and her harsh criticism of social backwardness, she had reinforced the perceptions of the colonial rulers who had expressed disdain for the weak-kneed Indians, especially Bengali men. Resistance of Indian men to the Indian Consent Act 1891, a colonial move towards prohibiting consummation of marriage by Indian men before their wives were twelve years of age, was cited as proof of their depraved nature, lack of self-restraint and self-discipline.[46] This kind of behaviour, the legislation argued, was associated with 'effeminate' men who are utterly inconsiderate, selfish and inhuman.[47]

The concept of 'motherhood' like that of 'masculinity' had also become the target of ridicule and merciless criticism at the hands of Christian missionaries, foreign medical personnel and the British administrators. The most damaging criticism had appeared in *Mother India* and it aroused a vehement nationalist outcry. Early motherhood, the consequence of child marriage, was perceived by the British as one of the major causes of the depraved character of Indian men as opposed to the English 'manly reserve' and 'self-control'. In fact, sexual incontinence was regarded as the basic cause of India's woes : material and spiritual poverty, sickness, ignorance, political immaturity, depression, ineffectiveness and feeling of inferiority. Commenting upon it, Mayo wrote:

> Force motherhood upon her at the earliest possible moment. Rear her son in intensive vicious practices that drain his small vitality day by day. Give him no outlet in sports. Give him habits that make him by the time he is thirty years of age, a decrepit and querulous old wreck and will you ask what has sapped the energy of his manhood?[48]

Despite being an exaggeration, this view had an element of truth. It provoked an outcry from the nationalists led by Mahatma Gandhi who dubbed Mayo as a 'mischief-monger'.[49]

Obviously, the relentless colonial offensive from the third decade of the nineteenth century onwards upon Indian society and culture, with constant focus on the degenerate character of its manhood and their callous neglect and exploitation of women, had generated a complex Indian response. It may be pointed out that the ideologies of social reform and the Indian national movement had gradually grasped the intricacies of the game of moral imperialism wherein woman's question, specifically her status and role in Indian society, was used as a crucial tool as well as a psychological ploy to demoralize the subject population and justify their enslavement. However, the emerging Indian intelligentsia from the first half of the nineteenth century onwards, who were involved in resolving the 'crisis' produced by an ideological and cultural encounter between India and England,[50] refused to accept the imperialist projections of the Indian society in toto. They gradually developed an obsessive concern with cultural questions while writing a new script for the past. Woman's question, especially the reformulation of the concepts of femininity and motherhood, became the crucial component in the process of redrawing the contours of historical consciousness, national and regional identities. Femininity had to be projected in such a way as would facilitate the Indian male's efforts to prove his 'masculinity' in the external domain as well as to preserve traditional patriarchal relations within the family and dominance of the male world view.

In their response to the colonial critique of the degrading position of Indian particularly Hindu women, the middle classes, who had supplied the bulk of the Indian intelligentsia and leadership for movements for social reforms and national liberation were obliged to project the positive aspects of Hindu culture. While asserting the superiority of their culture, the social reformers—Hindu, Muslim and Sikh—made a conscious effort to weed out the dead and outdated elements in their culture and tradition in order to make it more consistent with the Western ideas of liberalism and humanitarianism. These Western values were seen to be part of the 'material' domain, dominated by Western science, technology and method of state-craft. The rival of this domain was the 'spiritual' domain and woman was supposed to be its guardian.[51] While the 'material' domain of the non-

Europeans had been conquered and monopolized by their colonial masters, the 'spiritual' domain was still under the control of the Indian people, sympathetically interpreted by the Orientalists like William Jones. Hence, the inherent qualities of this realm, representing Indian cultural tradition, values and Indianness, had to be protected. However, this was not possible without sculpting new gender identities incorporating new ideas of equality and liberalism. Hence, the construction of 'new' woman more than 'new' man engaged the serious attention of the social reformers and the national leadership in the freedom struggle.

IV
SCULPTING NEW GENDER IDENTITIES: MYTHS OF PAST AND CONTEMPORARY REALITY

In the foregoing discussion, I have shown how the colonial offensive on Indian society and culture had provoked the perceptive social reformers and nationalist leaders to engage in an ideological debate, accompanied by the earnest heart-searching and introspection with their imperialist adversaries. Its major result was the formulation of a two-pronged strategy: first, intellectual defence of the intrinsic superiority and dynamism of Indian culture; second, the practical task of reforming those features of social life which they perceived to be obstacles in the way of the economic and social advancement of the educated middle class. In the course of this process of social reformation and national identity formation, a new image of the Indian woman had been carved. Herein, woman, as the representative of the 'spiritual' domain, was assigned a central role. Through the construct of 'new' woman, the national leaders, who were constantly accused of their unfitness to rule as a people, sought to prove their manliness as well as superiority of Indian (sometimes used synonymously with Hindu) culture as compared with alien culture.

In this context, sculpting of new gender identities, especially, the construct of 'new' woman assumed urgency. Indian women, though not merely passive recipients of this ameliorative activity, were presented with two identities: communitarian (sometimes bordering on communal) and transregional or nationalist. The former was more effectively forged at the regional level.

Communitarian/Regional Identity

The problem of identity formation of women from the communitarian perspective in the Punjab was complex as it has no single or coherent model for regenerating the Hindu or the Sikh male from the ignominy of 'effeminacy'. The kind of woman required for the present and future to suit the urges and needs of the Western-educated male in the Punjab, who was experiencing the contradictory pulls of the twin forces of cultural marginality and educationally-inspired alienation[52] and political subjugation, was to be fashioned in a communitarian/ sectarian mould. Punjabi women, who had internalized social subjugation through religious rituals, socialization process in the family and oral culture, were again invoked to become instruments for retrieving religion and culture from abysmal degradation and from the crippling foreign stranglehold. From the late nineteenth century to the early twentieth century, their social status was made the crucial component of the projects for reforming Hinduism and nature of the Sikh tradition. In other words, the tasks of redefining and reformulation of separate religious identities and boundaries focused on the role of women while retaining the existing family structure, gender roles and property relations grounded in the patriarchal ideology. In order to clarify my point, I shall draw my illustrations from the Arya Samaj and Singh Sabha ideologies on women's question and their image in social reform literature as the 'semiotic', cultural, affective and territorial universe of the Sikhs and Hindus had remained virtually identical until Kahan Singh Nabha proclaimed separate identity of the Khalsa through his Gurmukhi tract *Ham Hindu Nahin* (1897).[53]

These two regional social reform movements, spanning the last two decades of the nineteenth century and early twentieth century, instead of being mere religious manifestations, were an integral component of the socio-cultural complexities which constituted the historical processes during that phase. Being partly a continuation of the ongoing process of socio-cultural rejuvenation and definition of group identities, these movements articulated the fears and anxieties of the small number of the already settled urban professional and trading classes as well as of the first generation of the middle classes (drawn from landed elites, small land-holders and village literati, who sought jobs in the colonial administration and related professions) regarding their material fortunes in the unfamiliar colonial milieu shaped by the new agrarian, social and education policies.[54] This hybrid class felt even more insecure and unsure about the preservation of their respective cultural traditions, identities and stability of the institution of family in the face of aggressive evangelicalism often encouraged by the British rulers. The traditional guardians of Hindu and Sikh religious traditions—*Pandits, Babas, Bhais* and *Gyanis*—also experienced an acute sense of insecurity as their vested interests lay in status quo rather than in 'inventing' tradition and crafting new and standardized identities, the ambitious project of the restless new elites.[55]

Without going into the detailed history of any of these movements, I shall focus on the issue why the Arya Samaj and Singh Sabha reformers gave centrality to women's question in the course of their quest for new identity. The urgent concern for forging a positive and self-enhancing identity was not peculiar to one socio-religious group. The communal rivalry for image-building had been caused to a great extent by the social forces unleashed by the British colonial expansion into the Punjab—communications, commercialization, education, the incorporation of the province into the global economy and the electoral politics. Thus, the Punjab of the 1890s, wherein cultural environment underwent radical changes, saw various socio-religious groups locked in a fierce battle with each other;[56] sometimes all of them were ranged against their common enemy, the Christian missionaries. In this battle, the operational tactic adopted by each group seemed to be that the positive quality of one group could only be highlighted when the negative quality of another was juxtaposed. The debates that engaged Hindus, Sikhs and Muslims with the British rulers were focused on two major themes: *(i)* creation of a 'manly' race *(ii)* ethics of puritan morality which was subsumed under the banner of a rationalized and purfied religion, unfurled by these communities-in-making. However, it was Swami Dayanand who endowed the issue of the recovery of Indian 'masculinity'[57] with special significance while expounding his vision of a reformed Hinduism, the Aryan golden age, philosophy and social institutions as embodied in the *Rig Veda*. The crucial point in his thinking was his understanding of the unique role of women in the procreation and rearing of a special breed of men. In his view, motherhood was the sole rationale of a woman's existence. That was why the *Satyarth Prakash* lays down a variety of rules and regulations for ideal conception, child care and mother care.[58] Dayanand's insistence upon the eugenical perspective led him to advocate the appointment of a wet nurse in order to enable the mother to regain her strength. His concern for racial improvement was further reinforced by his directive to husband and wife to control their passion and preserve their reproductive powers in order to beget children of "high mental calibre, strong, energetic and devout".[59] Thus, Swami Dayanand, while retaining the traditional suspicion of female sexuality, "transformed it into a force which could be constructively channelized to serve the regeneration of Aryavarta".

In the historical writings and creative literature, the Aryan theme was developed with reference to the issue of identity unlike Dayanand who linked it with his theory of reformed Hinduism, society and Indian civilization : its growth, decline and plan for the restoration of its glory. Underlying their task of reconstruction of Aryan 'masculinity' was the consciousness of European representation of the Indians particularly Bengalis as effete, unmanly, slothful and slack people. To refurbish their negative image, the nationalist writers projected heroes from an earlier era. In order to construct an alternative heroic Hindu male identity, components from history and folklore were borrowed. In their ideal heroes, qualities of pride in Aryan heritage, a strong determination to reassert Hindu identity were combined with the martial qualities associated with particular regions and groups of people such as the Marathas, Rajputs and Sikhs. The process of the reconstruction of the heroic men and women as resisters to foreign rule (earlier Muslim rule) received considerable help from the detailed works of the mid-nineteenth century British writers such as Grant Duff on the Marathas, Tod on the Rajputs and Cunningham on the Sikhs.[60] However, it was the more popular historical writings like *Rajasthaner Ithihasa*[61] and *Sikh Yudher Itihasa*[62] which created awareness about the chivalric deeds of Rajputs and great battles fought by the Sikhs against the British. Above all, it was Rajani Kanta Gupt's *Arya-kirti*'[63] (reprinted in fifteen editions) containing the sketches of great historical figures of Hindu India among Rajputs, Marathas and Sikhs which contributed to the crystallization of the ideology of the emerging trend of militant nationalism. Valorization of martial values, perhaps, could be linked to the tradition of according high status to Kshatriya values in the ancient social order.

The significance of these writings lay in bringing search for pan-Aryan consciousness and trans-regional unified Hindu identity to a decisive stage. Through his novels, Bankim Chander completed the task of forging a self-enhancing Aryan (used synonymously with national) identity for both men and women characters who combined in their personality the militancy of the martial groups and spirituality of the sanyasi.[64] It is evident from Bankim's *Krishancharita*[65] and *Anandmath*,[66] that the regenerated Hindu 'national' identity excluded the foreigners (Muslims) and the low castes owing to their non-Aryan lineage.

This process of selective reconstitution of communal identities was not peculiar to Hindus, but Sikh and Muslim social-reform ideologues, propagandists and creative writers (also described as cultural nationalists) used a similar modus operandi in the nineteenth century. This approach has influenced the reformers in the construction of gender identity. For example, the Singh Sabha reformers, whose ideology was not expounded by one single charismatic individual like Dayanand but by a diversified leadership—a mix of landed elite and lower middle-class men, belonging to villages or small towns over a period of four decades[67] —had also reflected deep anxiety over the issue of physical degeneracy indirectly while resolving the problem of the rejuvenation of Sikhs as a community. The spokesmen of the Singh Sabha movement, namely, Bhai Mohan Singh Vaid and Bhai Vir Singh, had crystallized this concern in a cluster of virtues called Kshatriya virtues of fearlessness, courage and physical prowess underpinned by deep devotion to *Namu,* i.e. the Transcendent One. The Sikh heroes and heroines in Bhai Vir Singh's novels personify these virtues while fighting against their Afghan or Mughal persecutors in order to protect and preserve their cultural identity, women's honour, homes and land.[68]

The identity crisis of Sikhs acquired a new dimension with the loss of political power in 1849 when the British annexed the Lahore kingdom. In the hard-pressing and bewildering situation of the Western cultural onslaught on Hindus, Sikhs and Muslims, further complicated by their mutual competition and antagonism, the Singh Sabha reformers perceived the issue of 'manliness' in context with their conscious and concerted drive for Sikhizing the Sikhs and monopolizing the history, imagination and experience of the entire community. Their foremost purpose was to write a separatist Sikh history, reconstitute and demarcate their social universe and tradition from the Hindus, foster and standardize a distinct Sikh identity known as *Tatkhalsa* distinct from *Sanatan* Sikhs. The British recognition of their identity as a 'martial' race[69] had made the issue of establishment of the Sikh credentials for physical power less urgent as compared with the Hindus who had been branded as cowardly, weak and impotent. For example, heroic figures in Bhai Vir Singh's novels, especially *Baba Naudh Singh* (1921), which was set in a contemporary locale, agog with Christian missionary campaign for proselytising, were not required to prove the physical attributes of courage but the quality of mental and moral resistance. Though not dissimilar in motivation from his earlier and later novels such as *Sundari,* (1898), *Bijoy Singh* (1899) and *Satwant Kaur* (1927), *Baba Naudh Singh,* whose hero lived in a Punjab village during settled times, personified the rustic common sense, self-assurance, wit and Sikh virtue and piety. Bhai Vir Singh regarded the British *Raj* as a renewed challenge for test of faith. In contrast, qualities of martial valour and physical prowess were ingrained in the lead characters of the three novels set against the backdrop of the fluid political conditions and unsettled social life owing to the impending danger of marauding soldiers in the eighteenth century. While glorifying their chivalrous deeds and relentless struggle against the Afghan or Mughal marauders (who captured Punjabi girls and awakened the sense of pride and self-awareness of the Sikhs about their legacy through the exemplary heroes and heroines Sundari, Satwant Kaur and Bijoy Singh), they chose to be initiated into the *Khalsa Panth* and practise its ideals in daily life in all circumstances.

It may be pointed out that Sundari and Satwant Kaur, despite being detached from the domestic boundaries, continued to play their nurturing roles in the form of nursing their wounded brethren or arranging and preparing food for *langar.* However, Bhai Vir Singh did not project motherhood as the sole destiny of Sikh women, the theme often reiterated by Bhai Takht Singh, the Principal of Sikh Kanya Mahavidyalaya, and the Singh Sabha tract-writers. It may be said that the Punjabi spirit of resistance, republicanism and independence provided a common bond for the characters in this historical trilogy[70] which had exhumed the tragic memory of the abducted girls from the historical psyche of the people.

The foregoing discussion has shown that the discourse on the recovery of 'manlines' among the Arya and Singh Sabha reformers, which had aroused similar anxiety in the middle-class elites elsewhere in India, was frequently interlaced with concern for restoration of spiritual superiority and moral values. Towards the close of the nineteenth century, there was a distinct shift in the national idiom from exclusive emphasis on *bahubal* (physical power) to the glorification of moral power. With the discovery about the common Aryan origin of Indians and Europeans, there was a resurgence of self-confidence in self-worth, and issue of acquiring physical parity with the British rulers was relegated to the second place but not entirely discarded. Later on, Lala Lajpat Rai would take the equation of physical vitality and fitness for granted.

The Punjab of the 1890s saw the beginnings of this change in the social reform discourse. Despite the appearance of two pamphlets, Rama Shastri's tract entitled *Intermarriage of Hindus with Europeans and Other Non-Hindu Ladies* (1896) and Bawa Chajju Singh's tract *Brahamacharya Vs. Child-Marriage* (1895)[71] about the scientific methods of race perfection, the nationalists spent more energy in establishing the superiority of Indians in the spiritual-moral sphere in contrast to Western material society. The issue of the creation of a physically and intellectually virile race had led to the recycling of the ideology of motherhood while retaining the old Indian tradition of deifying the mother. Similarly, the symbolic value of 'moral' woman was utilized by Hindus, Sikhs and Muslims for constructing their superiority around moral issues.

Among the hotly debated issues which contributed to the creation of a new morality were included vegetarianism vs. non-vegetarianism, idol-worship vs. atheism, kine-killing vs. cow-worshipping, high tradition vs. popular culture and women's question.[72] The issue that generated maximum heat and intra-communal rivalry and factional fights within one reform group was the reconstruction of an ethics of puritan morality to which most middle-class groups adhered. The Punjab of the 1890s witnessed a fierce competition among these groups to project their own high standard of morality while downgrading the others in the scale.

The colonial state assumed the role of the final arbitrator in the disputes and controversies amongst various groups regarding the morality or immorality of the customs and the health or sickness of a religious community. While doing so, it often laid down the parameters for defining morality. For example, in the *Census of India 1901 for North-West Provinces and Oudh*, the colonial state tried to pass judgement on the moral standards of Hindus:

> The code of morality of the ordinary Hindu is much the same as that of most civilized nations, though, it is nowhere reduced to a code .... The influence of the caste is, however, of the greatest importance here, and some ethnographers have expressed their opinion that the *principal sanction attaching to a breach of morality is the fear of caste penalties rather than the dread of divine punishment.* ... Almost any moral law may be broken to save the life of either a Brahman or a cow.[73] (emphasis is mine)

By expressing its disapproval for the illogical 'religiosity' of every Hindu, the colonial state had constituted one ingredient of the code of morality in terms of Western rationalism.

A perusal of the debates in the social reform press in the Punjab shows that the condition and position of women was used as a measuring rod for the health and morality of a sect, community and nation. How do we explain the middle-class social reformers' obsession with creating the 'moral' woman? It is too complex a question to be answered by a mono-casual explanation. Its partial explanation is possible. The first and the foremost is the new elite's growing awareness of the arrogance and contempt of the Europeans particularly the British as a colonizing power, which had developed a comprehensive and damaging critique of social customs, institutions, traditions and 'barbaric' treatment of women in family and society through their systematic ethnographic researches and census reports.[74] It was repeatedly argued that their humane treatment of women proved the British claims of superior morality, integrity and sense of justice. For example, Christian missionaries were proclaimed as 'pioneers of civilization' because they were the first ones to open the eyes of Hindus towards their pernicious social customs like infanticide and sati. It was the initiative of missionaries like Alexander Duff that had persuaded the British government to inaugurate a policy of liberal education.[75] This was the standard argument of 'moral imperialism'.

Obviously, the British rulers used the argument of barbarity and social backwardness of Indians for state intervention in the form of legislation for the abolition of some of the social evils in nineteenth-century British India. It may be pointed out that the British administrators and Europeans, despite their deep faith in the *mission civilisatrice,* could not have succeeded in abolishing infanticide legally without the cooperation of those Punjabis (partly influenced by the fast-spreading colonial culture and partly by the ongoing process of experimentation and renewal within their own society) who were eager to fabricate a new civil society.[76] Through these forward-looking Punjabis, public opinion had been so strongly mobilized against infanticide that is was discontinued throughout the Punjab by the 1870s. However, the British rulers did succeed in hammering a sense of inadequacy amongst Punjabis regarding their treatment of women and in launching a Punjabi version of Orientalism through G.W. Leitner—the founder of Anjuman-i-Punjab (1865) in Lahore.[77]

Besides, the British functionaries and administrators utilized ethnography for constructing a selective picture of the organization and working of native societies in order to underline 'inherent' and 'intrinsic' divisions amongst them. The *Raj* created numerous stereotypes about various socio-religious groups and qualified the divisions among them not only in terms of religious but also in terms of their attitudes towards women. The following extract from the *Census of India, 1911* illustrates the point:

> As is well-known, the Hindus are less prolific than the Muhammadans, Buddhists and Animists, and other communities owing mainly to their social customs of early marriage and compulsory widow-hood. Girls are commonly married long before they reach maturity to men who may be much older than themselves, and a very large proportion of them lose their husbands while they are still of child-bearing age, or even before they have attained it. Apart from this, the Hindus have perhaps suffered more than their share from the vicissitudes of the decade. ... In the Punjab they have suffered an artificial loss by the removal of the restriction of the term Sikh to those who wear the *kes* and observe the other rules of conduct ordained by Guru Gobind Singh.[78]

This extract placed Hindus and Muslims in an antagonistic relationship and in a defensive position in relation to the British by constructing two stereotypes at one stroke: child-marrying Hindus and prolific Muslims. These myths were further elaborated. The notion that Hindus were weaklings was linked with the prevalent practice of child-marriage in various parts of India.[79] By using the cliché of 'ignorant' Muslim, the myth of 'multiplying' Muslim was validated.

Sikhs, who were gradually separated from Hindus through the application of arbitrary decisions, were no exception to this myth-making. Regarding them, two myths were constructed and sustained through almost the entire period of colonial rule in the Punjab. While the first projected them as a distinct *panth* and a young nation,[80] the second built their image as a martial race[81] and the British, being convinced of their fighting ability, were keen to utilize them as soldiers in the future imperialist wars as the First and Second World Wars would show. I need not go either into the question of contradictions creeping into the material and data in the official reports vis-a-vis their basic assumptions or into the issue of challenge posed to the colonial stereotypes by various groups. The relevant point for us is how the propagation of these myths by the *Raj* created an atmosphere wherein the perception of cultural differences among various groups was sharpened. Its bearing on the process of gender construction was no less significant because growing differentiation of social groups along lines of caste, tribe and religion pushed women's question to the centre-stage and set the tone for its debate.

Such a horrifying picture of the low status and maltreatment of women, believed to be true for the whole of northern India, had a special piquancy for the Punjabi society wherein cultural and moral values were deeply coloured by peasant mentality. In Section IV of this essay, an attempt has been made to demonstrate with illustrations from Punjabi agricultural proverbs, sayings and folk-songs that patriarchal values had governed the daily life and role of women. In such a social-set-up, male honour, prestige and happiness were perceived to lie in the control of a women's sexuality.[82] Protection of the virginity of an unmarried daughter was regarded as a ticklish problem for Hindus, Muslims and Sikhs. Woman's chastity, which has lost none of its social value even today, was highly prized in the nineteenth-century Punjabi society where bloody feuds over land and women spilled over many generations.[83] Any kind of misbehaviour was interpreted in terms of sexual misbehaviour, lack of character and morality. This is illustrated from the popularity of legends of Heer–Ranjha, Mirza–Sahiban, and Sasi–Punnu[84] whose young heroines were poisoned or forcibly separated from their lovers in the name of family honour, prestige and happiness but dubbed as betrayers by their lovers.

These patriarchal attitudes and notions about the control of women's sexuality, prevalent in the contemporary society, have been depicted in the memoirs of ambitious brothers and sons of landed-elite and rural literati who had joined the ranks of middle classes and rose to be army officers, bureaucrats, engineers, judges, lawyers, teachers and creative writers. For example, while describing the marriage customs in the nineteenth-century Punjab, Prakash Tandon focused on the value attached to a girl's modesty:

> If the boy's family came to suspect that the girl's parents had not taken enough care to guard her modesty, or if there was the smallest suspicion that the girl was immodest herself, the betrothal would immediately be broken off. Such girls brought shame upon their families.[85]

Prakash Tandon concedes that illicit sexual relationships were not too many and the society was "almost puritanical in its morals and conventions, but it was pragmatic in its approach to the odd lapse and infraction".

The Punjabi society was equally concerned about controlling the sexuality of widows, especially those in the child-bearing age. After the death of her husband, a woman was supposed to de-sexualize herself.[86] A young widow was regarded as a problem and burden for both her parents and husband's family. The ritual of *kanyadan* as a part of the marriage ceremony, especially among the high-caste Hindus seemed to have absolved the married woman's parents from any further responsibility. Debarred from pleasures of life, the Hindu widow had to live literally like a bonded slave in her dead husband's family or bow to the custom of self-immolation i.e., sati. The rural areas of central Punjab and south-east Punjab, where the widow-remarriage had social sanction in the form of *Chaddar Andezi* or *Karewa* among Jats, women had no choice but to marry the elder or younger brother or even the cousins of her husband, in order to avoid division of land and other property. However, no section of the middle classes in this region would accept widow-remarriage at any cost before Arya Samaj ideology had validated it through their re-interpretation of the *Vedas*.[87]

Obviously, Dayanand's ideas about the amelioration of women's condition were novel for the Punjabi society wherein social reform activity had remained perfunctory up to the 1870s. His formulations about the new role-models for women, necessitating education, marriage reforms especially widow-remarriage and *niyoga* (levirate marriage), unleashed long-drawn out controversies among Hindus, Sikhs and Muslims in Punjab. They were confronted with the dilemma to choose between two alternatives: whether to protect their honour as Punjabis in the eyes of their tradition-bound *biradari* and to face the ridicule of the colonial officials, Christian missionaries, etc. or to modernize themselves. As nationalists, their task was to strike a compromise between tradition and modernity as both were required by the nationalists and the social reformers. In such a problematic situation, women became the ideological battleground where these complex issues had to be contested and resolved. It became alarming and demanded immediate attention with the intrusion of active *zenana* missions into Punjabi homes whose stability depended upon women's unquestioning subservience to patriarchal values. As women were perceived to be the most vulnerable part of society, humanizing women's life and renewing their commitment to religion, and cultural traditions in the light of elementary knowledge imparted in the two premier Arya Samaj and Singh Sabha educational institutions–Kanya Mahavidyalaya, Jalandhar and Sikh Kanya Mahavidyala, Ferozepore–became urgent for the social reformers.

Trans-regional/Nationalist Construct

I shall discuss only those features of this construct which are relevant for understanding its linkages with the communitarian constructs of 'new' woman, put forth by Arya Samaj and Singh Sabha reformers, who had reformulated the separate Hindu identity and Sikh identity. Each one of these constructs drew elements from a space inhabited by an urbanized middle-class upper caste Hindu male's perception of the ideal woman[88]. Gandhi had added a dynamic concept—political role—in his model of social role for woman without revolutionizing assumptions on which these middle-class reformers had based their construct. He had redefined politics to reconcile it with the space of home.

The Arya Samaj, Singh Sabha and other nineteenth-century reformers had reaffirmed the doctrine of 'separate spheres' rooted in biological differences. Differences between sexes were used to legitimize different social and cultural roles for women in society and prescribe a moral code for their interaction with each other.

Conceptualizations of these two spheres as separate dichotomized the area of activity for men and women. It implied confinement of a woman in private space inside the house and free movement of a man in public space but entry into private space according to his need and convenience. While family socialized boys and girls for these gendered roles, marriage as a social institution articulated these differences within an ideological framework. The male was the 'bread winner', the 'provider' and the 'protector' and thus 'superior'; woman was the 'mother' and 'nurturer', the 'giver' and she possessed the quality of tolerance, patience, self-sacrifice, humanity and moral courage; man could be 'selfish', 'possessive', independent but lacking in real strength and 'intuition'. Thus, language was used as a tool to initiate women into the process of imbibing cultural ideas and values that shaped their images of themselves and inform the visions they entertained about future.[89]

The concepts of femininity and motherhood were given centrality in the construction of the modernized version of woman, whose subjugation seemed less galling because of the high projection of her spiritual role. In the Indian tradition of deifying the mother, representations of Durga, Saraswati, Sita and Vaishno as mothers were held up as examples of the deep veneration for women in Indian society. The centrality of *mattabhav* (motherhood)[90] was used to imprint the idea of an ancient, vigorous and superior civilization upon the British mind. In the framework of this definition, 'motherhood' implied love, caring, suffering, sacrifice for children, moral strength and creative energy. Its major consequence was the formulation of the ideology of motherhood and the crystallization of the image of a moral, powerful, nurturing and spiritual Mother India—symbolizing the essence of the cultural superiority of Indians.

The eugenical perspective was incorporated in the image of the mother who nurtured a race of supermen—physically strong and morally superior. In this ideology of motherhood, procreation was given a place of honour as in the Indian tradition. Idealization of motherhood in the nationalist construct was shared by the urban reformers. Whereas the utilitarian purpose of nurturing a generation of Indians fit for self-governance was articulated with sophistication by the reformers and national leaders, the peasant society in central and south-east Punjab expressed the male preference through popular sayings in the typical folk idiom. The overall thrust of these formulations was to emphasize the instrumentality of women in cultural, socio-economic and political life.

The nationalist construct of 'new' woman, which tended to treat gender as a homogeneous category, was based on mythology, history and literature. The mythical figures of Sita, Savitri, Draupadi and Gargi were projected as the epitome of the virtues of Indian womanhood. Uma Chakravarti has rightly commented, "Women of the past were valorized in two separate ways for their spiritual potential and their role as *Sahadharminis* (partners in religious duties) in ancient times, and as heroic resisters who cheerfully chose death rather than dishonour".[91] From elements out of history and folklore, representing images of glorious women of the golden past, was fashioned a new identity of women to suit the ends of present and future. The choice of aspects of tradition and the proportion in which these were mixed varied from each reformer to each nationalist leader.[92] However, there was considerable agreement on certain essentials. On the issue of the fundamental characteristics of Indian womanhood, more specifically Hindu womanhood, the liberal-revivalist divide was minimal.

Reformers of all hues and the nationalist leadership proposed to enhance the social presence of women and focus on refashioning their minds and personality. Despite the fierce debate on the content and level of female education, there was no doubt about its efficacy in equipping them with qualities of intelligent comprehension, habits of cleanliness, orderliness and self-discipline. All these virtues were added to the baggage of traditional womanhood in order to improve family life without threatening patriarchal hierarchy, male control of sexuality and stability of social order.

Both the nationalist construct and the reformers' image of woman gave certain freedom and autonomy to her. In order to qualify this freedom and to contain it within the parameters of patiarchal ideology, the nationalist leadership formulated a 'common' woman construct.[93] This construct covered prostitutes, nautch girls, street vendors, fishermen and washerwomen. By projecting them as coarse, vulgar and promiscuous by virtue of being somewhat independent as wage-earners, the nationalist leaders had drawn boundaries of moral space for 'new' woman's movement and a code of conduct for her behaviour. This differentiation between the 'common' woman and the much valorized 'new' woman was used as an argument for confining women to spinning and swadeshi, later giving reluctant legitimacy to their participation in dharnas and processions.

Another interesting and common point in the nationalist and communitarian construct of new woman was the valorization of widowhood which gave social legitimacy to the remarriage of child-widows and thus an oblique approval to peasant custom of widow-remarriage with variations in pragmatic concerns. For example, Gandhi's construct of woman was modelled on the basis of received notion of the noble qualities of the Hindu widow. Projecting it as Hinduism at its best, Gandhi regarded the "... widow's life as a reflection of Hinduism. When I see a widow, I instinctively bow my head in reverence. Man is but a clod before her. A widow's patient suffering is impossible to rival".[94] Thus, he had created a god like woman who was an asset for social welfare and national service.

It may be pointed out that the obsessive concern for a woman's chastity and honour was shared by reformers, national leaders, high caste Hindus and peasants. Their valorization of widowhood and their sanction to widow-remarriage with riders were motivated by their keen desire to preserve social order, patriarchal control over female sexuality and monopoly of control over property. However, compromises had visibly been made to make a woman's role more valuable in family, society and politics in the colonial milieu.

Did these visions of womanhood, constructed by the reformist and nationalist leadership, relate to the reality of women's lives, their experiences and actions in contemporary society? There is enough evidence to indicate that many women had internalized the constructed and 'invented' notions of the 'golden' age and believed in the model of superwoman possessing qualities of learning, heroism, spiritual power and high-mindedness of *Sahadharmini* of the Vedic times. For the 'new' Singh woman, Sundari was the 'paradigm' of Sikh ethics encapsulated in the maxim—*Kirt Karna, Vand Chhakna, te Namu Japna*—to labour for one's keep, to share with others, and to practise the recitation of the Divine name.[95] As the spokesman of Singh Sabha, Bhai Vir Singh articulated his anxiety that women were more vulnerable to superstition, idolatry and forgetfulness of the Transcendent One.[96] The ideologies of both the social reform groups shared the belief that rejuvenation of Hindus and Sikhs was possible only through the creation of a 'moral' woman. Thus, they sought to create model women through careful socialization in schools and homes.

In order to evaluate the extent of their conformity or deviation from the models of 'new' woman, let us briefly review the career of three women: Sarla Debi Chaudharani from an urban, educated, liberal and highly-placed family, Laxmi Arya from an orthodox and rural background and Rameshwari Nehru having an aristocratic upbringing.

Sarla Debi Chaudharani[97] (grand-niece of Rabindra Nath Tagore and the daughter of a well-known former Secretary of the Congress, J.N. Ghoshal and the Bengali novelist Swarna Kumari Debi) has been eulogized by the Bengalis as well as the Punjabis for her contribution to the nationalist movement in both these regions. A cursory glance at her autobiography shows that this phase had virtually ended with her marriage in 1905 to Ram Bhuj Dutt Chaudhari, an Arya Samajist and a nationalist leader. At the age of thirty-three, Sarla Debi had been emotionally blackmailed to marry this widower by her mother who pleaded that their high-caste family's social prestige would be damaged in case their daughter remained single. Her conformity with the existing patriarchal norms offers a significant contrast to her behaviour as an unmarried girl.

For example, Sarla Debi had defied her parents by taking up a job away from home when she was barely nineteen years old. She had also been actively involved in setting up a secret society, *Suhrid Samiti* at Mymensingh in 1901. Apart from organizing physical training camps for Bengali youth, she had mobilized them for participation in revolutionary activities through her credentials and articles in *Bharati* (earlier edited by her mother). After her marriage in 1905, the centre of her political activities shifted from Bengal to the Punjab. Nevertheless, she continued to exert a powerful influence upon the Bengali youth and to coordinate their activities from Lahore. Apart from organizing the Punjabi women under the banner of Arya Samaj, Sarla Debi was also a founder-member of the Bharat Stri-Mahamandal. Neither her activities as a Congress worker up to 1945 nor her writings, including patriotic poems, had taken up the issue of womens' rights and problems.

In 1919, Sarla Debi became Gandhi's ardent follower and admirer. Owing to her dynamic personality, she became one of the leaders of the *swadeshi* movement and of the campaign against Dyerism in this region. In the course of their long association, Sarla Debi and Gandhi developed a bond of mutual regard and affection. While the former hailed her mentor as the "innermost soul of India", the latter regarded his admirer (Sarla Debi) as his "spiritual wife".[98] It may be pointed out that their relationship never occasioned any controversy. Besides, the elite response to the entire spell of Sarla Debi's activities illustrated the current perception of gender roles. It is significant that neither the communitarian nor the nationalist construct disapproved of her militancy and high visibility in the mass movements from the 1920s to the 1940s as it tended to reinforce the 'invented' notion of 'heroic' and 'moral' urban woman.

My second example, Laxmi Arya, [99] despite her deviation from the accepted code of conduct for a widow in an orthodox peasant society, has been valorized for her role as a freedom fighter in the form of an award of *Tamra-patra* and a pension by the state government. A brief review of her life story is instructive. Born in December 1893 in a *Jat* family of a small village Rohra in district Rohtak (South-east Punjab, now known as Haryana), Laxmi Arya became an important participant in the Gandhian movements from the 1920s to 1940s. Brought up as an orphan by her grandparents, she became the victim of the then prevalent custom of child marriage. Married at the age of eleven to Chaudhari Rati Ram, she was ill-treated by her mother-in-law for bringing inadequate dowry. Laxmi Arya, who lost her husband in 1921, had to suffer more humiliation and physical torture at the hands of her mother-in-law as she refused to conform with the normal practice of widow re-marriage in the rural society.

Her brother Balwant Singh, who was a staunch Arya Samajist, rescued her from the sad fate of a child widow and urged her to educate herself. Despite stiff opposition from her relatives, Laxmi not only began her self-education from scratch but also joined the *swadeshi* movement in 1921 along with her brother and adopted *khaddar* as her dress. Very soon the villagers began to call her a regular Gandhiite. In 1924, when her brother died, Laxmi was again obliged to carve out her own destiny. She decided to join Kanya Maha Vidyalaya in order to continue her education She lived in *Vidhwa Ashram* (widow's home) which was an integral part of the institution. Owing to economic hardship, she could not continue her education beyond the eighth class and took up a job as teacher in Kanya Gurukal, Khanpur for one year and six months.

From 1930 onwards, when she joined Sabarmati Ashram, Laxmi participated in constructive programme and political activities such as picketing liquor shops, no-tax campaigns, salt satyagraha and individual satyagraha against India's enforced participation in the Second World War. She suffered imprisonment for varied terms in jails and was fined a number of times as a picketer. Being illiterate, she was given 'C' class as a political prisoner. Besides her active participation in the campaign for uplift of Harijans, Laxmi donated her agricultural land for this cause.

In her own way, Laxmi had worked to redefine women's self-image and role in the rural society through her personal conduct. After Partition she accompanied Bibi Amtus Salaam and Laxmi Trikha (ardent disciples of Gandhi) to Pakistan in order to bring back the abducted women as part of the rehabilitation work. It can be said that these women had become somewhat ambivalent to the prevalent notion of female worth, adjudged in terms of physical chastity which had been violated without their consent.

My third example comes from Rameshwari Nehru's life and career.[100] Her brief life sketch is likely to give us an idea of the process of her transformation from a subdued girl into an articulate and critical woman. Born in 1886, Rameshwari Nehru belonged to a Kashmiri Brahmin family which had settled in the Punjab during the reign of Maharaja Ranjit Singh. Her father, Raja Narendra Nath, despite his strong inclination towards Arya Samaj, disapproved of its ideal of 'new' woman and its campaign for female education. Obviously, Rameshwari, after being given somewhat informal training in reading and writing but more intensive schooling in domestic arts befitting a purdah family, was married to Brijlal Nehru, an officer in the Accounts Department. Soon after their marriage, the newly married couple shifted to Anand Bhavan (Allahabad) where her husband had been brought up by his Western-educated and liberal-minded uncle Pandit Motilal Nehru. As a result of her constant exposure to new ideas, discussions about current socio-political trends in Europe and heated debates on the extensive involvement of women in the ongoing national struggle for freedom and as a champion of social classes especially as a founder-editor of *Stree Darpan* (Allahabad), a Hindi magazine for women in north India.

As one of the early crusaders for Indian women's movement, she utilized *Stree Darpan* (started in 1909) for initiating a dialogue between diehard traditionalists and liberals on vital socio-cultural and political issues.[101] It is not surprising that the journal should have targeted and addressed its message to the bulk of Hindi-knowing middle-class women throughout north India. As a social-action journal, it had sought to inculcate a critical temper among its readers and to project a new image of Indian women which certainly did not resemble the model of an uncompromising rebel as presented by Pandita Ramabai. Without disowning their nurturing roles, these sensitive and critical women had argued that they sought to acquire the qualities of alertness, courage, fearlessness, truthfulness, experience in world affairs and an intelligent as well as enlightened outlook in order to perform their nurturing and public roles efficiently. A new sense of self-respect and pride in their identity as women and awareness of their power in their roles as daughters, sisters, mothers and wives had exuded from articles, poems, stories and editorials in the columns of *Stree Darpan*.

Besides, contributors to *Stree Darpan* had demanded the reformulation of a more rational and equitable code of conduct and scrapping of discriminatory social regulations and *shastric* prescriptions regarding the socialization of male and female children, nature of their education and distribution of socio-economic power among them. As crusaders for social reform and national freedom, they accused Indian men of blatant hypocrisy which was exposed by their demand for Home Rule from the British rulers and by their persistent denial of autonomy and human rights to Indian women. It may be pointed out that these women had also urged their sisters to do self-introspection and to liberate themselves from their obsession with ornaments, ignorance, supersititions and blind faith in outdated social customs, rituals and fake religious men.

Keeping in view Rameshwari Nehru's work as a crusader for women's movement both as an editor and an activist in the All-India Women's Conference as well as her extensive work for the uplift of Harijans, should she be categorized as a conformist or rebel? It may be conceded that she had followed the negotiatory path between the male social reformers' and Western feminists' prescriptions for restructuring female lives, ideals for Indian womanhood and their roles on domestic and public terrain. Obviously, she had represented the values of new patriarchy which advocated mobility within the existing institutional framework but resisted any structural changes. Broadly speaking, the spirit of accommodation shown by her generation had grown out of tactical reasons and not for lack of intelligent awareness of the grim experiential reality of women's lives. Thus, internalization of values and role models was selective but not mechanical or wholesale.

Rameshwari Nehru was a progressive woman who had effectively used the print media, i.e. *Stree Darpan* for bringing about a qualitative change in the self-image as well as social and intellectual outlook of Indian women, particularly Hindi-educated women. They were equipped to forge new bonds and loyalties beyond their kinship networks in the course of their interaction through the columns of the journal which had helped them to carve out new spaces and roles for themselves. In fact, Rameshwari Nehru had activated them, to use Herman's phrase, for 'seizing speech', i.e. expressing their anger, silence or gaps in their consciousness. Rameshwari Nehru enabled readers and contributors of *Stree Darpan* to hone and utilize their articulation skills to penetrate the hegemonic male discourse and forced men to listen and respond to their voices. I may add that Sarla Debi and Laxmi Arya, who had neither grappled with the issues of gender subordination and exploitation in writing nor launched campaigns for women's uplift, had experimented with new roles.

V

Conclusion

In conclusion, I wish to underline three points relating to the process of gender construction in the colonial Punjab. Firstly, the bulk of middle classes in this region, having their hearts and minds firmly anchored in peasant ethos but their material interests tied to the urban colonial world, perhaps consciously assumed the role of an improvised bridge between the rural and fast-expanding urban culture. In their perception of gender relations, the patriarchal ideology continued to dominate. The institution of patriarchal family remained a common denominator of the socio-economic and even political networks between rural and urban areas. Similarities in patriarchal practices in rural and urban areas were visible in the maintenance of caste and class basis of marriage as well as norms of sexual morality particularly chastity in the case of woman. In fact, the paradigm of the new 'moral' woman, posited as the opposite of the 'common' woman who was coarse, loud, vulgar, quarrelsome, sexually promiscuous and devoid of superior moral sense, was shared by the nineteenth-century middle-class social reformers, Hindu and Sikh landed elite in this region and the nationalists and it continues to shape the image and consciousness of women.

Secondly, the rural elites turned middle class, who were questioning the existing pattern of gender relations and seeking solutions to the concrete problems arising out of the rapidly changing external and internal situations, found their answers from a variety of sources. These could be described as reinterpreted classical tradition, modernized folk forms, the legal idea of equality in a liberal democratic state, the utilitarian theory of bureaucratic and industrial practice and the new kind of patriarchy. It is in the context of reconstituting patriarchy, wherein the Arya Samaj and Singh Sabha's model of 'moral' and 'spiritual' woman (essentially rooted in the values of a peasant society) became relevant. The 'new' woman was subjected to public in addition to family patriarchy. In order to establish a standard pattern of social behaviour for women, conduct books were published and circulated by the Arya Samaj and Singh Sabha. These books contained guidelines for each aspect of a middle-class woman's life.

A close perusal of the normative literature for women showed that the middle classes had contrived a conscious interlocking of the selective elements of Western and Eastern patriarchy through the sex-differentiated formal education in order to create the model mother and wife to suit the new circumstances and also to absolve themselves of the charge of being primitive, cruel and selfish. Projected as a symbol of cultural superiority, the new image of the middle-class woman combined the bourgeois virtues of orderliness, thrift, cleanliness, personal sense of responsibility, literacy, accounting and hygiene with the traditional feminine virtues of chastity, self-sacrifice, service, submissiveness, devotion, patience, etc. Complicity, not resistance, was a desirable attitude. Thus, the most prized component in the standard version of urban 'moral' woman, whether Sikh or Hindu, was her ability to imbibe the ideology of subordination vis-a-vis men. The aim of socialization process in the family and educational programme for men was exactly the opposite: internalization of their hegemonic position and active role in the public domain. In the new patriarchy, however, the ideal of *Sahadharmini* or companion in a monogamous marriage was glorified and thus by implication discarding the prevalent norm of sexual promiscuity in rural society.

In the reconstituted patriarchy, a qualified concept of freedom for women was propagated. The social reformers and national leaders had reached a tacit agreement on this issue. As long as women demonstrated the so-called feminine/spiritual qualities including submission to the new norms of social behaviour, existing pattern of gender hierarchy and roles, they could go to school, travel in public conveyance, watch public entertainment programmes, participate in nationalist agitations, fund-raising campaigns and take up jobs. However, empowerment of women through education and social and legal reforms was not sought either by the nineteenth-century social reformers or by the nationalist leaders like Lala Lajpat Rai and only to a limited extent by Mahatma Gandhi. The fear that some of these reforms being advocated for women, might eventually lead to their emancipation, made the issue of social reform particularly marriage reforms and higher education a source of friction and factional disputes among the liberals and conservatives.

Thirdly, the colonial state and the middle classes seemed to share a common terrain but not goals regarding the project of reconstituting patriarchies and reinforcing the subordination and deprivation of women from access to the resources of economic, social and political power. The processes, which made the definition of gender crucial to the formation of class and gender ideologies during the colonial period, were activated in the agrarian economy of Punjab by the British policies. The colonial state had to formulate new land revenue policies for extracting surplus and resort to selective modernization of economy as exemplified in the Canal Colonization of barren lands in the West Punjab. It had also to create classes and win allies among the landed elite and peasantry to bolster its image and fight its wars as well as to establish its hegemonic rule in India.

Apart from strengthening the existing unequal gender relations, these changes were favourable for reconstituting patriarchies which further helped in the exclusion of women from ownership or control of means of production prevalent in the pre-colonial agrarian structure. Among the measures adopted to ensure the economic subordination of women included putting individual property rights primarily in the hands of men with women having only ancillary rights—dependent on their subordinate relationships with men— transforming existing matrilineal systems into patrilineal patterns of succession, etc. A further marginalization of women from public life took place due to the impersonal bureaucratic rule of law and by bringing them under its control, which helped to intensify their dependence on men.

Even through the laws which were codifications of the customs of the dominant land-owning and other rural groups, juridical sanction was given to certain patriarchal practices regarding marriage, succession and adoption. Thus, the statutory Hindu law was actually a codification of high-caste Hindu norms, which were privileged over customary law. This could only be to the disadvantage of both urban and rural Hindu women.

In the end, it may be stated that the process of construction of gender identity was suspended before the social and mental personality of 'new' woman and her consciousness could be infused with inner dynamism which would enable her to become autonomous to choose her own destiny. Perhaps, the reason underlying the diversion of the male leadership's attention from women's question was that the emerging middle classes had succeeded in their primary aim of creating a well-defined and strong political identity underpinned by their assertive and separate cultural identities. They had also been able to standardize their distinct identities as religious communities and construct undifferentiated Hindu and Sikh social universe and brotherhood, bound by bonds of a purified or rationalized religion, a set of common *rites de passage* and high tradition of new elite. Put at the centre-stage in the late nineteenth century, the 'new' woman was pushed back to the sanctuary of home when the time came for sharing political, economic and social resources and power after 1947. The new patriarchal approach is crystallized in the comments of the eighty-year-old woman-freedom fighter, Savitri, whose husband Comrade Ramkishan became the Chief Minister of Punjab in independent India. She said:

> *Jaloosan which naare lagaan layi sadi lor si. Jadoan rajnitik takat wandan da waqt aaya sanu kya gya 'tusi tan ghar di rani ho! Iss kichar wich hath gande karan di ki tuq!'*
>
> (We were useful for raising slogans as volunteers in nationalist agitations. When the time came to share political power, our husbands, who were active in politics, told us, "You are the queen of the domestic realm. Why do you soil your hands in dirty politics!")

REFERENCES

1. For a detailed exposition of the theory of capitalist world system see Immanuel Wallerstein, *The Modern World System,* (New York: Academic Press, 1974). For its interpretation from neo-Marxist or unequal exchange conception of development see Samir Amin, *Unequal Development,* (New York: Monthly Review Press, 1976). E. Laclau, 'Feudalism and Capitalism in Latin America', *New Left Review,* 67, (1971), pp. 19–38. A.K. Bagchi has argued that colonial rule de-industrialized India. For example, see his article, 'De-industrialization in India: Some Theoretical Implications', *Journal of Development Studies,* 12, 1975–76, pp. 136–64.
2. Marilyn French, *Beyond Power: On Men, Women and Morals,* (New York: Summit, 1985). Also Susan Griffin, *Women and Nature: The Roaring Inside Her* (New York: Harper Colophon, 1980). There is growing literature challenging the association of reason and masculinity. See for example, Mary Hawkesworth, 'Knowers, Knowing, Known: Feminist Theory and Claim of Truth', presented at the Women Studies Resource Centre, Ontario Institute for Studies in Education, Toronto, Ontario, January 12, 1987.
3. Alison Jagger, *Feminist Politics and Human Nature,* (Totowa, New Jersey: Rowman and Allen Helm, 1983), p. 344. Also O'Brien, *The Politics of Reproduction* (London: Routledge and Kegan Paul, 1983), pp. 1–15, 18. Understanding it as the role of the individual, John Money had described gender role as everything that a person says and does, to indicate to others or to the self the degree in which one is male or female or ambivalent. It includes but is not restricted to sexual arousal and response.
4. John Money and Anke. A. Erhardt, *Man & Woman, Boy & Girl: The Differentiation and Dimorphism of Gender Identity from Conception to Maturity,* (Baltimore: The Johns Hopkins University Press, 1972), p. 284.
5. *Ibid.,* p. 146.
6. John Money and Patricia Tucker, *Sexual Signatures: On Being a Man or Woman,* (Toronto: Little Brown & Company, 1975), p. 40. Transvestism is a clear example of this mixed-up sense of gender. A man with a sense of being feminine while cross-dressing is excitedly aware of being a male.
8. Money and Erhardt, *Man & Woman, Boy & Girl,* p. 146.
9. *Ibid.* Money laments the 'semantic handicap' of not having a single term to refer to 'gender-identity-role'. He is concerned that without such a term we may slip into the logical and conceptual confusion to think that one can juxtapose identity and role. The term 'gender-role-identity' has been used in I. Frieze, J Parsons, P. Johnson, D. Ruble and G. Zellman,

Women and Sex Roles, (New York: H.H. Norton and Company, 1978).

10. Robert Dahl, *Preface to Democratic Theory,* (Chicago: University of Chicago Press, 1956), pp. 12, 13, 79–81.
11. *Census of Punjab 1881, Report,* (Calcutta: Superintendent of Government of India Press, India, 1883), p. 7.
12. *Ibid.*, p. 2.
13. *Census of India, 1911, Report,* p. 20.
14. For the exposition of the concept and features of 'dominant caste' see M.N. Srinivas, 'The Dominant Caste in Rampura', *American Anthropologist,* 61, (1959), pp. 1–16. In his *Caste in Modern India and Other Essays,* (Bombay: Asia Publishing House, 1962), p. 90. Srinivas specifies Jats as the 'dominant caste' in the Central Punjab and South-east Punjab (now called Haryana).
15. Denzil Ibbetson, *Punjab Castes,* (First published in 1881; reprinted, Patiala: Language Department Punjab, 1970), p. 109.
16. Prakash Tandon, *Punjabi Saga,* (1857–1987). Pt I, *Punjabi Century* (1857–1947), (Delhi: Penguin Books, India, 1988), pp. 73–75.
17. *Census of India 1901, Report,* p. 80.
18. Denzil Ibbetson, *Punjab Castes,* p. 218.
19. Prakash Tandon, *Punjabi Saga,* p. 38.
20. Richard G. Fox, 'Urban Class and Communal Consciousness in Colonial Punjab: The Genesis of India's Intermediate Regime', *Modern Asian Studies,* 18.3 (1984), p. 465. Indu Banga, *Agrarian System of the Sikhs: Late Eighteenth and Early Nineteenth Centuries,* (New Delhi: Manohar Book Service), 1978.
21. Discussion in the four foregoing paragraphs is based on Richard G. Fox, *Lions of Punjab: Culture in the Making,* (New Delhi: Archives Publishers, 1987), pp. 56–60.
22. N. Chodorov, *The Reproduction of Mothering; Psychoanalysis and Sociology of Gender,* (California: University of California Press, 1978), pp. 38–39.
23. Jainarayan Verma. *Hariyanvi* Lokoktiyan: Shastriya Vishleshan, (Delhi: Adarsh Sahitya Prakashan, 1972), p. 30.
24. Kishan Singh Bedi, (trans.), *Agricultural Proverbs of the Punjab,* (Chandigarh: Public Relations Department, Punjab), p. 19.
25. Informal chat with my grandmother Parmeshwari Devi and her peer group.
26. Jainarayan Verma, *Haryana Ki Lokoktiyan,* p. 123.
27. For details of these factors and other contributory causes see *Census of India 1931 Punjab, Report,* Vol. XVII, pt. 1, p. 156. Also E.A. Gait, *Census of India, 1911,* Report, Vol. 1, pp. 214-9.
28. Kishan Singh Bedi, *Agricultural Proverbs of the Punjab*, p. 55.
31. *Ibid.,* p. 77. Two proverbs cited in the next three paragraphs have been extracted from the book under reference, pp. 38, 68.

32. *Ibid.,* p. 110.
33. H.M. Rattigan, *Digest of Civil Law for the Punjab Chiefly Based on the Customary Law as at Present Ascertained,* (First Published 1880; reprinted, Allahabad: The University Book Agency, 1966), p. 747.
34. Kishan Singh Bedi, *Agricultural Proverbs of the Punjab,* p. 98.
35. *Ibid,* p. 28.
36. For the effects of Customary Law and Hindu Law on widows and the remarriage question see Lucy Carrol, 'Law, Custom and Statutory Social Reform' in *Indian Economic and Social History Review,* 24, 4 October–December (1983), pp. 363–89.
37. Jainarayan Verma, *Haryana Ki Lokoktiyan,* p. 127.
38. *Multan District Gazetteer,* 1901–02, p. 98.
39. Prakash Tandon, *Punjabi Saga,* p. 38. Also Ved Mehta, *Daddyji,* (Delhi: Vikas Publishing House Pvt. Ltd., 1972), p. 8.
40. Ved Mehta, *op. cit.,* p. 10.
41. Richard G. Fox, 'Urban Class and Communal Consciousness in Colonial Punjab', 465.
42. Ved Mehta, *n.* 39, p. 40.
43. *Ibid.,* p. 56.
44. James Mill, *The History of British India,* with notes by H.H. Wilson, (London: James Madden, 1840), pp. 312–13.
45. Katherine Mayo, *Mother India,* (London: Howard Baker, 1917), p. 16.
46. *Ibid.,* pp. 33.55. In these pages, Mayo has reviewed the debates on Indian Consent Act 1891. Also Mrinalini Sinha, 'Colonial Policy and the Ideology of Moral Imperialism in Late Nineteenth Century Bengal' in M. Kimmel, *Changing Men: New Directions in Research on Men and Masculinity,* (New Delhi: Sage Publications, 1987), p. 224.
47. Mrinalini Sinha, *Supra,* p. 226.
48. Katherine Mayo, *n.* 45, p. 48.
49. *Collected Works of Mahatma Gandhi,* Vol. XXXV, 1927–28, (New Delhi : Ministry of Information and Broadcasting, 1964), pp. 235, 441. In order to rectify the one-sided picture, containing palpable falsehoods with exaggerations and suppression of facts, he urged US-based Dhan Gopal Mukherjee to arrange a lecture tour of Sarojini Naidu. Through her eloquence, the poetess would certainly draw crowds and dispel the wrong impressions created by Mayo's *Mother India.*
50. Himani Bannerji, 'Fashioning a Self: Educational Proposals for and by Women in Popular Magazines in Colonial Bengal', in *Economic and Political Weekly,* 26, 43, 26 October 1991, pp. 45–42. In Himani's view, the language of social reform in the 19th century and the early years of the 20th century is inscribed with the discourse of 'crisis'. Allusions to 'continuity and change', 'tradition and modernity', all involve the management of gender roles and division of labour outside and within the family, in terms of the needs of the new times. For example, Tapan

Ray Choudhary in *Europe Reconsidered: Perceptions of the West in Nineteenth Century Bengal,* (Delhi: Oxford University Press, 1988), pp. ix–x, makes this idea of 'new times' and encounter between 'the East' and 'the West', the point of departure of his whole interpretative and historical exercise. The "encounter", he points out, meant "revolution in their world view".

51. Partha Chatterjee, 'The Nationalist Resolution of Women's Question', in Kumkum Sangari and Sudesh Vaid, eds., *Recasting Woman: Essays in Colonial History,* (New Delhi: Kali for Women, 1989), pp. 238–39.
52. Kenneth W. Jones, *Arya Dharma: Hindu Consciousness in 19th Century Punjab,* (New Delhi: Manohar Publications, 1976), p. 314.
53. For a detailed discussion of the shared cultural tradition, language and social customs, see Harjot S. Oberoi. 'From Ritual to Counter-Ritual: Rethinking the Hindu–Sikh Question 1884–1915', in Joseph T. O'Connel, Milton Israel, Willard G. Oxtoby, eds. with W.H. McLeod and J.S. Grewal, visiting eds., *Sikh History and Religion in the Twentieth Century,* (Toronto: S. Asia Studies, University of Toronto, 1988), pp. 139–147.
54. Ruchi Ram Sahni, "Self Revelations of an Octogenerian", unpublished manuscript in the possession of Prof. Ashok Sahni, his grandson who is currently teaching in Punjab University, Chandigarh, pp. 127–40. His memoirs give a fascinating account of the socio-economic changes in Punjab. Kenneth W. Jones, *n.* 52, pp. 313-15.
55. Harjot S. Oberoi, *The Construction of Religious Boundaries: Culture, Identity and Diversity in the Sikh Tradition,* (Delhi: Oxford University Press, 1994), pp. 207–27.
56. Kenneth W. Jones *n.* 52, pp. 16–20, 135–53.
57. For an excellent elucidation of the concept of 'masculinity' or manliness see J.J. Campbell, *Honour, Family and Patronage: A Study of Institutional and Moral Values in a Greek Mountain Community,* (New York, Toronto, Bombay : Oxford University Press, 1964), pp. 260–70.
58. Swami Dayanand, *Satyarth Prakash,* trans. Chirajniv Bhardwaj, (Agra: Arya Pratinidhi Sabha, 1915), p. 22.
59. Uma Chakravarti, 'Whatever Happened to the Vedic Dasi', in Kumkum Sangari and Sudesh Vaid, *n.* 51, p. 57. I have borrowed this perspective from Uma Chakravarti.
60. Grant Duff, *History of Marathas,* (London: Longmans Green, 1826); James Tod, *Annals and Antiquities of Rajasthan,* 1828–30, ed. William Crooke, (London: Oxford University Press, 1920); J.D. Cunningham, *A History of the Sikhs,* (London : John Murray, 1849).
61. A.R. Malik, 'Modern Historical Writings in Bengali', in C.H. Phillips, ed., *Historians of India Pakistan and Ceylon,* (London: Oxford University Press, 1961), p. 451.

62. *Ibid.,* p. 449.
63. *Ibid.* The same author wrote a book on the Mutiny entitled *Sipahi Yudher Itihasa* (1876) which glorified Rani of Jhansi, Kunwar Singh and Nana Sahib for their heroic exploits.
64. T.W. Clark, 'The Role of Bankimchandra in Development of Nationalism', in C.H. Phillips *n.* 61, pp. 435–37. In Bankim's view, Indians had been enslaved because they were weak and effeminate and they lacked the consciousness of nationhood. He advocated the creation of a strong militant race. In order to attain this objective, it was essential to restore national unity and pride through a reinterpretation of the past which showed Aryan awareness of nationhood at some stage.
65. For an interesting analysis of *Krishan Charita* see Sudipta Kaviraj, 'The Myth of Infinity: The Construction of the Figure of Krishna in Krishnacharita'', *Occasional Papers,* 1987, (Nehru Memorial Museum and Library, Delhi).
66. Jasodhara Bagchi, 'Positivism and Nationalism: Womanhood and Crisis in Nationalist Fiction: Bankim Chandra's *Anandmath',* in *Economic and Political Weekly,* 20, 43, 26 October (1985), pp. 60–61.
67. For an excellent analysis of the nature of Singh Sabha leadership and its concerted drive to evolve a separate Sikh identity, universe, tradition and ideology see Harjot S. Oberoi *n.* 55, pp. 244–52, 286–92, 306–77.
68. I have based my description and analysis of the Singh Reformers' view of 'mainliness' on Bhai Vir Singh's novels *Sundari* (1898), *Bejoy Singh* (1899) and *Satwant Kaur* (1927).
69. Nikky-Guninder Kaur Singh, *The Feminine Principle in the Sikh Vision of the Transcendent,* (Cambridge, New York: Cambridge University Press, 1993), p. 188.
70. Harbans Singh, *Bhai Vir Singh,* (Delhi: Sahitya Academy, 1972, 1984), p. 52.
71. B. Rama Shastri, *Intermarriage of Hindus with Europeans and Other Non-Hindu Ladies,* (Lahore : Sant Singh Luther Oriental Press, 1896); Bawa Chajju Singh, *Brahmacharya Vs. Child Marriage,* (Lahore : Arorbans Press, 1895).
72. Kenneth W. Jones, *n.* 52, pp. 94–119. For the contest between Popular Culture Vs. High Tradition see Harjot S. Oberoi, n. 55, pp. 351–60.
73. Robert Burn, *Census of India, 1901, North-West Provinces & Oudh Report.* Vol. VI, pp. 75–76.
74. For a detailed discussion of this aspect see Kamlesh Mohan, 'Construction of Colonial Ethnography: Imperial Pursuit of Knowledge for Hegemony in British India', in *New Perspectives on Empires and Science* (forthcoming).
75. *Selections from the Vernacular Newspaper Reports, Punjab, for the*

Year 1899, (New Delhi: National Archives of India), p. 98. *The Nur Afshan,* Ludhiana, 10 February 1899.

76. For a first-hand account of the response of young Punjabis to the process of transformation in the Lahore of the 1880s see Ruchi Ram Sahni, *n.* 54. pp. 127-40. Also M. Das, 'The Measures to Abolish Female-infanticide in the North-West Provinces and the Punjab', in *Studies in Economic and Social Development of Modern India,* 1854-56, (Calcutta: K.L. Mukhopadhyay, 1959), pp. 323–61.
77. For a detailed study of Punjabi Orientalism see J.P. Perill, 'Punjabi Orientalism: The Anjuman-i-Punjab and Punjab University 1865–68' (Unpublished Ph.d. dissertation, University of Missouri-Columbia, 1976), pt. I, pp. 182–93. Cited in Harjot S. Oberoi, *n.* 55, p. 2323.
78. E.A. Gait, *Census of India, 1911, Report,* Vol. 1. pt. 1, p. 120. Also *Census of India,* 1901, n. 73, pp. 116–17.
79. Khan Ahmad Hasan Khan, *Census of India, 1931; Punjab Report,* Vol. XVII, pt. II, pp. 181–85.
80. J.D. Cunningham, n. 60.
81. Sir George MacMunn, *The Martial Races of India,* (First printed in 1912; reprinted London: Sampson Law, Marston Co., Ltd. 1933), p. 254. R.W. Falcon, *Handbook on the Sikhs for the Use of Regimental Officers,* (Allahabad: Pioneer Press, 1896), p. 94.
82. Prakash Tandon, *Punjabi Saga 1857–1987,* p. 101.
83. *Ibid.,* p. 55.
84. For the text of these legends see R.C. Temple, *The Legends of the Punjab,* Vol. I, II & III, (First printed in 1881; reprinted, Patiala: Department of Languages, Punjab, 1963), Waris Shah, *Heer Waris,* 1967, ed. Jeet Singh Seetal, (Patiala: Pepsu Book Depot, *n.d.*).
85. Prakash Tandon, *Punjabi Saga 1857–1987,* p. 55.
86. *Ibid.,* p. 102. Also Anshu Malhotra, *Gender, Caste, and Religious Identities: Restructuring Class in Colonial Punjab* (Delhi : Oxford University Press, 2002), pp. 84–115.
87. *Ibid.*
88. Sujata Patel, 'Construction and Reconstruction of Women in Gandhi', *Economic and Political Weekly,* 23, 8, 20 February 1988, p. 378.
89. I have borrowed these ideas from Sujata Patel, *Ibid.,* pp. 378–89.
90. Margaret Cousins, 'Women and Oriental Culture', *The Leader,* 9 January 1930.
91. Uma Chakravari, 'Whatever Happened to the Vedic Dasi?' in Kumkum Sangari and Sudesh Vaid, *n.* 51, p. 52.
92. *Ibid.*
93. Suruchi Thapar, 'Women as Activists. Women as Symbols: A Study of the Indian Nationalist Movement', in *Feminist Review,* 44, Summer 1993.

94. *Collected Works of Mahatma Gandhi,* Vol. XII, 1924, (New Delhi: Ministry of Information and Broadcasting, 1924), p. 524.
95. Nikky-Guninder Kaur Singh, *n.* 69, pp. 192–93.
96. *Ibid.,* p. 190.
97. My observations on Sarla Debi's life and career are based on her autobiography *Jibaner Jhara Pata,* (First printed in 1922; reprinted, Calcutta, 1925), pp. 123–29, 140, 186–86. Also the *Modern Review,* June 1913 and June 1953; Home Department, Political A, Proceedings May 1909, nos. 135–147.
98. *Collected Works of Mahatma Gandhi*, Vol. XIX, pp. 138–39.
99. Personal interview with Laxmi Arya on 14 June 1988.
100. Om Prakash Paliwal, *Rameswari Nehru: Patriot and Nationalist,* (Delhi: National Book Trust, 1986).
101. For an evaluation of Rameshwari Nehru's contribution to the recasting of women's consciousness see Kamlesh Mohan, 'Fashioning Minds and Images: A Case Study of *Stree Darpan* 1909–1928', in this volume.

New Images, Identities and Roles

3

Fashioning Minds and Images

A Case Study of Stree Darpan (1909–1928)

I

The issue of the image of women in *Stree Darpan* (a Hindi magazine launched in 1909 at Allahabad) was linked with India's dominant and urgent concern for recasting its own identity and historical consciousness from the early nineteenth century onwards. The print media, especially vernacular magazines in the various provinces of British India, played a major role in the self-defining project for Indian men and women. With the emergence of women as a rudimentary intelligentsia in the early twentieth century, there was a qualitative change in the approach to the ongoing search for a new woman—Brahmo, Arya, Sikh and Muslim, with special focus on the refashioning of their self-image and world view in keeping with the demands of the colonial milieu and the material needs of the urban middle classes.[1] In contrast to the nineteenth-century social reformers, who treated women as objects for reform or uplift, these radical women, (not in the sense of subverters of tradition but sensitive, intelligent and eclectic interpreters of tradition), used media for projecting the persistent social blindness to the contentious issue of gender relations and nature of women's oppression, especially institutionalization of male control of female sexuality, fertility and labour in the name of *shastric* wisdom, tradition and family honour. However, they went beyond social reform and improvement of familial relationships. They sought to carve out not only new spaces and roles for women but also to fashion a new image and mental personality.

The main argument of this essay is that gender consciousness and activism among the Hindi-educated women in northern India flowed from their growing awareness of discrimination, social tyranny, oppression, economic dependence and low status owing to their biological identity. The influence of Western feminist discourse remained marginal in Bihar, Uttar Pradesh, Madhya Pradesh and Punjab owing to the dominance of either feudal values or peasant culture coupled with widespread female illiteracy.

In this context, it is relevant to underline two points. Firstly, the Indian women's movement in the Hindi region, unlike the male-led social reform movements in the nineteenth century, did not look up to the West as the sole source of new ideas for the regeneration of a 'backward' nation like India. While locating its *raison d'etre* and substance in India's rich cultural heritage, the crusaders of women's cause like Rameshwari Nehru and others tried to shake off the burden of the past. Their ideology of social transformation, it may be conceded, was less influenced by interaction between the British feminists and the Western-educated Indian women but more by their realization that dependence upon male 'charity', 'benevolence' and 'spiritual' concern would not bring them autonomy, rights and power. However, the dominant orientation and strength of Indian women's movement accrued from its prolonged and active association with the anti-colonial struggle in India. In fact, all the progressive movements in India—social, political, cultural or literary—shared the common goal of liberation from foreign rule. Of course, they carried on their fight against caste-oppression, gender injustice or feudal exploitation through their separate fora.

Secondly, I want to point out that the Indian women's movement sought to mobilize that section of social world which Edwin Ardener has described as 'muted' groups.[2] Women's journals in Hindi, especially *Stree Darpan,* undertook to give visibility and voice to their target group who had internalized the social compulsion of silent suffering and self-effacement as little girls.

II
HINDI JOURNALS IN ALLAHABAD

In this essay, I have chosen *Stree Darpan* for analysing women's image on two counts. Firstly, it was unlike the other women's magazines, namely, *Saraswati, Chand, Grihlakshmi* (Allahabad) *Panchal-Pandita* (Jalandhar), *Tehzeeb-e-Niswan* (Aligarh), *Sharif Biwi* (Lahore), *Punjabi Bhain* (Ferozepur), whose male editors had some times co-opted their wives as editors while it [*Stree Darpan*] had been founded and edited by a woman named Rameshwari Nehru from 1909 to 1924. Born on 10th December 1886, she had spent the formative period of her life under the dominant influence of her orthodox father Raja Narendernath. Despite being an Arya Samajist, he did not share its reformist views regarding the role of education in recasting men and women. Her constant exposure to the liberal Westernized atmosphere of Anand Bhawan as the daughter-in-law of Pt. Motilal Nehru's elder brother late Nand Lal, whose son Brij Lal Nehru married her in 1902, had enabled Rameshwari to enrich her social vision and formulate progressive views on women's role in home, society and polity. It was under these socio-cultural constraints that Rameshwari Nehru undertook the unusual task of cultivating women's mind and crusading against those customs, which imprisoned her mind and body. Even more daring and ambitious was her endeavour to redraw and extend contours of social consciousness of not only the majority of purdah-bound women over a long period but also of the self-centred men through the rational process of dialogue and interaction.[3]

Secondly, this magazine had gradually become the nucleus of women's movement not only in the Hindi heartland but also in the entire north India. In this connection, a significant fact may be mentioned that the establishment of the Prayag Mahila Samiti by Rameshwari Nehru in Allahabad in 1909[4] had coincided with the launching of *Stree Darpan* which sought to offer wide social and communication space to women and helped to locate their issues in the mainstream perspective of the national struggle for *swaraj*.[5] Obviously, these early thinkers perceived the immense value of coordination between *mahila samitis* (women's associations) and women's journals if these were to be used as catalysts and mobilizers.

It is worthwhile to survey briefly the spectrum of journalistic activity in Allahabad during the first three decades of the twentieth century[6] which witnessed the growth of *Stree Darpan* from a fledgeling into one of the most prestigious and representative of women's journals in Hindi. Bhartendu Harish Chandra, apart from discussing women's issues in his writings, was the first to start a women's journal, *Balbodhini* in 1874. Three and a half decades elapsed before this question gripped the social imagination with such a force as to turn it into a major theme in literary and journalistic writings.

Out of the numerous women's journals published during the period under reference, three attracted special notice: *Grihlakshmi, Stree Darpan* and *Chand.* All the three were published from Allahabad, the focal point of nationalist and Indian women's movement. While *Grihlakshmi* and *Stree Darpan* began to publish in 1909, *Chand* brought out its first issue in 1922. Both *Grihlakshmi* and *Stree Darpan* had looked at social problems from the women's angle. However, the former tended to reinforce the traditional roles of mother, sister and daughter. Qualities of a model daughter-in-law and her code of conduct were frequently discussed by its contributors. However, *Stree Darpan* chose to dilute social obsession with women's domestic role and project the urgency of utilizing their potentialities for social and national work.

The three magazines under reference were extremely critical of the prevalent evil social customs of child marriage, inhuman treatment of widows and female illiteracy. The Hindi journal *Chand,* which had male editors and a woman manager, gave more space to these pressing problems as was evident from its three special issues on widows, child marriage and women's education. It linked social reform with its comprehensive agenda of revolution. Its various issues revealed that its crusade for changing of social attitude towards women was far more radical than its proclaimed objective "to make the Indian woman into an ideal housewife".

As this essay is primarily concerned with the role of women's Hindi journals in recasting their image and mindset during the period under reference, *Stree Darpan* is more suitable for an indepth analysis. Belonging to a later period, *Chand* is beyond the scope of this study.

III
AIMS AND POLICY

In order to understand the new image of women in *Stree Darpan*, it shall be helpful to discuss its aims and policy. Its aims were influenced by its editor's perception of the urgent problems of Indian society and politics, and her belief that contemporary magazines including the one run for the benefit and in the name of women, though making an admirable contribution, were not fully alive to their concerns and social agony, their point of view and their changing self-image. Hence, *Stree Darpan* was launched with a view to presenting not only women's perception of existing social mores, problems and current national issues but also the common man's opinions and aspirations. It undertook to sculpt a new model for the Indian woman: self-reliant, confident and capable of securing her rights and her independent economic and social status. However, its major aim was to cultivate the minds of women and to make them conscious of their own predicament growing out of their socialization and conditioning within the patriarchal value-system. It also proposed to accelerate the pace of the then ongoing socio-cultural and political changes in India and manifold developments in the world.[7]

Acutely conscious of tensions and clashes between different points of view, she proposed to utilize her magazine for initiating a dialogue between the upholders of two points of view on every issue—social, cultural and political.[8] While the diehard traditionalists regarded new ideas and trends as destructive and obstructive, the protagonists of a liberal approach and Western values viewed new light as a happy sign. For the formation of an enlightened public opinion, the magazine followed the policy of generating discussion and debate between both the groups. The editor had argued that the readers would benefit more intellectually if the opposite points of view on various issues and problems were juxtaposed.

By serving as a forum for creative dialogue and exchange and circulation of ideas, *Stree Darpan* proposed to enable its readers, especially women, to understand and identify the roots of social problems and participate in the process of social change and also to harness the heat of ideological friction for recreating or 'inventing' tradition[9] and recasting gender relations. Its successful career of one decade had won the admiration and approval of a number of contemporary newspapers and magazines such as *Pratap, Vanketeshwari* and *Swarajya* which had not only endorsed the editor's bifocal strategy of social change and the magazine's policy, but also issued appeals for more subscriptions.[10]

Being primarily a social-action journal, *Stree Darpan* from its inception (its first available issue dated 1911), directed its discourses towards women from the families that were undergoing a process of modernization. It was meant to cultivate the minds of these women with two major goals in view. One was to raise them to a level where they could be suitable companions for their husbands. The ideal of *Sahadharmini,* consciously cultivated and espoused by Indian women,[11] was a useful construct for the middle-class men who had entered professional careers and were required to interact with the British administrators and officials. The latter's perceptions and attitudes no longer reflected the positive Orientialist view[12] of Indian civilization and society but the negatively critical paradigm of Utilitarians.[13] The second goal was to prepare them mentally to play their dual role as active crusaders for social reform and fighters in the nationalist struggle for independence.

Stree Darpan was divided into two sections: *(i)* for adults, especially women and *(ii)* 'Kumari Darpan' for teenaged school and college-going students. In its section for adults, the journal used to publish articles on various socio-political issues, prayers, patriotic poems, serialized novels penned by a number of socially aware women, some of them being politicized as well. Male writers, too, made useful contribution. Among the well-known names were included left-wing writers namely, Radha Mohan Gokul Ji, Satyabhakt, Ramashankar Awasthy, the famous Hindi poet Sridhar Pathak and the journalist Ramrikh Sehgal, Hukma Devi, Abadi Bano, Satyawati, Uma Kumari Nehru, Roop Kumari Nehru nee Wanchu and several others. Rameshwari Nehru's editorials moderated the clashing points of views of these writers who hailed from Uttar Pradesh, Bihar, the Punjab and Central Provinces (now called Madhya Pradesh), West Bengal and Sindh. From 1926 onwards, Mahatma Gandhi's messages and letters to women figured frequently in this journal.

The second section of *Stree Darpan* began to be published from 1916 onwards with Roop Kumari Nehru as the Assistant Editor. The latter had addressed its message to the impressionable teen-aged girls who were to be trained not merely as prospective housewives and mothers but more as propagandists and active participants in Gandhi's Non-co-operation, Civil Disobedience and Quit India Movements.

Its editor, Rameshwari Nehru, while underlining the non-commercial character of the journal—run on no profit no loss basis, frequently issued appeals to the public, through its own columns and other nationalist vernacular newspapers, for adding to the number of subscribers to a women's journal. In spite of the price-hike of stationery and printing, she had expressed her determination to continue the publication of *Stree Darpan* without compromising on its quality and reducing its size of over sixty pages.[14] It was remarkable that *Stree Darpan* managed to publish almost all its issues on time barring three months during the problem-filled first seven years.

IV
MAJOR ISSUES AND THEMES

Let us turn to issues and themes in the columns of *Stree Darpan*. The major issues such as education, purdah system and mismatched marriages, which sparked off debates and discussions among the readers and contributors, had been taken over on its agenda by the Indian Women's Movement in due course.

Education figured propminently on the agenda of the crusaders for women's upliftment. In order to demolish the deep-rooted social prejudice, oppressive customs and male resistance against women's education, Rameshwari Nehru launched a fierce campaign for creating awareness among men and women through the columns of *Stree Darpan* from 1911 onwards. In its January issue, her article 'Stri Shiksha Se Desh-unnati', she cited the example of Japanese women who made a positive contribution to each aspect of national life. Similarly, education would enable Indian women to play an active and valuable role in public life. Besides, it would train them to discriminate between right and wrong. Obviously, education also had an instrumental value in recasting gender relations, balance of power and authority in the patriarchal family set-up. Numerous articles and a few poems on this theme highlighted the practical reasons, apart from the human rights perspective, for mobilizing public opinion in favour of opening schools and colleges and vocational courses for women. The most compelling argument was the growing demand for the educated girls by the Western-educated young men of the middle-class families who wanted drawing room companions and not tradition-bound, illiterate wives.

Related with this was the social agony of illiterate women who suffered daily insults and humiliations as wives at the hands of their educated husbands owing to their genuine problems of communication coupled with their ignorance. The following extract from Kailash Rani Baatal's article 'Strion Ka Mahatav Tatha Purushoan Ka Kartavya', which appeared in the December 1915 issue, illustrates the point:

> *Sabhyata ki poshak ke ander abhi bahut se sankiran bhaav ke hariday chhupe rahte hain jo ki antekaran se stri jaati to paon tale rakhna pasand karte hain.*
> (Even today, a number of men hide their narrow and reactionary views about women behind their civilized appearance. It is their heartiest desire to keep women under their foot).

The readers and contributors to the journal were drawn into the fray as a result of the editor's ceaseless campaign through the publication of their articles and poems in the various issues especially the May–June, 1911. Braj Rani's poem 'Vidya Parho', apart from sounding a note of protest, exhorted women to develop an urge for education because India had an honoured tradition of women's education. Madaalsa, Gargi and Maitreyi are well-known names in the galaxy of scholars. In the same issue, Yadunandan Prasad deplored the indifference to women's education in the twentieth century which was otherwise marked by rapid strides in the field of education all over the world.[15] Pursuing this point further, Krishna Kumari (Lahore) had linked national degeneration with the neglect of women's education.[16] Both of them had advocated an intensive campaign for their education for similar reasons: efficient motherhood, acquisition of skills for performing wifely duties and *pativrata dharma.* In its August 1918 issue, Rameshwari Nehru's editorial, 'Desi aur Vilayati Nari Shiksha' added to the list of benefits of educating them saying that it would enable women to develop a sense of pride in being Indians. A more liberal angle surfaced in Vishwanath Prasad Gupta's article 'Stri Shiksha' in the November 1928 issue which underlined the similarity between the aims and objectives of the lives of both men and women. Hence, the real purpose of education was to develop physical, mental and moral potentialities and capabilities of all Indians irrespective of their sex.

Another important point in this ongoing debate, initiated by the nineteenth-century social reformers, was the nature and content of education. The question of the content of their education was linked with the broad issue of role and position of women in the social and family structure. In spite of broadening of the scope of women's activity from domestic to public life and enhancement of their personal dignity and status, the image of their traditional nurturing roles still dominated the social psyche. It is illustrated by the general thrust of poems, articles and stories in the various issues of *Stree Darpan* from 1911 to 1928, which underlined the need of giving liberal education to women for sharpening their intelligence. It would enable them to acquire skills in needle-work, cooking and in any of the domestic arts which ought not to be the major subject of teaching. This argument was highlighted in an article titled 'Stri Shiksha' by an anonymous patriot which appeared in the July 1916 issue of *Stree Darpan*. The anonymous writer, who described himself as a humble patriot, observed:

> Our most important concern, while imparting the highest education to young girls, is that it should not blunt their talent to become an ideal housewife.

The writer also advocated the need of training women for employment in various professions such as teaching, medicine, journalism, social work and politics, but without any compromise regarding the ultimate role of woman as the ideal housewife. In practice, obviously, teaching of domestic arts continued to remain a major subject in the premier institutions for girls in North India: Crosswaithe Girls School (Allahabad), Aligarh Zenana Madrassa (Aligarh), Kanya Maha Vidyalaya (Jalandhar) and Sikh Kanya Vidyalaya (Ferozepur).

Through her editorial commentaries, Rameshwari Nehru not only informed her readers regularly about the establishment of new educational institutions with boarding facilities for girls and the expansion of existing schools and colleges in north India but also issued appeals for donations to support them. One of the most pioneering and dynamic institutions was Kanya Maha Vidyalaya (Jalandhar), founded by Lala Devraj in 1889. It was highly honoured for its self-reliance in financial matters and thus independence in policy and management by the sympathizers of the women's movement as was evident from Magan Divedi Gaupuri's article in the September 1910 issue of *Stree Darpan*. Rameshwari Nehru had drawn public attention to Lala Devraj's success in creating a band of selfless teachers out of its former students, namely, Mangla Devi, Anandi Devi, Lajjawati Devi and Savitri Devi. The last two students served as the Principals of Kanya Maha Vidyalaya for varying terms.

The other educational institutions also received special notice in the columns of the Hindi magazines. The first was the Besant Kanya Maha Vidyalaya (Benaras), founded by Dr. Annie Besant, in the course of her educational experiments from 1913 to 1919. Perceiving the interdependence between women's education and national rejuvenation, she had emphasized the need to train girls in Sanskrit and vernacular literature so as to awaken their pride in their own heritage.[17] The second was the Crosswaithe Girls High School (Allahabad), which was an important centre of nationalist activity. Its reputation for high standard in education and management attracted students from Lahore, Jalandhar, Calcutta, Santhal Pargana, Rangoon, etc. It must be pointed that the contributors to *Stree Darpan* did not notice an important institution like Aligarh Zenana Madrassa[18] (established in 1906 by Sheikh Abdulla and Wahid Jahan Begum under the banner of Mohammedan Educational Conference and later expanded into a women's college) which played a crucial role in promoting education among the purdah-bound girls belonging to Sharif Muslim families in India, particularly Aligarh.

The second important theme of *Stree Darpan* was a vigorous campaign against purdah, which Patricia Jeffery has characterized as 'sexual apartheid'.[19] Women writers like Satyawati and Bhagyawati demonstrated their ability of understanding the complex issue of purdah in context with the larger issue of systematic and organized social oppression of women. While analyzing its harmful consequences, Satyawati pointed out the futility of the abolition of purdah in isolation when women were deprived of education, real knowledge, wealth and personal freedom. It would acquire meaning in relation to the total removal of all oppressive social customs and practices.[20] Criticizing it as a major obstacle in a girl's education, Satyawati went a step further when she linked it with the women's right to good personal health like every other human being. These budding intellectuals, who had erroneously attributed the popularity of purdah to the influence of Muslim rule,[21] campaigned for its abolition for pragmatic reasons. For example, Bhagyawati's article 'Adhunik Purdah Pranali' in the August 1918 issue argued that it was not possible to make arrangements for the education of girls in the Zenana as majority of Indians were too poor to afford a private lady or male tutor. The crux of her argument lies in the following extract:

> If India is to recapture its past glory and to progress, women's potentialities ought to be given full scope for development. In order to achieve this objective, the custom of *purdah*, the

inveterate enemy of women's health, has to be discarded for ever.

In the same issue of *Stree Darpan*, a teenaged girl, Kumari Chandravati Gupt reiterated the much discussed arguments for the abolition of purdah. Going a step further, she urged her sisters to get education, claim their personal autonomy and rights without losing any time.

Evidently, an acute consciousness of deprivation of their rights as human beings as a result of their enforced segregation had provoked anger, which was visible in the columns of *Stree Darpan*. In the December 1918 issue, Rajdulari's article 'Purdeh ki Visham Vedna' reflected not only collective awareness of their agony caused by daily humiliations and oppression but also a resolve to end gender discrimination and to work for the reformulation of the norms and code of conduct for men and women, framed by society. She urged men to change their rigid attitudes and orthodox views in keeping with the progressive trends of the world. While emphasizing the vital need for uprooting pernicious social customs particularly purdah, child marriage, mismatched marriages and dowry exchange, she pointed out that women possessed as much intelligence as men for deliberating upon the issue of national welfare and implementing plans for achieving these objectives. She also raised the important question of training women for various jobs in order to enable them, especially widows, to earn their own livelihood instead of being destitutes and dependents.

As a result of this relentless campaign against purdah through the columns of *Stree Darpan*, a vigorous movement for its abolition was launched in Bihar during 1928. Kanhaya Lal Nigam, who became the new editor of the journal when Rameshwari Nehru shifted to Delhi, voiced his hope for its success in north India. A number of Hindu families influenced by the Arya Samaj movement against oppressive social customs, had already discarded purdah from 1880s onwards. Rameshwari Nehru, who rose to be one of the prominent leaders of All India Women's Conference, had also pursuaded women of her natal family to give up this practice despite stiff opposition from her orthodox father Raja Narendra Nath. The significant point is that she had enlisted women as active participants in their own liberation. The growing band of rudimentary intelligentsia among north Indian women was gradually developing emotional bonds and a new concept of sisterhood as a result of the circulation of new ideas and opinions and proxy interaction facilitated by *Stree Darpan.* Their membership of Ladies' associations, formed under the wings of various social reform organizations and later as components of Women's Indian Association and All India Women's Conference, was indicative of their expanding gender-consciousness, their changing self-view and world-view.

The debate on mismatched marriages, which figured frequently in the columns of the journal, highlighted the growing resentment of critical women against the discriminatory social norms of the patriachal family system in India which subjected women to mental agony and denied them control over their sexuality and fertility. Especially, the increasingly popular practice of widowers' remarriage greatly agitated their minds because it was responsible for adding to the number of child-widows and thus posing a grave social problem. *Stree Darpan* became the forum for a creative dialogue between the supporters and opponents of widow-remarriage. In this debate both the issues of social health and fundamental right of women to satisfy their natural sexual urge within the institution of marriage remained alive in the contributions to this journal. In its January 1911 issue, debate was sparked off by the publication of the text of Savitri Devi's lecture in Prayag Mahila Samiti. Manglanand's commentary had not only questioned social sanction to remarriage of widowers and advocated widow remarriage but also redefined *pativarata dharma.* He said *pativarata dharma* did not imply devotion to the dead husband but observance of fidelity to the man whom the widow married. In his view, widow-remarriage would certainly not lead to moral corruption among women.

The women contributors and readers expressed their views forcefully. In the February 1918 issue, Gulab Devi Chaturvedi's (Kota) letter on this issue was widely recommended for reading and serious thought by the editor Rameshwari Nehru. The crux of her message was that women themselves have to assume the role of saviours against the organized social oppression including the galore of widowers' remarriages. However, stories by women-writers did not show their heroines taking the radical step of ending their miserable plight as widows through remarriage. The stories entitled 'Prem Bindu' in June 1917 issue and 'Aradhana' in the May–June 1919 issue illustrated the stronghold of the traditional image of a self-sacrificing and suffering woman. As a result, the impression gained ground that the battle of widow-remarriage was more keenly fought by male-writers than women. It lent credence to the uplift perspective of women's movement at least on this issue. Men's projection of their role as saviours of widows remained dominant even during the second and third decades of the twentieth century, when women's movement was vibrant and the agitation for their rights, stridently vocal.

There was also the prevalent tendency to valorize widowhood among the orthodox Hindus. Despite her sincere advocacy of the right of widows whether little girls or young adults to remarry, Rameshwari Nehru was inclined to glorify the moral stature and social value of ascetic widowhood, perhaps under the Gandhian influence. For illustration see the English translation of an extract from her editorial comment in the June 1919 issue:

> Indian women have always been honoured and given the highest status in society for their sexual chastity and pure life as well as devotion to their husbands. ... Those widows, who have chosen to inculcate and personify these qualities and to engage themselves in religious duties selflessly, are to be worshipped by the whole world. But the problem arises in the case of those widows who fail to control their sexual desire. Among them are included the teenaged girls and young adults. We can not understand our leaders' logic when they sanction remarriage for one category and prohibit it for the other. Widows, belonging to both categories, fall in different age-groups but they suffer from the same mental sickness.

In fact, valorization of widowhood and desexualisation of these women remained a dominant feature of the middle-class ideology underlying the process of the construction of 'new' woman from Swami Dayanand to Mahatma Gandhi. While the former had advocated widow-remarriage for the improvement of Hindu race,[22] the latter had sanctioned it for child-widows only on compassionate grounds and for adult widows as a measure against moral corruption. Generally speaking, Gandhi had created a godlike woman in the person of widow whose potentialities were an asset for social welfare and national service.[23]

However, the majority of the contributors of *Stree Darpan* and readers, who were young housewives, middle-aged mothers with teenaged daughters, sisters-in-law and a small number of highly educated working women, tried to locate the problem of social resistance to the remarriage of widows in the context of the broad issue of the position of women in Indian society. For example, Hukma Devi, the Principal of Girls' School, Dehradun, had openly advocated the formulation of new social norms, which gave an equal right to widows to resume conjugal life. In the August 1917 issue in her article 'Stree Unnati Kaise Ho' she had focused attention upon the devaluation of women as indicated by the alacrity of widowers to remarry. Even during their lifetime women suffered neglect when sick. Neither their beauty, nor their accomplishments nor their lifelong devotion to their husbands entitled them to their (husbands) fidelity and love as well as dignified status in the family. In fact, it could be said that these women showed acute awareness of the gap between the scriptural status of women and the harsh reality of their existence in the patriarchal system. 'Paon Ki Jooti', an expression used by Hukma Devi in her article 'Ardhangini Ya Paon Ki Jooti' in the issue of March 1918, became a recurring symbol of shame and humiliation for Indian women. The metaphor 'dumb cattle' reinforced the image of the faceless identity of women.

Its positive outcome was a deep concern with the issue of gender discrimination which had been voiced through poems, articles and stories throughout the period under reference. In the December 1915 issue of *Stree Darpan,* an anonymous writer in her personal account of 'Ek Vidhwa Ki Jiwani' presented a comparative view of the privileged position of a widower and the abject status of a widow. While criticizing the patriarchal social system for practising gender discrimination, she lashed out at women for their submission to injustice and oppression. Her observations on this issue revealed the keen ability of the writer to discuss problems dispassionately:

> In the mistaken perception of Indian society, men are seen to be more useful than women. It may be conceded that men have been unjust to women. But the question is why women did not protest against this injustice. Why did they not assert their individuality and rights? Women share more responsibility for their own degradation. ·

Smt. Suryadevi's poem 'Nari Vilap', published in the December 1918 issue of the journal, gave a heart-rending description of the humiliating treatment meted out to the submissive and devoted wives by their educated husbands. The following extract illustrates the point:

Pati pass hai B.A., M.A par ghar
mein patni nipat ganwar
Aise ghar mein prem kahan hai
machta hai nit hahakar
Din bhar karti kaam, nahin par
babu ko hota santosh
Hui zara bhi deir kaam mein
aa jata jhat unko rosh
Bahut log shikshit ho kar bhi
yun karte naari satkaar
Dosh nahin hum ablaon ka
Kyon ham rakhi gayin ganwar?

(The husband is a B.A, M.A. The wife is utterly illiterate. In such a home, there is no love but bickerings and tensions. His wife toils the whole day, yet the gentleman is unhappy. A woman's delay in her work rouses his anger. Many educated men honour their women in this way. Why blame women for lapses when they are illiterate?)

These women's acute awareness about their wasteful lives gradually surfaced as a voice of organized social protest against the duplicity of male nationalists who demanded more educational institutions and right of self-government for themselves while suppressing the human rights of their wives, daughters and sisters.

Hukma Devi as one of the select band had articulated this turn in women's movement in the April 1918 issue of *Stree Darpan.* She proposed the organization of Kanya Hitkarni Sabha (A Society for Welfare of Young Girls) which had a list of fourteen objectives including a united front for 'active resistance', *Sakriya Pratirodh* and the publication of a newsletter called *Kumar aur Kumari.* The fact of the rising level of feminist consciousness was proved by Hukma Devi's suggestion to the editor to present a petition to the British Government seeking the imposition of legal restriction upon the practice of widowers' remarriage. It was also attested by the enthusiastic responses to Hukma Devi's proposals in the form of a score of letters whose writers had offered her sustained cooperation in the coming years. The impact of *Stree Darpan's* active campaign on this issue had positive implications for the Indian women's movement, not only in India but also for its advocates abroad. In 1917, its editor

Rameshwari Nehru was invited to help the organization of *Kanya Hitkarni Sabha* in Rangoon. Thus, the majority of contributors to this journal had played an active role in raising the level of Indian women's consciousness as well as in consolidating movement for their social and political rights without demanding structural changes.

Let me evaluate the widely-accepted 'uplift' perspective on Indian women's movement, as articulated through the columns of *Stree Darpan* before turning to the second, i.e. ultra-progressive views of the firebrand Uma Nehru. Displaying an interesting inter-twining and interplay of relational-individualist argument for women's rights, the advocates of the participatory strategy for women's upliftment had focused on social reform agenda rather than restructuring of gender relations and institutions, women's education and their substantial share in public life. These educated upper middle-class women activists demanded self-hood, more visibility, and other channels of self-expression and fulfilment through varied social and political roles without relinquishing their domestic responsibilities. Their explicit insistence upon the retention and reinforcement of the identity of women did not imply inimical gender relations but complementary and cooperative companionship. It was this spirit which informed their struggle for emancipation from social, economic and political servitude.

Both Rameshwari Nehru and Sarojini Naidu, despite their different educational backgrounds and value-orientations, represented the new version of uplift perspective in the Indian women's movement. They differed from the nineteenth-century social reformers' goals and expectations. Believing with Gandhi that women were not objects of reform and humanitarianism but self-conscious subjects who would, if they chose, become arbiters of their own destiny. Neither of them had demanded or worked for changing the patriarchal familial relations and discriminatory and hierarchical social structure. They believed that the existing social system, specifically the Hindu society could accommodate women's aspirations for self-hood, development of their talent, intellectual potential and assumption of new social, economic and political roles.

The second perspective on Indian women's movement, reflected in *Stree Darpan*, had been projected by radical-minded Uma Nehru, who was the daughter-in-law of Nand Lal Nehru—the elder brother of Motilal Nehru. Despite their exposure to the Western intellectual currents and liberal atmosphere in their in-laws' house, Rameshwari Nehru and Uma Nehru were poles apart in their views on the reform of the contemporary Indian society, gender relations, political and economic problems as well as in their vision of a new world order. The fact, that the latter's radical value-orientation and feminist arguments were communicated without prejudice to the readers of *Stree Darpan,* indicated the editor Rameshwari Nehru's open mind, an essential requisite for a moderator. Take for example, Uma Nehru's article 'Hamare Samaj Sudharak' in the March 1918 issue of *Stree Darpan*. She ridiculed social reformers' obsession with the retrograde search for golden age in the *Ramayana* and *Mahabharata* when the historical forces were pushing the world in a different direction. She also criticized them for their double standards which were evident from their exhortation to Indian women to emulate the Sita-Savitri ideal while they were busy acquiring English education, Western lifestyle and values. Commenting upon the contradictory logic and behaviour of the Western-educated Indian men, she wrote:

> *Sita aur Savitri banane ke liye Ramchander, Krishan, Bharat aur Yudhishter ki aavashakta hoti hai. Coat, patloon, aur necktie-collar shareer par aur pashchimi aarthik adarshoan ki tarang dil mein lekar aisi stri jati ke utpann karne ki abhilaasha akaashpushap dhundne ke samaan hai.*
>
> (The task of producing model women like Sita and Savitri seems incongruent with a social situation which does not oblige men to become a Ramachander, a Krishan, a Bharat or a Yudhishter. Dressed in coat, pant and necktie and inebriated with the ambition to emulate Western economic ideals, Indian men's craving for such ideal women is akin to a search for the proverbial mythical flower).

In her article 'Hamare Hridya' in the May 1918 issue of *Stree Darpan*, she had underlined another aspect of this contradiction in the behaviour and hypocrisy of Indian men who lamented the loss of national liberty but betrayed utter insensitivity to the enslavement of women's body, soul and spirit.

Unlike Rameshwari Nehru, Uma Nehru bitterly challenged the validity of discriminatory gender relations legitimized by the institutions of family and marriage whether among the Hindus or the Muslims. In her article 'Hamare Samajik Dhanche' in the April 1918 issue of the journal, she dubbed this traditional model as master–slave relationship between man and woman, and pleaded for enduring companionship based on love, friendliness and mutual respect. In her writings, Uma Nehru had exposed the hypocrisy of the male contention that learning, independence and strenuous mental and physical work spoilt the beauty of women. Her article, 'Haamari Soortein', published in two parts in the July 1918 issues of the journal under reference, pinpointed the selfish mentality of the Indian men who controlled women's sexuality and fertility and exploited her labour by hailing her as *grihlakshmi.* She mounted a frontal attack on the patriarchal ideology which glorified strength as the essence of masculinity and beauty as the hallmark of femininity. In her view, the only way to sensitize men to the suffering, drudgery and injustice they had inflicted on women for centuries in the name of tradition and feminine virtue, was to reverse the gender roles and deny men access to knowledge and power.

The most remarkable thing about Uma Nehru's writings was her insight into the causes of the low status and socio-economic enslavement of women. She had blamed the 'procrustean' Indian society which used three patriarchal moulds—the ancient Hindu, the Turkish and modern or Western—to subjugate and oppress Indian women. This understanding had helped her to project the issues of Indian women's movement in the context of the fast-changing material conditions of India and Europe which had set in motion new socio-economic forces. In her view, changes in the position of European women had been brought about by their new economic and political system. As Indians aspired to organize their national life on the basis of these very economic and political principles, it is difficult to neutralize its consequences. Hence, Indian women, so far ill-equipped to play any meaningful role in India's liberation struggle, needed to be trained for new roles in social, economic and political struggle against the British colonial exploitation and imperialist subjugation of India. Pursuing this line of argument, Uma Nehru demanded an independent identity as well as social and political rights for women as these were based on the natural human urges, especially the need for self-expression. This explains her vehement support to Sarojini Naidu's proposal for women's right to vote, passed in the August 1918 session of the Indian National Congress. These views were expressed in her article 'Strion Ke

Adhikar' in the 1918 issue of the Hindi journal *Maryada*.

As the formulations of both the Nehru women—Rameshwari and Uma—had been articulated through the columns of *Stree Darpan,* their role in bringing about attitudinal change among women towards the institutions of family and marriage and finally in their notions of femininity and *Stridharma* shall best be discussed in relation with the journal's impact as a social-action organ in Section V.

V
IMPACT UPON WOMEN

How far did *Stree Darpan* succeed in its mission of transforming the consciousness, i.e. self-image, world-view, ideals, aspirations and goals of the urban Indian women especially of the Hindi-educated in the north? What was the extent of its effectiveness as a social-action journal? Could it create an enlightened public opinion through creative dialogue and debate between two points of view on contemporary controversial social and political issues? In order to evaluate this journal's multi-faceted contribution, I shall focus on changes in these women's self-view and world-view, values, attitude towards marriage, conjugal relations and traditional roles, triggered by the encounter between the East and the West.[24]

The editor Rameshwari Nehru had chosen to utilize its communication potential and space in the service of this long-term and arduous national mission of recomposing the mental ethos and refashioning the notions of Indian womanhood among the Hindi-educated. Their acute realization about the irrationality of dichotomization of space and values on the basis of sex had injected a sense of urgency in the middle classes which shouldered the crucial responsibility for evolving patterns of adjustment or confrontation with the colonial state, society, and economy. It was coupled with the task of reinvigorating and 'inventing' tradition in order to rebut the charge of social backwardness and unfitness for self-government.

Consequently, the first and second decade of the twentieth century witnessed major alterations in their self-image and perception of womanhood. The Hindu view of feminine nature and norms for their conduct, drawn from two separate though related sources: male-oriented classical literature and folk oral tradition, was regarded as the product of patriarchal ideology.[25] The prescribed norms of submissiveness, obedience, devotion to husband in all circumstances and chastity for the ideal woman had grown out of the male belief in her inherent evil nature—fickleness, heartless disposition and irrepressible sexual disire.[26] The new generation of rational and somewhat radical women from the urban middle-classes regarded this cluster of womanly virtues as a unilateral construct, legitimized by religious scriptures and cultivated in the family. That was why contributors to *Stree Darpan* as well as its editor continued to dispel such popular notions about women.[27]

Instead, a positive image of women was projected through the columns of *Stree Darpan*. The liberal feminists like Uma Nehru argued that women, like men, ought to acquire the qualities of alertness, independent thinking, self-confidence, competitive spirit, courage, fearlessness, truthfulness, experience in worldly affairs, organizational skills and an intelligent as well as enlightened outlook in order to perform their nurturing and public roles efficiently.[28] Both men and women attached great value to the habit of self-discipline, compassion, tolerance, politeness and sympathy.[29] Thus, the separating line between female virtues and male qualities became increasingly fluid.

The growing consciousness about women's worth even among ordinary housewives had surfaced in their severe criticism of the prevalent social trend of lamentation over the birth of daughters, who have been regarded as liabilities. A new sense of self-respect and pride in their identity as women and awareness of their power in the roles of daughters, sisters, mothers and wives exuded from their writings.[30] These sensitive and critical women openly expressed their contempt for those narrow-minded but so-called civilized men who believed in the subjugation of women and treated them as 'beasts of burden', 'dumb cattle' and 'paon ki jooti'.[31] Their fervent faith in their own intellectual ability to discriminate between right and wrong and in their keen sense of duty was reflected in the editorial comment on Manohar Prasad Mishar's article 'Strion Par Dabau' published in the August 1919 issue. The patriarchal ideology of disciplining women, through the denial of learning by experience, and imposition of control or restrictions over their minds, body and spatial movement in order to keep them on the path of dharma, was ridiculed by Rameshwari Nehru, Uma Nehru and many other sympathizers of Indian Women's movement. The English version of the extract from this editorial in Hindi illustrates the point:

> Our Misharji [a male writer] not only favours limited freedom for women in their domestic activities but also their progress at a slow pace. He wishes to introduce them to good things. Evidently, he regards women as children. *The goal of Indian women's movement is not showing 'good and nice things' but to secure their rights.* Undoubtedly, they may sometimes make mistakes but nobody has the right to punish them for their lapses.[32] (emphasis is mine)

The substitution of the feeling of helplessness and dependence by an action-oriented outlook marked a new and positive turning point in the transformation of women's consciousness. Its first indication became visible in the appreciative reaction of one of the male readers to the bold step of a young wife who had used the columns of *Stree Darpan* to project her predicament and warn her community (in this case Aggarwal) of her determination to become a convert to another religion in case they failed to save her from maltreatment and beating by her mother-in-law.[33]

Stree Darpan, which had assisted in the emergence of rudimentary intelligentsia among women, had enabled them to articulate their awareness of harsh reality of their lives and institutionalization of their social oppression. For those, who had been conditioned to glorify their silent suffering and self-sacrifice as the essence of womanhood, the frank expression of their centuries'-old mental agony and longing for a dignified life was a prelude to their active involvement in their own upliftment and the broader movement for social reform as well as a crucial component in their changing self view.

These critical women had tried to broaden the scope of social reform and enrich its meaning and content. The real social reform means actual restructuring of the social institutions and not merely lukewarm efforts in this direction. It also means the substitution of narrow selfish individual concerns with total commitment to the strengthening of community structures and networks for promoting general welfare. Its ultimate goal was not only the amelioration of the status of women, the downtrodden and the poor but also the inculcation of love for freedom, equality and justice in each member of society, and qualities of courage and self-respect among the weaker sections as well as the shaping of a catholic social vision. These women believed that a healthy social reform process and programme ought to be correlated with the nature and pace of contemporary worldwide changes while balancing individual development with a happy and prosperous corporate social life.[34]

In the role of budding ideologues and relentless crusaders for social reform, these women bluntly exposed Indian men's blatant hypocrisy which was shown by their demand for Home Rule from the British rulers and by their own denial of autonomy and freedom to the women folk. Published in the December 1918 issue of *Stree Darpan*, a satirical poem 'Kya Home Rule Loge' by Gyan Devi, elucidated the point:

> *Parishram nahin karenge, aapas mein khoob larenge,*
> *Aisi dasha mein rehkar, kya home rule loge?*
> *Vivah jaldi kar ke, Vidhwa bahut bana kar,*
> *Un par rehm na kha kar, kya home rule loge?*

> (You shall not toil but fight with each other and yet you hope to get Home Rule? Live apart as Moderates and Extremists and live in mutual hostility. And yet you hope to get Home Rule? Marry off little girls, add to the number of widows. Be cruel to them. And yet you hope to get Home Rule?)

Earlier in her editorial comment 'Strian aur Vote' in the September 1918 issue, Rameshwari Nehru had criticized Pt. Madan Mohan Malaviya's opposition to the resolution demanding votes for women on the pretext of their being *purdah-nashin*. This resolution had been tabled in the Bombay session of the Indian National Congress, held from 23 to 31 August 1911.

The changing self-image of Indian women and their questioning finger towards the continued monopolization of public roles by men were well-epitomized by Haridya Mohini's rebuttal of Padam Singh Sharma's article 'Stree Shiksha Par Akbar Ke Vichar' (reproduced from *Grihlakshmi*). For example, see the following extract in the June 1917 issue of *Stree Darpan:*

> *Publick mein kya zaroor ki ja kar tane raho,*
> *Parh likh kar apne ghar hi mein ishwar bane raho,*
> *Tum ko bitha ke taak par pooja karenge hum,*
> *Bhogo jo ghar mein baith, na latton ko koye gam.*

> (Why is it obligatory for you to project yourself as public men? Get knowledge and stay like gods at home. We shall place you

as idols in the nook and worship you. If you choose to enjoy the domestic pleasures you will cause no anxiety to Sahebs.)

On the basis of their shared experiences of subordination, victimization, repression, humiliation, emotional and economic dependence on the family (both natal and husband's home), these critical women—majority of them being ordinary housewives—questioned the justification of double moral standards and privileges of polygamy and divorce for men. They also demanded the reformulation of a more equitable and rational code of conduct and scrapping of discriminatory social regulations and *shastric* prescriptions governing upbringing of male and female children, especially the content and level of education, (or no education at all), access to and distribution of socio-economic power, property rights and social status.[35]

It was a sign of their maturity that these women had graduated from the stage of bold and unsparing criticism of patriarchal structures, ideology and discriminatory social practices to self-introspection and self-reform. Arguing that no section of society or community could achieve real progress, reform and secure their rights through initiative by others, the women writers urged their sisters to become self-reliant. Their real liberation consisted in breaking shackles of ignorance, superstitions, blind faith in social customs and rituals. The habit of squandering huge amounts of money on gold ornaments, expensive clothes, undeserving licentious and wily *pandas, shamans* and fake *sadhus* and *fakirs* was the sign of immaturity. Real charity consisted in giving education to the poor and in becoming foster-parents of orphans.[36]

Let us discuss briefly their changed expectations from marriage and views on gender relations. Although the new crop of women had not expressed disapproval of arranged marriages, they resented mismatched marriages. A number of women and male writers had lashed out at the arbitrariness of the majority of parents (especially Hindus) who, in order to earn merit of *Kanyadan*, married their innocent little daughters to any man—widower, drunkard, licentious, chronically sick, mentally unsound or advanced in age. Once married, she was callously denied either help, support or shelter even when she was maltreated or widowed.[37]

Aware of the changing mental ethos of the young girls,

Rameshwari Nehru decided to reprint prize-winning articles on the almost taboo theme 'Pati Kaisa Ho' from the June-July issues of *Chand* (originally published in the English magazine *Physical Culture*) in its December 1916 issue. It became the pointer of intelligent and imaginative women's desire to choose their future husbands or at least to envisage certain essential qualities in them. Some of these were mental compatibility (subsuming an equal level of intelligence and educational qualification if not higher), sound health, good physique if not exactly handsome body, generous, sincere and affectionate disposition. These rational and wordly-wise girls from middle-class families expected to share common ethical values, intellectual interests and marital bliss of companionship.

Despite the slow pace of attitudinal change in traditional families, a new perspective emerged on gender relations. Expectations of these young women changed from one-sided devotion and fidelity, master–slave relationship between husband and wife to a more humane and personal equation based on mutual self-respect, romantic love and a sense of camaraderie. Obviously, the conventional ideal of *sahadharmini* or *ardhangini,* which relegates wives to the position of mere promoters of their husbands' interests and an instrument to fulfil their social and religious obligations, was reconstituted and refurbished (being a blend of old and new virtues) to serve as a useful construct for the Western-educated ambitious middle-class Indian men. Factually speaking, their womenfolk had shown remarkable adaptability and readiness to assume their new responsibilities as cultured and intelligent wives, and well-trained mothers who could rear healthy progeny.[38] In spite of being a replica of Victorian woman, this role-model was accepted (though with some reservations and modifications to suit the Indian tradition) by these progressive women because it gave recognition and importance to women's feelings, concerns, intellectual potentialities and dignity as individuals.[39]

The contentious issue of recasting gender relations, leading to an improvement in the quality of conjugal life and in the treatment of the young daughters-in-law in the traditional joint families, was thrashed threadbare in the various issues of *Stree Darpan*. The select band of the enlightened urban women (not necessarily highly educated and exposed to the feminist movement in Europe) questioned the unilateral imposition of *pativrata dharma* which demanded total surrender of a wife's mind, body, soul and worldly possessions to her husband, unquestioned obedience and service like a slave, i.e. *dasi karma,* and blind faith in husband's infallibility.[40] They voiced their sharp disapproval of Ram's cruel treatment and banishment of Sita in deference to ill-informed public opinion which was cited as an example of male insensitivity and injustice. Unless women were given the right to choose their husbands in *Swayamvara* and equal opportunities of education and self-development, they had no obligation to observe *pativrata dharma,* i.e. duties towards their husbands. Husbands, too, were expected to realize and perform their duties towards their wives, i.e. *patnivrata dharma.*[41] Thus, reciprocity in conjugal relations was the new social norm, equally applicable to men and women. Both husband and wife could retain their identity and personal freedom in the new equation of gender relations.

A major alternation in women's perception of their sexuality was reflected in the columns of *Stree Darpan.* Some of them seemed to have got rid of their feeling of guilt, associated with physical pleasure. However, they resented being treated as sex objects and as factories for production of children.[42] A change in male attitude to the female body was part of the new perception of gender relations. It was reflected in the writings of liberal and enlightened men, who dubbed the sex-hungry males as brutes, even wolves as they used women for satisfaction of their carnal desires. In fact, these men were held responsible for pushing helpless women into flesh trade. The following extract in English translation illustrates the point:

> I regard men as beasts or even wolves. Men should not feel provoked by my sharp abuse. Unfortunately, as a male myself, I am aware of the inherent wolfish cruel tendency in our mentality. I concede that men are wise, powerful, learned, courageous and pioneers but why should others bother about these qualities? If males use these capabilities and talent for exploiting and enslaving the fellow human beings they ought to be shunned and condemned.[43]

Let us analyse these women's views about their traditional roles. Despite their loud protests against women's confinement to nurturing roles and tyranny of household drudgery, these rebellious women had cherished and glorified motherhood. How can this contradiction be explained? Subjugated and degraded as wives and decimated as individuals, women perceived the acquisition of motherhood as a harbinger of honour, status and power in the family as well as society. They also perceived it as a sign of divine happiness, the ultimate fulfilment of their destiny and socio-religious obligations. In the popular imagination, motherhood was associated with self-sacrifice, compassion, benevolence and boundless love. It was believed to purify the soul from dross.[44] These images had been buttressed by the Indian classical tradition of deifying the mother wherein representations of Durga, Kali, Saraswati, Sita and Vaishno were held up as examples of the deep veneration for women in Indian society.[45]

The nationalist leadership utilized the concept of *mattabhav* (motherhood) to imprint the idea of an ancient, vigorous and superior civilization upon the arrogant British imperialists[46] who denigrated Indians for their social backwardness, especially oppression of women.[47] The nationalist definition of 'motherhood' which implied love, caring, suffering, self-sacrific, moral strength and creative energy was extended to include eugencial function— the production of the race of morally, physically and intellectually equipped supermen. Its major consequence was the formulation of the ideology of motherhood and the crystallization of the image of the morally powerful and nurturing spiritual Mother India. These formulations were reiterated in the columns of *Stree Darpan* from 1911 to 1928.

In projecting the key role of mothers in the progress or decline of individuals, nation or mankind, Indian men and women sought to establish a new equation between the functions of mothers and the project of nation-building. While placing new demands on women as awakeners, mobilizers and active crusaders for *swaraj* and a comprehensive programme for social reform including their own uplift,[48] the nationalist leadership did not underplay its stake in healthy and enlightened mothers.[49] The women activists and ideologues endorsed this new orientation.

A significant indication of the value attached to Indian women's multiple roles was the growing awareness and concern among men about the amelioration of health of wives, mothers and children, especially daughters.[50] Their perception of the vital link between the physical fitness of mothers and national health was articulated by schoolgirls, married women and progressive men. It was reflected in their writings, which urged the readers to observe principles of health—hygienic living, nutritious food as well as balance between mental and physical labour.[51] For example, two poems, 'Purdah' and 'Nari Vilap', representing the anguished cries by the *purdah-nashin* women against their enforced imprisonment in the unhealthy surroundings, were published in the June 1926 issue of *Stree Darpan*. Being family-reading material, *Stree Darpan* had the strategic advantage of disseminating health awareness even among the purdah families whose women had been kept ignorant of their potentialities and new roles in the changing socio-political conditions. Thus, even ordinary housewives became sensitized to this important aspect of their personalities in addition to the mental awakening created by a number of vernacular journals.

As a result of substantial changes in their self-view and world-view coupled with their recent heady experience of social bonding outside the family and kinship network and newly acquired mastery of communication skills as contributors and readers of the *Stree Darpan*, the highly educated women and the ordinary housewives were equally eager to assume a variety of roles in public life. While graduating from apprenticeship under male reformers to independent organization and activity these women had chartered their roles in three broad areas of public terrain: *(a)* Women's movement, *(b)* National freedom struggle *(c)* and Professional employment.

(a) Women's movement

For the early architects and participants of women's movement in north India, one component of their work was the formation of *mahila samitis* or Ladies' Clubs at the local level. Rameshwari Nehru, who had founded Prayag Mahila Samiti (1909) Allahabad, gradually matured as an ideologue and activist to project women's issues and problems in the total socio-political context by the 1920s when all-India women's organizations, were first formed. Composed of women from different religious groups, communities and social backgrounds, these organizations, namely, Bharat Stree Mahamandal (1901), Women's Indian Association (1917), National Council of Women (1925) and All India Women's Conference (1927) made it possible for them to define their own interests and problems, purpose, solutions and plans and finally implement them.[52]

The second component was their active campaign for legislative reforms in the form of resolutions, reports and deputations to the periodically constituted committees for constitutional reforms, negotiations with the Congress leaders and protest meetings to intensify the pressure of women's organizations on the recalcitrant ruling power. The shift from demand for social reform to legislative reform with regard to the grant of political rights for women, especially right to vote, was based on the notion of social equality[53] and their right to participate in the political and administrative process. Basically conservative in nature, the demand for vote was a symbol of equality and not a means of bringing about change in the structure of society. Rameshwari Nehru had explicitly stated that women did not want the right to vote from personal or selfish motive but from a desire to discharge their personal responsibility. The complexity of modern life necessitated that women should have political rights to enable them to control the environment in the interests of their home and children.[54] Rameshwari Nehru and other representatives of women's organisations had emphasized that the presence of women in public life would help to improve the moral tone of society and elevate the standard of political life.

Apart from familiarizing its readers with the case and arguments for women's franchise, each issue of *Stree Darpan* discussed progressive stages in their struggle. The first stage included sending a special delegation to the Montagu–Chelmsford Committee on Constitutional Reforms (1917) and its evidence before the Joint Parliamentary Committee which recommended the removal of sex qualifications.[55] The second stage of the demand for 'votes for women' was launched with the appointment of Simon Commission in 1927, when women asked for representation on it. Between 1917 and 1930, they had not opposed the idea of reserved seats and nomination and after 1930, the plea for reservation in local bodies was continued.[56] It must be pointed out that their campaign for women's political rights had deepened their understanding of the national struggle for administrative reforms[57] as a prelude to independence.

(b) National freedom struggle

Stree Darpan had carried on a relentless campaign for the induction of women in the political struggle as it had believed with Gandhi that mobilization of this major segment of society was a sure way of converting each home into a battle ground thus making Indian freedom struggle mass based. Gandhi's advocacy of personal dignity and autonomy for women as well as of their natural fitness as *satyagrahis* had provided a *raison d'etre* for their entry into public life. From 1919 onwards, contributions to the journal reflected the new turn in the aspirations of the average house-bound women to serve their motherland. Regarding national enslavement as the result of social stagnation, inferior status and degrading position of women young, unmarried as well as married women wrote songs and prayers expressing their desire to enlighten the Indian men about Mother India's glorious past and exhort them to serve the motherland and restore its exalted status.[58] Their role-models ranged from the traditional ideal women like Sita, Savitri, Shavya, etc. to the more dynamic and enterprising English, Japanese and American women who had distinguished themselves as educationists, teachers, engineers, nurses, political agitators, suffragettes, etc. *Stree Darpan* had published not only the life stories of Miss Clark, Mary Carpenter, Annie Besant and a number of other prominent women[59] but also *Nari Ratan Mala* (containing the biographies and achievements of women) for the benefit of its readers and reviewed worth-reading books in its various issues.[60] The dominant theme in the editorials, articles and poems, published in *Stree Darpan* from 1918 onwards, concerned the urgency of bridging the gap between public and private world, and integrating nurturing roles with the new task of national liberation and development.[61] Sarla Debi Chaudhrani, Sarojini Naidu and a few others were cited as the models of dynamic Indian women, who had ably combined their domestic roles with their new responsibility as patriots in the service of *Bharatmata*.

By the early 1920s, *Stree Darpan* became the sounding board for Gandhian views and strategy of non-violent struggle against imperialism, economic exploitation and social oppression of women.[62] Rameshwari Nehru, an ardent Gandhian, acted as his interpreter and mobilizer of women's sympathy and active support for the ongoing socio-political movements. By her campaign for the core programme of the Non-cooperation Movement—*swadeshi,* particularly *khadi*, throughout 1921 and later on, too, in *Stree Darpan,* she had aroused the interest of its readers and contributors as illustrated by their writings including comments and letters to the Editor. She had not only helped them to understand the concept of *swadeshi,* its polyvalent symbolism, its implications for the national purification and training of the potential recruits in the ongoing fight for economic self-reliance and political freedom but also to debate these and the most contentious issue of the entry of women into public roles for national development and expansion of their social and communication spaces.[63] The positive impact of motivation is evident from the articles, poems, prayers, biographies, stories and letters contributed by the Hindi-educated women and teenaged girls, namely, Kailash Rani Baatal, Smt. Kalindi Narayan Verma, Gian Devi, Savitri Devi, Vishweshwari Devi and Miss Shishayar, who exhorted women to participate in the Non-cooperation movement, spin regularly for the manufacture of khadi clothes for their family, use *swadeshi* and inculcate patriotism and the nationalist spirit in their families and broaden the scope of their work gradually.[64]

Even more significant was their ceaseless effort for removal of mental block and prejudice against women's participation in the gigantic task of national development, progress and India's liberation from the foreign yoke. Their impassioned assertion of equal rights as Indians to work for this noble cause was tempered by the assurance that they would continue to be good wives and mothers.[65] These radical women justified their participation in the political struggle. For example, in her acerbic comment upon 'Stree Jati aur Swadhinta' by Deshbandhu, in the issue of August 1921, Rameshwari Nehru had demolished the male insistence upon shackling women to nurturing roles alone through the entire span of their life on the basis of three arguments. Firstly, men and women possessed the same degree of sensitivity, mental and physical capabilities, as well as souls and hearts. Secondly, European women's participation in public roles, instead of harming societies and nations, had promoted national development, progress and status. Thirdly, Indian men were not in such a deplorable mental and moral state that they would perpetually be in need of inspiration from their wives; and children, too, would eventually outgrow their dependence upon their mothers.

(c) Professional employment

The entry of women into the national liberation struggle, primarily with a view to making it mass-based, did not imply acceptance of their economic roles. That was why Rameshwari Nehru raised the issue of professional employment for women in order to enable them to lead an honourable life without servile dependence upon men. In her article 'Strian aur Dhanoparjan' reprinted from *Chand* in the December 1915 issue of *Stree Darpan,* she had ridiculed the glorification of women's economic dependence by male writers on the plea that it had social approval and religious sanction and ensured domestic peace and harmony. She argued that entry of women into professional employment would neither demand any radical change in social norms nor vitiate and upset the even keel of domestic life and family relationships. While justifying the need for vocational training for every young girl, Rameshwari Nehru observed:

> Hence, it is the duty of the far-sighted parents to give such vocational training to their daughters from early childhood as would enable them to become economically independent. Their ability to earn would help them to lead a dignified life instead of becoming destitutes in case of a mishap or misfortune.

The crux of Rameshwari Nehru's argument was that it was the moral duty of wise parents to equip their daughters with such training and vocational skills as would enable them to get jobs for earning livelihood. She had discussed advantages of assumption of economic roles by Indian women. Firstly, it would bring joy in the lives of widows who would no longer have to tolerate humiliation and exploitation owing to their independent economic means of income. The second but the most important gain would be in terms of its positive change in the personality of women—growth of a sense of self-respect, dignity, autonomy and the habit of taking decisions independently. Thirdly, it would enable the nation to utilize the vast potential of its women-power for promoting prosperity, development of arts and crafts as well as raising her status. In her article 'Stri Jati aur Swavlamban' in the December 1916 issue, these arguments were reiterated. Rameshwari Nehru had also discussed the availability of suitable jobs in various professions. Indian women could be trained to take up jobs as teachers, governesses, nurses and *charkha* spinners. In order to reinforce the case for economic independence for Indian women, she had used statistical data about the large-scale employment of European women in various professions.

The contributors to *Stree Darpan* had frequently referred to the economic dependence of women as an important factor for the degradation of women. Some of them had dubbed it as a major handicap in the process of social revolution wherein Indian women were required to play a catalytic role. Lack of independent economic means would prevent them from initiating constructive changes in the patterns of living including food habits and standards of cleanliness in the domestic sphere and modernization of society.

It may be pointed out that neither the thinking women like Rameshwari Nehru nor the other activists of Indian women's movement had raised the demand for the economic empowerment of women—right to access and control of economic resources of the family. This was, perhaps, a strategic consideration for securing rights for women step by step and gradually creating favourable public opinion for radical changes in the patriarchal institution of property. Quite a bit of awareness about the advantages of the induction of women into economic roles had been created. But it would take another three or four decades before women-force would become visible in job market even in the educationally advanced provinces of Madras, Bombay, and Bengal. In the Hindi heartland, which comprised educationally backward areas of Bihar, Uttar Pradesh and the Central Provinces (now Madhya Pradesh), employment of women proceeded at a painfully slow speed.

VI
CONCLUSION

The project of cultivating women's minds and refashioning their image had inevitably involved pruning, recreating and 'inventing' Indian tradition. It is not an undifferentiated past which leaps up from the issues of *Stree Darpan.* In its reconstruction, voices of women emerge as more radical and more significant than the liberal or orthodox male voices, which tended to carve out role models for women within the framework of glorious Vedic tradition and patriarchal value system. The ideal of competent domesticity for wives and nurturance of a healthy progeny for mothers were regarded as the basic constituent of Indian womanhood which was stretched to include their public roles as agitators and picketeers. A number of women writers rejected the assumption of high status of women in the glorious past. They differentiated between illusions of status, real authority and empowerment, e.g. prefixing wife's name to that of husband, deceptive courtesies, etc. Impelled by the new urgency of scrutinizing the romanticized model of super woman, some of them even questioned the idealization of Sita, who suffered indignity at the hands of her husband. While trying to understand gods and goddesses in new contexts and scriptural prescriptions for wifely roles from an angle sharpened by experiential knowledge, these radical women had underlined the dangerous tendency: how examples from classics were used for prejudicing the common man. They identified the root-cause of their oppression even before Gandhi had formalized his views on the nature of oppression of women and their personal dignity.

The image of women, as projected through the columns of *Stree Darpan,* is complex, multi-layered and multi-dimensional. The nationalist construct of a super woman, which mixed images of the learned Gargi, the heroic Luxmi Bai, the self-sacrificing Sita, the powerful Savitri, and the self-reliant Draupadi, persistently and subtly haunts the reader. There is also her more humane image— intelligent, critical, assertive, demanding social reforms, conscious of social and political rights. It becomes gradually visible as the creative dialogue progresses between the diehard traditionalists and the advocates of modern values, personal dignity, rights for human beings and not exclusively for men. Another picture is of a more aggressive new woman, projected by the Western-educated Uma Nehru, whose ultra radical views were not understood by the average Indian woman. This resembles the model of a liberated, sometimes anti-male woman.

Where does Rameshwari Nehru, who shared a liberal marital home with Uma Nehru, fit in? An eclectic interpreter of Indian tradition, she chose to incorporate the humanitarian values of the West in reformed social norms and code of conduct for gender relations for all Indians irrespective of the consideration of religion. It may be said that she had represented the values of new patriarchy which advocated mobility within the existing institutional frame-work but resisted any structural changes. Her radicalism, despite its occasional sting, had not aroused male hostility as she had often emphasized that the suffragette movement in India was a fight against orthodoxy, ignorance and reaction and not against the other sex.[66]

The new patriarchy, which evolved the nationalist resolution of women's question by modifying and reinforcing the existing structures, had co-opted women as the helpmate in the fulfilment of socio-political and economic aspirations of middle-class men under the colonial rule. In order to blunt the radicalism of feminists like Uma Nehru, its ideologues had approved of limited incorporation of the material culture of the West without compromising their passionate belief in the preservation of the self-identity of the national culture itself. As an extension of this position, they identified home as the site to retain the 'inner spirituality of indigenous life' through the agency of women. In order to enable themselves to discharge this responsibility, Indian women were urged to cultivate the virtues of "chastity, self-sacrifice, meekness, patience, devotion, kindness and love for selfless service". As long as they emulated this ideal, they could go to school, travel in public conveyance, watch public entertainment programmes and in time even take up employment in public.[67]

Broadly speaking, it was the internalization of these new patriarchal values by Rameshwari Nehru's generation of women that had facilitated the bridging of gulf between domestic and public terrain leading to their large scale entry in the Indian freedom movement and slow change in the social orientation and the conventional male view about women's nature (*Stri Swabhava*) and role. However, their spirit of accommodation had partly grown out of their strong belief in the humanistic values of Indian cultural system. Speaking to students in one of the colleges in the U.K., Rameshwari Nehru said that the concept of equality between man and woman was contained in the Hindu philosophical and religious literature.

Even more significant for this attitude were the tactical reasons. Firstly, the Indian social system lacked the basic input for a militant feminist movement—an urbanized middle class with a large number of educated women trained in professional skills and unhappy to waste their talent in domestic drudgery.[68] Secondly, the confrontationist perspective for Indian women's movement, vociferously and vigorously articulated by a few Western-educated upper middle-class women, had a limited relevance for the material conditions in India under the British rule. Owing to the male insistence on the 'cult of the genteel lady' as a mark of high social status[69], the British feminists had experienced relative deprivation despite expanding opportunities of employment and economic prosperity in the era of industrial capitalism.[70] However, the long-drawn out struggle for national freedom proved to be a more powerful catalyst of Indian women's consciousness than the demand for economic rights. Besides, the formulations of the prominent leaders of Indian women's movement namely, Rameshwari Nehru and Kamla Devi Chattopadhyay (who were also influential figures in politics) aligned with the beliefs and value-system of new patriarchy without much tension. Thus, the broad consensus on the reformulation of social values and morality, affected under the umbrella ideology of nationalism, strengthened the spirit of mutual accommodation and tolerance among Indian men and women. This positive orientation was reflected in the columns of *Stree Darpan*. Rameshwari Nehru had effectively used the print media, i.e. *Stree Darpan* for bringing about a qualitative change in the consciousness, social and intellectual outlook of Indian women, particularly the Hindi-educated women. They were equipped to forge new bonds and loyalties beyond their kinship networks in the course of their ideological interaction through the columns of the journal which had inducted them as crusaders for women's rights. Besides, she had enabled women to carve out new social and communication spaces for themselves. To use Hermann's phrase, she had activated them for 'seizing speech', i.e. expressing their anger, silence or gaps in their consciousness. Through *Stree Darpan*, the Hindi-educated women could hone and utilize their newly-found articulation skills to intervene in the hegemonic male discourse and forced them to listen. Thus, Rameshwari Nehru was instrumental in the emergence of a rudimentary intelligentsia among women who would gradually mature and become a pressure group in the 1940s.

Rameshwari Nehru's chief contribution as an editor was the skilful use of the technique of juxtaposition of different images of women and opposite points of view, of long term as well as current social and political issues for shaping enlightened public opinion incorporating the hitherto suppressed reactions, carefully hidden perceptions and insights of inarticulate women. One of its significant outcomes was the projection of the various dimensions of issues under reference through debates and discussions among the rival protagonists thus facilitating their mutual ideological interaction and indepth understanding. Rameshwari Nehru acted frequently as the moderator—occasionally intervening to clarify or to summarize the long-drawn out debate or dialogue with a view to enabling its target groups, especially women, to evaluate the issues under discussion with reference to the specificity of the Indian situation.

The second fallout of this creative dialogue was the generation of heat, enthusiasm, spiritedness and determination among women to fight their own battle through the collection of funds, formation of women's awareness-groups comprising girl-students from schools and colleges as well as educated married women at the local, district and national levels. These highly educated women of the middle classes were conducting their battle in the higher echelons against outdated social mores, customs, institutions and suppression of rights. But their less fortunate sisters, who had mastered the vernacular languages, were equally eager to participate in the early women's groups to improve their family life and their position. Formation of Prayag Mahila Samiti and Mahila Parishad in the remote towns of Mirzapur proved the continuity and simultaneity of organizational work among elite and ordinary women.

It may be conceded that *Stree Darpan* had been effectively used to bring about major alternations in the perceptions of middle-class women. However, their resulting mental reorientation had not equipped these women to declare either a total break with the past or evolve a militant strategy to defy and dismantle the existing social system. In this context, it may be emphasized that there was uneven transformation of the consciousness of middle-class women whose self-view and world-view continued to be influenced by differential standing of their families within the same economic class. The contributors as well as the editor also failed to analyze the heterogeneity of women's oppression which was complicated and mediated by caste, religion and geo-economic conditions.

Nevertheless, the significance of this self-defining project of *Stree Darpan* must not be underestimated. No doubt, Rameshwari Nehru had followed the negotiatory strategy between the nineteenth-century male-reformers and the British feminists' prescriptions for restructuring family lives, ideals of Indian womanhood as well as roles in domestic and public terrain. Turning it into an asset in the form of general social goodwill including somewhat grudging tolerance of the orthodox camp, she had activated a sizeable number of intelligent and socially committed women to coordinate and intensify their efforts for reducing gender discrimination and oppression as well as changing their disadvantaged position in relation to patriarchy. She had enabled them to respond to emancipatory calls and integrate their nurturing responsibilities with new roles as activists and organizers in public life.

REFERENCES

1. For an interesting discussion on the reformers' search for 'new woman' see Uma Chakravarti, 'Whatever Happened to the Vedic Dasi', in Kukum Sangari and Sudesh Vaid, eds., *Recasting Women: Essays in Colonial History,* (Delhi: Kali for Women, 1989), pp. 52–89.
2. Edwin Ardener, 'The Problem Revisited', in S. Ardener, ed., *Perceiving Women,* (London: Dent, 1975), pp. 21–23.
3. Rameshwari Nehru, *Gandhi is My Star: A Selection of Her Writings and Speeches,* (Patna: Pustak Bhandar, 1950), Introduction; Om Parkash Paliwal, *Rameshwari Nehru: Patriot and Nationalist;* (Delhi: National Book Trust, 1986), pp. 2–17; Kusum Pant, *The Kashmiri Pandit: Story of a Community in Exile,* (Delhi: Allied Publishers Pvt. Ltd., 1987), pp. 171–173; interview with Gulab Pandit on June 24, 1991, who was the Secretary and a close associate of Mrs. Rameshwari Nehru.
4. Somnath Dhar, 'Rameshwari Nehru Passes Away', in *Modern Review,* February 1967, Vol. CXXI, No. 2, p. 107.
5. Rameshwari Nehru's editorial articles in the issues of *Stree Darpan,* October 1915, July and December 1916, and December 1919 discuss the aims and objectives of this journal.
6. The information regarding journalistic activity in Allahabad has been drawn from Vir Bharat Talwar, 'Feminist Consciousness in Women's Journals in Hindi 1910–1920', in Kumkum Sangari and Sudesh Vaid, *n.* 1, pp. 207, 217–21.
7. *Ibid.*
8. *Stree Darpan,* October 1915, Editorial.
9. Eric Hobsbawm, 'Introduction: Inventing Traditions', in Eric Hobsbawm and Terence Ranger, eds., *Invention of Tradition,* (Cambridge: University of Cambridge Press, 1983), pp. 1, 13. In Hobsbawm's view, 'invented' traditions are highly relevant to comparatively recent "historical innovations, the nation with its associated phenomenon: nationalism, the nation-state, national symbols, histories". Construction of gender identity, i.e. womanhood may as well be included in this list. Social engineering, which is often innovative and purposely undertaken, gives them a definite character.
10. Cited in *Stree Darpan,* December 1919.
11. Sonal Shukla, 'Cultivating Minds: 19th Century Gujarati Women's Journals', *Economic and Political Weekly,* XXXI, 43, October, 1991, pp. 45, 63.
12. Uma Chakravarti, *n.* 1.
13. Eric Stokes, 'The First Century of British Colonial Rule in India : Social Revolution or Social Stagnation', in Thomas R. Metcalf, ed., *Modern India: An Interpretative Anthology,* (Delhi: Sterling Publishers, Pvt. Ltd., 1990), pp. 173–98.

14. *Stree Darpan,* July 1916, Editorial; also its issue of December 1919, Editorial.
15. Yadunandan Prasad, 'Stree Shiksha Aur Bhavishya Ka Sansar', in *Stree Darpan,* May–June, 1911.
16. Smt. Krishna Kumari, 'Bharat Ki Yeh Dasha Kyon Hui', in *Stree Darpan,* February 1918.
17. Annie Beasant, *Hindu Reform on National Lines,* (Adyar: Theosophical Publishing House, 1932), p. 11.
18. For a detailed discussion about the establishment of Aligarh Girl's School see Gail Minault, 'Sheikh Abdullah, Begum Abdullah and *Sharif* Education for Girls at Aligarh', in Imtiaz Ahmad, ed., *Modernisation and Social Change Among Muslims in India,* (Delhi: Manohar Book Service, 1983), pp. 207–36.
19. Patricia Jeffery, *Frogs in a Well: Indian Women in Purdah,* (New Delhi: Vikas Publishing House, 1979). Patricia Jeffery has used 'sexual apartheid' as the title of Chapter I, dealing with the issue of seclusion of women.
20. Smt. Satyawati, 'Striyan aur Purdah', and Smt. Bhagyawati, 'Adhunik Purdah Pranali Tatha Us Se Haniyan', in *Stree Darpan*, August 1918.
21. Smt. Rajdulari Devi, 'Purdeh ki Visham Vedna', and Kumari Chandravati Devi, 'Strian aur Samajik Swatantarta', in *ibid.,* December 1918.
22. For the Arya Samaj's conceptualization of womanhood and its role see Swami Dayanand, *Satyarth Prakash* Trans. Chiranjiv Bhardwaj, (Agra: Arya Pratinidhi Sahba, 1915), pp. 22–32.
23. *Collected works of Mahatma Gandhi,* Vol. XII, 1924, (New Delhi: Ministry of Information and Broadcasting, 1974), p. 524.
24. Tapan Ray Chaudhary, *Europe Reconsidered: Perceptions of the West in Nineteenth Century Bengal,* (Delhi: Oxford University Press, 1988), pp. ix–x. Tapan makes this idea of 'new times' and ecounter between 'the East' and 'the West', the point of departure of his whole interpretative and historical exercise. The 'encounter', he points out, means 'a change'. "It is a part of modernisation", "the revolution in their world-view". Allusions to 'continuity and change', 'tradition and modernity' involved the management of gender roles, division of labour outside and within the family in terms of the needs of the 'new times' in the social reform discourse in India.
25. Doranne Jacobson and Susan Wadley, *Women in India: Two Perspectives,* (New Delhi: Manohar Book Service, 1977), p. 120. This view found expression in Manohar Prasad Mishar, 'Stree Par Dabau', in *Stree Darpan,* December 1919.
26. I.J. Leslie, *Strisvabhava: The Inherent Nature of Women,* Vol. I, pt. II, N.J. Allen, R.F. Gombrich, T. Ray Chaudhary, eds., (Delhi: Oxford University Press, 1986). This paper is a commentary on

Tryambakayajavan's *Stree Dharmapdhiti,* an 18th-century document.

27. The contributors to *Stree Darpan,* particularly women, had tried to remove wrong notions about women's nature. For example, see comment of Yadunandan Prasad, 'Stri Shiksha aur Bhavishya Ka Sanskar', 'Pativrata Dharma aur Swatantarta', August 1921. The writer of this article took Prameshwar Dyal, Vakil, to task for his contention that women without patriarchal control tended to become licentious.
28. Uma Nehru 'Pashchatya Strian', in *Stree Darpan,* December 1915.
29. Nar Haridass, 'Abala Vinay', in *Stree Darpan,* December 1915. Phulkumari, 'Ek Manohar Aabhushan Sahansheelta', in *ibid.,* April 1919. Phul Kumari gave a comprehensive definition of tolerance subsuming goodness, patriotism and love for social service, etc.
30. Kailash Rani Baatal, 'Strion Ka Mahatva Tatha Purshoan Ke Kartavya', in *Stree Darpan,* December 1915. C.Y. Chintamani, 'Strion Ki Dasha', May 1911, Rameshwari Nehru, 'Mata Ka Uttardayitav', March 1918. Also Rama Shankar Visharad, 'Ramani Mahatav', September 1918.
31. *Ibid.* Baatal referred to those who treated women no better than domestic animals. Hukma Devi, 'Ardhangini Ya Paon Ki Jooti', March 1918; Kesari Devi, 'Ashaant Grih', July 1921. She accused men of treating women as 'cattle'.
32. Rameshwari Nehru, 'Strion Par Dabau', in *Stree Darpan,* August 1919.
33. Om Prakash Aggarwal, 'Aggarwal Bandhuaun Tatha Anaya Pathakgan: Reply to a letter', in *Stree Darpan,* May 1928.
34. Kumari Pyari, 'Man Ki Baat – Letter to the Editor', in *Ibid.* May–June 1920. Smt. Rajdulari Devi, 'Purdeh Ki Visham Vedna', December, 1913. This article was, originally, read in the Stree Dharam Sammelan, Fatehgarh, 1918.
35. These ideas are scattered in Letters to the Editor, articles and poems, contributed by both male and female writers to *Stree Darpan*, 1911–1928. For example, see Sant Charan Khanna, 'Bhartiya Strian Aur Unke Sudhark', January 1918. This article highlighted the dichotomy between public utterances and private life on the issue of uplift of women; Gulab Devi Chaturvedi, 'Letter to the Editor', February 1918; Kumari Chandravati Gupta, 'Strian Aur Samajik Swatantarta', and Surya Devi 'Nari Vilap', December 1918. Their theme is victimization, oppression and denial of personal dignity, autonomy and education to women. Also Kumari Raj Kishori, 'Bhari Achraj', April 1919. This poem expresses scepticism and bewilderment over unilateral expectations and imposition of double standards on women; Kumari Pyari, 'Man Ki Baat – A Letter to the Editor', May–June 1920. Deshbandhu, 'Stree Jati Aur Asahyog', August 1921. It focused upon division between male and female spaces.
36. Surya Kumari Devi, 'Stri Jati Mein Dhan Ka Durupyog', December 1918; Girija Kumari Ghosh, 'Bhushan Bhavna', August 1911.

Satyabhakt, a Communist leader in Uttar Pradesh and a champion of women's movement, highlighted another aspect of reform in his article 'Bharat Mein Ashleelta Ki Vridhi', October 1919. Obscene and abusive songs (*sithne*) at marriages even in respectable families was the target of attack.

37. Ayurvedacharya Chatursen Shastri, 'Stri Shakti', June 1926.
38. Kumari Chandravati Gupt, 'Strian Aur Samajik Swatantarta', August, 1918; Mahatma Gandhi, 'Strion Ke Nam Chithi', August 1921.
39. Rameshwari Nehru, 'Stri Jati Aur Desh Ki Swadhinta', August 1921.
40. Surya Devi, 'Nari Vilap' December 1918; Dharampatni Kalindi Narayan Verma, 'Pativrata Dharm Aur Swatantarta', August 1921. The fact that the author articulated her radical ideas under the name of her husband showed the deep-rooted impact of the social norm of the merger of wife's identity with her husband's identity.
41. Smt. Hira Devi, 'Stri Vrat', July 1910. In her articles, Kailash Rani Baatal, a regular contributor to *Stree Darpan*, often drew attention to the contradiction between the public postures and private behaviour of Indian men who flaunted the liberal ideal of 'duties towards women' as a rhetoric. Her article, 'Strion Ka Mahatava Tatha Purushoan Ka Kartavya', December 1915, was an eloquent articulation of these ideas; Uma Nehru, 'Hamara Samajik Dhancha', April 1918.
42. Rameshwari Nehru, 'Bebyahi Mata', Editorial, 1 April 1919; Dharampatni Kalindi Narayan Verma, 'Pativrata Dharma Aur Swatantarta', August 1921. Editorial, May 1926.
43. Ayurvedacharya Chatursen Shastri, *n.* 37. Dev Narayan Upadhyay, 'Nari Jeevan', August 1921. In the same issue see Deshbandhu. 'Stri Jati Aur Swadhinta'.
44. Rameshwari Nehru, 'Mata Ka Uttardayitav', in *Stree Darpan,* March 1918. The Editor had delivered this lecture at the Bharat Mahila Samiti Conference (Rangoon) on 25th January 1918.
45. Susan S. Wadley, 'Women and the Hindu Tradition', in Doranne Jacobson and Susan Wadley, *n.* 25, pp. 114–17, 124. Rameshwari Nehru, *n.* 44. While Susan Wadley has focused on the quality of female nature as projected in the Hindu classical and folk tradition, Rameshwari Nehru reminded its readers about the honourable status and benign nature of motherhood.
46. Margaret Cousins, 'Women and Oriental Culture', *The Leader,* 9 January 1930.
47. For the typical colonial view of Indian culture and women see James Mill, *The History of British India* with notes by H.H. Wilson, (London: James Madden, 1840), pp. 312–13. Mill's indictment of degenerate Indian civilization and the abject position of women, who required 'protection' and 'intervention' on humanitarian grounds, was ingrained in the colonial ideology. Almost eight decades later, Mill's line of

argument would reappear in Katherine Mayo, *Mother India,* (London: Howard Baker, 1917).

48. Gian Devi, 'Kya Strian Yug Yugantar Kar Sakti Hain', January 1919; Surya Narain Agnihotri, 'Narian Avem Jagatvyapi Kranti', May 1928; Mahesh Prasad, 'Strian Kya Nahin Kar Saktin', Jai Rani Rohtagi', Asahyog Aur Strain', August 1921, Uma Nehru, 'Strion Mein Swadeshi Prachar', November 1921.
49. Hemant Kumari Chaudhari, 'Matri Samaj Ka Sudhar' in *Stree Darpan,* December 1915. This article was reprinted from *Navjivan.*
50. Rameshwari Nehru, *n.* 44; Hemant Kumari Chaudhari, *n.* 49; Krishan Verma, 'Stri Samaj Mein Sharirak Sudhar Ki Aavashayakta', September 1921.
51. *Ibid.;* Shakuntala Devi Gupta, 'Unnati Kya Hai?', April 1925; Raj Rani, 'Suswasth Ki Kunji', November 1928; Raj Rani, a teenaged poetess, defined the five principles of health.
52. Geraldine Forbes, 'From Patronage to Partisanship: The Beginnings of the Women's Movement in India', in Margaret Case and N. Gerald Barrier, eds., *Aspects of India,* (New Delhi: American Institute of Indian Studies, 1986), pp. 99–115. For a detailed account of the Women's movement in India See Jana Everett, *Women and Social Change in India,* (New Delhi: Heritage Publishers, 1981).
53. For an understanding of Rameshwari Nehru's notion of social equality see her editorial 'Stri Jati Aur Swadhinta', August 1921; also Kumari Chandravati, 'Strian Aur Samajik Swatantarta', December 1918.
54. *Rameshwari Nehru Papers* – Copy of her speech delivered at a women's college in England, (New Delhi: Nehru Memorial Museum and Library).
55. For a critical review of women organizations' campaign for vote see Geraldine Forbes, 'Votes For Women', in Vina Mazumdar, ed., *Symbols of Power: Studies on the Political Status of Women in India,* (Bombay: Allied Publishers, 1979), pp. 3–39. For an idea of Rameshwari Nehru's role in this campaign see various issues of *Stree Darpan,* January-June 1918, May–June and August 1919, August 1921.
56. Geraldine Forbes, *n.* 55, pp. 14–15.
57. The Montagu–Chelmsford Report, which had sparked off a controversy between the supporters, opponents and critics of the Reform Scheme, was also discussed in the columns of *Stree Darpan.* For an optimistic view of Reforms see Kailash Rani Baatal, 'Bhartiya Sudharon Par Kuch Vichar', August 1918. For the criticism of the Report see Rameshwari Nehru, 'Upar Vaale Lekh Par Sampadakiya Vichar', August 1918. In order to clarify doubts, raised by the Editor on the issue under reference, Kailash Rani Baatal wrote another article entitled 'Bhartiya Shasan Sudhar Par Kuch Vichar', September 1918.
58. Savitri Devi, 'Desh Prem', May 1911; Braj Kishori Devi, 'Desh Bhakti', August 1918; Shishayar, 'Bharat Mata', December 1918, January 1919.

59. For the glorification of the conventional ideal of womanhood incorporating the additional quality of patriotism see 'Balikaon Ka Jivan-run Gaan', August 1918. In the same issue see also Kumari Chandravati Gupt, 'Strian Aur Samajik Swatantarta'; Vishaveshwari Devi Bajpeyi, 'Swadeshabhiman', January 1919. Admiration for the talented and spirited European women was expressed in a number of articles, published in the various issues of *Stree Darpan.* Kailash Rani Baatal, 'Japani Lalnaon Ki Unnati', August 1911; Gopal Prasad Sharma, 'Vayaparin Mahilayen', October 1915. This article was printed from *Swadesh Bandhav,* July 1915; Kumari Sujata Devi, 'Niswarth Jivan Ka Chitran – Mary Carpenter', December 1918; Miss Helen Keller, 'Bhartiya Strion Ko Sandesha', September 1919.
61. Rameshwari Nehru, 'Stree Jati Aur Asahyog', August 1921; also her editorial, 'Stri Jati Aur Desh Ki Swadhinta', in the same issue.
62. *Stree Darpan* reprinted a number of Gandhi's articles, letters and his comments from *Navjivan, Young India* and other journals on various aspects of women's degraded position which had an important bearing on the reform of Indian social system, man–woman relationship and their role in the ongoing struggle for *Swaraj,* both economic and political. See for example, 'Stree Jati ke Sambandh Mein Gandhi Ji ke Vichar', March 1918; 'Strion ki Unnati ke Vishay Mein', July 1919; 'Mahtama Ji ka Kathan' and 'Strion ke Nam Gandhi Ji ki Chithi', August 1921; 'Hamari Patit Behanain', November 1921.
63. Editorial 'Satyagraha', May–June 1919; also see editorial of August 1921.
64. A number of articles on the theme of Non-cooperation and *swadeshi* were published during the year 1921. For example, see Rameshwari Nehru, 'Charkhaon Ka Prachar', July 1921. The August 1921 issue published Rameshwari Nehru's editorial 'Swadeshi'; it was a comment on Deshbandhu's article, 'Stri Jati Aur Asahyog'; another editorial article 'Stri Jati Aur Desh ki Swadhinta'; Jai Rani Rohtagi, 'Asahyog Aur Strian', in *ibid.* In this issue, poems also appeared. For example, see Anup Sundari Rohtagi, 'Asahyog Tarang', and Gauri Shankar Sharma, 'Mahatama Gandhi Aadesh'. Shri Nischal 'Charkhe Par Gaan', September 1921. Vishambharnath Jijja 'Strion Ka Kartavya', November 1921 indicated a more positive approach. The author urged women to form their own independent separate organization and mobilize contribution to the ongoing non-violent struggle under the leadership of Mahatama Gandhi.
65. Rameshwari Nehru, 'Stri Jati Aur Desh Ki Swadhinta', August 1921. Her editorial, 'Veer Strian', November 1921, cited Bi Amman's message which urged both Muslim and Hindu women to join hands with the Congress in order to make Swadeshi Movement successful. In the same issue see Uma Nehru's article 'Strion Mein Swadeshi Prachar'; Kesari

Devi, 'Ashant Grih', July 1921. This writer argued that men could not secure *swaraj* without the whole-hearted co-operation of women. Until women were treated as dignified and autonomous individuals, they would never lend their sympathy and active support.

66. *Rameshwari Nehru Papers, n.* 54.
67. Partha Chatterjee, 'The Nationalist Resolution of the Women's Question', in Kumkum Sangari and Sudesh Vaid, *n.* 1, p. 247.
68. Romila Thapar, 'Looking Back in History', in Devaki Jain ed., *Indian Women,* (New Delhi: Ministry of Information and Broadcasting, Government of India, 1975), p. 14.
69. Barbara Walter, 'The Cult of True Womanhood 1820–1860', in the *American Quarterly,* No. 16, 1966, pp. 151–74; Catherine Hall, 'The Early Formation of Victorian Domestic Ideology', in S. Burman, ed., *Fit Work for Women,* (Canbera, London: Australian University Press, 1979), pp. 15–31.
70. For a competent analysis of the impact of industrial capitalism on women in the 19th-century Great Britain and America see William O'Neill, *Every One Was Brave,* (Chicago: Quadrangle Books, 1969). For an analysis of the impact of capitalism on the institution of family see Alizaresky, 'Family and Personal Life', *Socialist Revolution,* 3, January–April, 1973, pp. 79–123. Also Ivy Pinchbeck, *Workers and Industrial Revolution 1750–1850,* (New York: Augustus M. Kelly, 1909), pp. 282–316.

4

Jallianwala Bagh Tragedy
The Catalyst of Indian Women's Consciousness

The iron-fisted Punjab administrators in 1919 unwittingly performed the bloody baptism of the 'muted groups' in the vocation of politics. Edwin Ardener, the first to propose the theory of 'muted groups', has argued that the 'dominant groups' in society generate and control the dominant models of expression and if the 'muted groups' wish to express themselves they are forced to do so through the dominant modes of expression whether colonial or indigenous.[1] As far as Ardener is concerned, the problem of muting is a problem of frustrated communication. Until the end of the nineteenth century, the majority of Indians, especially women and masses, remained 'muted' because their model of reality, their views of the world, could not be realized or expressed in the dominant structures and cultural idiom. Even the English-educated Indians, despite their valiant efforts to participate in the colonial discourse, were eventually forced to restructure their self-image, world-view and attitudes towards the colonial connection because the racist Western projections of India and Indians gradually stood exposed in their narrowness, bias and overblown sense of superiority. Their growing knowledge of the nature of British imperialism and the experiential reality of the colonial social world and politics transformed their consciousness which was predominantly anti-colonial but not strictly nationalist; the latter presupposes change in perspective from opposition to colonialism to the problems of unity and integration within the country.[2]

In this essay, I will try to show how the colonial state's negative response to the agitation against the Rowlatt Bills, its veiled defence of the Jallianwala Bagh massacre, the subsequent British attempts to whitewash and gloss over the indiscretions of the dictatorial civil authorities and misuse of power by the Martial Law administrators in the Punjab, has altered the mindset of not only the politically—conscious minority in this region as in the rest of India but also that of the 'muted groups', especially the poor illiterate masses and women. In the latter case, the dichotomy between domestic and public space was to become increasingly fluid, less restrictive and stifling as the national movement graduated from elitist circles to the nationalist arena.

History-writing from this angle adumbrates an inner view of historical process. The source material for this article is found more in interviews, statements before non-official bodies and vernacular literature on the Jallianwala Bagh tragedy and biographies and autobiographies than in government records and documents.

I
NATURE OF THE COLONIAL STATE IN PUNJAB

The Punjab was a Non-Regulation province and its administrative structure, dominated and controlled by the colonial state on account of the region's crucial importance for the solvency and military security of the British *Raj*, was a curious mix of authoritarian, paternal and democratic elements. The unique character of the state and its polity had influenced the development of the people's attitudes and mental orientation towards the colonial connection as well as the form of political and social movements. The process of the construction of its governmental structure, legal institutions and codes, and revenue system which spread over more than six decades, was characterised by 'masterful attempts' to prolong the atmosphere of military conquest up to late 1850s[3]. John Lawrence mitigated the harshness of this autocratic phase by his respect for indigenous customs and intimate contact with the people, especially peasantry, which may be termed as 'paternal utilitarianism', fired by evangelical zeal and underpinned by a Platonic conception of being a wise guardian. The long-term authoritarian and domineering mentality was determined by the self-image of the early British conquerors-cum-administrators and functionaries in Punjab who were faced with a three-fold task; *(a)* to convert 'the sullen and bitter resignation of the vanquished into honest, contented and hearty loyalty'; *(b)* infusion of the elements of civilized administration; and *(c)* to convert the Punjab into not only a secure but also a profitable possession.[4] Such a perception of their role was reinforced by the cataclysm of 1857.

The self-image of the Punjab administrators as saviours of the *Raj* was moulded by a number of assumptions about the potential threat from a high-spirited and martial local population and the border tribes. Imbued with imperial consciousness, they pursued their mission 'to subdue, administer, convert and improve without halting and without question'.[5] A sense of *angrezi dharma* provided justification and direction to the functionaries of the *Raj.* Above all, these officers were keen to carve out their image as decisive, strong and efficient rulers who were also sensitive, fair and accessible to the people.

In other words, the legitimacy of their rule was the major concern of the British who secured it through various strategies such as the cultivation of goodwill and support of those institutions, social groups, religious elites, landed aristocracy, *jagirdars,* prominent families and war-like tribes, whose help was regarded as vital for social and political control. This major compulsion was highlighted in a document on 'Social and political intercourse with Punjabis', distributed amongst young officers.[6]

In the next phase, dominated by Fitz James Stephen (the Law Member 1869–72), the paternal element was replaced by an authoritarian tendency in utilitarianism, but evangelical zeal still energized the imperial mission. Believing that the foremost function of government in India was 'to protect peaceable men and to beat down wrong doers, to extort respect and to enforce obedience',[7] he highlighted the positive role of law, backed by power. Following this logic, law constituted the most significant basis of legitimacy for colonial officials. The phase of aggressive legislation during the 1860s and 1870s, which was a direct outcome of this belief, had stripped the Punjab of its distinction of being a 'Non-Regulation' province and brought it close to the pattern of the other parts of British India. Unlike the Benthamite period, when the movement for modernization had been regarded as a co-operative effort between the English and the Indian middle class, the Punjab school of administrators "forced reform at the sword-point believing that benighted people had to be compelled towards light".[8] Now, reform was carried out in the spirit of racial conquest that characterized the post-mutiny period coupled with the strong-handedness of the Punjab school but none of its Lawrencian kindliness, and general harmony between the paternalist and modernizing currents. Despite the increasing advocacy of 'rule of law' through its definition and codification for the modernization of 'despotic and Oriental societies', particularly Indian, the reactionary and high-handed military mentality remained operative through the regimes of Denzil Ibbetson and Michael O'Dwyer. Such a perception of the colonial state has been projected by a few scholars who have argued that the colonial state based its power on coercive domination rather than consent or hegemony.[9]

Recent writings have shown that the colonial state cannot be described merely as a coercive institution.[10] Undoubtedly, the power of the colonial state rested on its monopoly over instruments of force and violence. However, after the conquest of the country, demonstration of coercive power and judicious intervention of repressive measures were regarded essential for creating an awareness of the power of the *Raj* but not in managing the day-to-day affairs of the state. In the formulation and implementation of policies and laws, the element of forcible imposition was moderated by the desire to secure consent and conciliate opposition. In other words, legitimization of colonial rule remained a major preoccupation of the colonial state. It is in this context that the concepts of consent of the colonial people for legislation or the use of force and collaboration, with the potential supporters of the *Raj* acquired significance.[11] While consent implied a certain degree of willingness on the part of the state to concede space to public opinion and flexibility of approach to the problems of administration in a foreign country, 'collaboration' offered 'a share in the government' in the form of important appointments in bureaucracy to landlord and princely classes at the price of unqualified support to the British rulers and endorsement of their policies. In the imperialist hegemonic discourse, neither 'consent' nor 'collaboration' was entitled to the privileges available to the people in a representative government.

Obviously, the British-Indian State was semi-hegemonic—an amalgamation of authoritarian and liberal elements. Despite the imperialist content of its policies and essentially exploitative functions and goals, it had replicated many characteristics of the modern state in western Europe. The nature of democratic freedoms and civil liberties guaranteed in colonial societies certainly differed from those in Europe. While retaining its authoritarian core, the colonial state was obliged to concede "a semblance of civil liberty in keeping with the democratic practice at home because it has made some constitutional commitments in India".[12]

The nature of colonial state was influenced by one major development: transfer of authority and power over the Indian empire from the hands of the East India Company to the British Parliament under the Government of India Act of 1858. The British approach to the empire, projected as primarily utilitarian by Eric Stokes, is now regarded as a product of the collective application of four doctrines. These may be described as the Burkean doctrine of imperial trusteeship, the Benthamite theory of state activity as propagated by Mills (James Mill and his son J.S. Mill), the Platonic concept of a ruling elite in the role of wise guardians, and the evangelical zeal to spread the Christian gospel, so as "to save the souls of a perversely irresponsive people". Despite the obvious mutual contradictions and affinities in the course of their interaction, the cumulative impact of these doctrines was transmuted into a continuing motive force of the British imperial policy.[13] Its long-term but strange impact on Indian polity was the evolution of colonial constitutionalism without dismantling the autocratic form of imperial government in India.

It may be pointed out that the role of the European ideas, especially these four doctrines, was important in the crystallization of the hardcore of the colonial state and its hegemonic discourse but the response of the colonial society in a given situation and its specific needs were crucial to the entire process. Both the elite colonial administrators and policy-makers[14] and the nationalist leadership recognized the dependence of the colonial state for ruling India upon the consent of the subject people to accept its moral authority, its laws and policies for the regulation of their social and property relations. For example, Gandhi rejected the interpretation of consent as merely passive acquiescence, apathy, submissiveness and unquestioned obedience to state apparatus. While conceding the fact that the colonial state was militarily too powerful to be dislodged with violence, he proclaimed the active role and autonomy of an enlightened public opinion in his book, *Hind Swaraj:*

> You have great military resources. Your naval power is matchless. If we wanted to fight you on your own ground, we should be unable to do so, but if the above submissions be not acceptable to

> you, we cease to play the part of the ruled. You may if you like cut us to pieces. You may shatter us at the cannon's mouth. *If you act contrary to our will, we shall not help you and, without our help, we know that you cannot move one step forward.*[15] (emphasis is mine)

However, he acknowledged that the development of such a critical temper and consciousness of the people's strength among the thirty crores of human beings demanded a psychological transformation. It implied the removal of a 'slavish and defeatist mentality' underpinned by fear, caused by use of brutal physical force and psychological onslaught.

Gandhi's first major countrywide experiment of cultivating a critical temper among Indians and mobilizing their moral resistance was occasioned by the British imperialist government's decision to curb elementary civil liberties of the people through the legislation of the Rowlatt Act despite nationalist opposition. In this context, it is important to analyze the nature of Indian consciousness with special reference to the Punjab which became the centre of display of physical force, coercive power and repression by the new breed of authoritarian functionaries led by its Lieutenant Governor Sir Michael O'Dwyer.

II
MINDSET OF THE COLONIZED

Despite the timelag in terms of the Punjab's encounter with the colonial rule and its legitimizing discourse, its people covered various turns in colonial consciousness in the short span of seven decades, i.e. 1849–1919, when the Jallianwala massacre was perpetrated. Whether in Bengal, where the actual process of imperial expansion had been set in motion as early as 1765 with the Battle of Plassey, or in the Punjab which became the last but the most valuable outpost of the British empire, the British were constantly haunted by the fear that military conquest had only won them a 'precarious hegemony'. The most enduring and the most profitable conquest was the one over mind. By the mid-nineteenth century, when not plagued by any rivals and threats, the rulers abandoned their majestic aloofness and compromising and beseeching tone but focused their energies upon forging tools and strategies for legitimizing the presence of the colonial state, its hegemonies, authority and *raison d'etre* of its economic exploitation.[16]

The colonial state had used two strategies: the first one required the new rulers to adopt the political structure as well as the cultural discourse of the existing Mughal regime, which had a practical utility for the Company Government during the period 1765 to 1813, when it had not possessed real political authority and economic power to enforce social reforms, to restructure social relations and manufacture identities. But more relevant to our purpose is the second strategy which stipulated that the structure and discourse of Indian polity and society be remodelled through a serious missionary effort for the spread of Western education. Its direct implication was that the British potentates became seriously engaged in increasing colonial consciousness and intensified their drive for the spread of Western education with a twofold purpose: utilitarian and ideological. For its first, i.e., utilitarian purpose, the colonial state was to train an army of English-knowing Indians who would fill in the lower rungs of various administrative departments and that too on meagre pay. Its second purpose but its main premise underlying the introduction of English education in India was the 'colonization of consciousness'. It was through the dissemination of Western education that the so-called 'moral' mission or 'civilization' mission in India was to be accomplished. It was given the utmost importance for moulding India into a replica of England—the best model of social, political and material progress—in order to enable her to serve the needs of industrial England and the British Empire.

The first generation of the Indian intelligentsia in the nineteenth-century Bengal had eagerly assimilated this ideological perspective. As this theme has been fairly well researched, I shall let it go and focus my attention on other related aspects of the transformation of colonial consciousness in the context of the Jallianwala Bagh tragedy. However, I would like to make one general comment on its nature. The colonial consciousness, which may be called the essence of Indian response towards the early phase of colonial encounter, reflected an uneasy ambivalence—a knotted combination of an acute awareness of subjection, which was caused by worsening socio-cultural and political decrepitude coupled with a sense of grateful loyalty to the 'intrinsically good' British rule.[17]

Despite regional variations owing to the nature of political consciousness, exposure to English education, new political ideas and institutions, the evolution of colonial consciousness reflected certain common characteristics. One of its major features was the cultural co-optation, which had implied the "internalization of the colonial role definitions, the language of homology between sexual and political stratarchies", imperialist perceptions of Indian history with its 'golden age' in the past and positive projection of the colonial state and its policies by the British rulers and the urban-educated sections of Indians.

Crucial to this exercise was the identification with the aggressor in the terminology of psycho-analysis.[18] As an end-product of the colonization of consciousness, many Indians began to see themselves as crypto-barbarians who ought to civilize themselves and learn to be manly through the agency of the *Raj* which possessed a vigorous rationalist tradition, superior scientific knowledge and modern political system and theory.[19] It was not surprising that they perceived salvation in becoming more like the British in friendship or enmity. Without fully sharing the British concept of martial races, the hyper-masculine, manifestly courageous, superbly loyal Indian castes did resurrect the ideology of the martial races embedded in the traditional Indian concept of statecraft. This explained the new meaning attached to *kshatriyahood* as a symbol of authentic 'Indianness' in the nineteenth-century socio-religious and political reform movements. New identity made them demand an honourable relationship between the rulers and the ruled.

At this point of time, the colonized, while playing the game within the rules set by the colonizer, rejected bisexuality and perceived femininity-in-masculinity as the final negation of man's political identity. It is not surprising that almost all protest movements before 1919 sought to redeem the Indian masculinity by defeating the British in violent conflict. Thus, the vanquished and enslaved Indians legitimized the concepts of manliness in a dominant culture: aggression, achievement, competition and power.[20]

However, the nineteenth-century response to the growing Western politico-cultural and economic domination, which had accepted the colonial state as a public authority (responsive to popular sentiments and demands while making laws and policies) and its advertised credentials of being a just and firm ruler as well as the image of India as a supine, sick, prostrate and 'effeminate' polity and civilization, could not remain representative of colonial consciousness from the beginning of the twentieth century onwards. Gandhi's insightful and creative reading of Western and Indian tradition in the context of contemporary imperialist scenario produced a "transcultural protest against the hyper-masculine world-view of colonialism".[21]

With the induction of women in his experimental satyagraha in South Africa, Gandhi had begun to construct his theory that activism and courage were perfectly compatible with womanhood, particularly motherhood. By restating the concept of androgyny (i.e. manliness and womanlines were equal, but the ability to transcend the man–woman dichotomy is superior to both because it is a signifier of godly and saintly qualities), Gandhi had not only rejected the colonial culture's ordering of sexual identities: *purusatva* (the essence of masculinity), *naritava* (the essence of femininity) and *kalibtava* (the essence of hermaphroditism) but also its argument of racial superiority.[22] Even more important was the implication that the colonialism and its culture, which were rooted in violence and aggression, stood negated and discredited. Gandhi seemed clear in his mind that activism and courage could be liberated from aggressiveness and recognized their compatibility with Indian womanhood. Thus, began his search for a coherent concept of femininity and empowerment of women for social and political change.

Gandhi's project of the redefinition of 'femininity' and its new role was interlinked with his serious concern (as of other national leaders and social reformers) for retrieving Indian 'masculinity' through the rebuttal of Katherine Mayo's mischievous charge of 'effeminacy' against his countrymen as it was an indirect endorsement of the British imperialist view about their [Indian] unfitness to rule.[23] Obviously, women's status, which had become a political issue and a point of debate and controversy under the *Raj,* became a crucial component in the process of the transformation of Indian consciousness, especially for liberating it from 'psychological and ethical complexes', also described as 'slavish or defeatist mentality' by the nationalist leadership.

III
WOMEN IN ROWLATT AGITATION TO MARTIAL LAW

Despite his first encounter with woman-power as *satyagrahis* in the course of agitation against the Black Act of 1913 (which declared

Hindu, Muslim and Parsee marriages invalid) in South Africa, Gandhi made the first explicit connection between women and their role in nation building in his speeches, campaigning for recruitment of Indians in the army during the First World War.[24] It is only with his emergence as a political leader when he confronted the problem of mass mobilization that he became increasingly aware of women, not only in terms of their problems, but also as a powerful potential force in society. Refusal of the British Government to concede his request to drop the Rowlatt Bills, which had been consistently opposed in the press and in Imperial Legislative Council by the non-official members as well as the elected members right from its introduction to its final disposal as an Act,[25] obliged Gandhi to mobilize all Indians for nationwide protest against the 'devilish legislation'.[26] Gandhi issued his famous *Hartal Manifesto* on 23 March 1919 and fixed 6 April 1919 to be observed as All India Hartal Day and a day of 'humiliation and prayer'. It was entirely based on fasting, prayer and penance for the purification of the soul.[27]

Gandhi made a special appeal to the women of India to join the satyagraha movement in large numbers and cooperate with men in their constitutional struggle which they had launched against the Rowlatt legislation.[28] As he realized that no mass movement could be successful without the participation of the 'muted' sections of society, he thought it fit that the women of India should not be kept ignorant of the prevalent political situation and resentment against injustice in the country. Even if they were not educated, they could cooperate in national constructive work like *swadeshi.* Instead of reiterating the earlier reformers' equation between education and uplift of women, Gandhi had valued their attitudinal change and contribution as practical thinkers and actors in the nationalist politics. Indian women's consciousness, which had already been awakened by social reformers, particularly Arya Samajists, was given a new direction by Gandhi. While urging women to shoulder their new responsibilities as nation builders, he said, "They have to suffer more than men and so long as they do not take equal part with men in the affairs of the world and in religious and political matters we shall not see India's star rising".[29] A large number of Indian women such as Raj Kumari Amrit Kaur, Sushila Nayar, Bibi Amtus Salaam, Mani Behn Patel, Sucheta Kriplani and Rehana Tayyab acknowledged the powerful impact of Gandhi in moulding their personal lives, attitudes and aspirations.[30] However, it was their own direct participation or of their menfolk in the anti-Rowlatt agitation which had transformed their perceptions and attitudes. For the purpose of analysing the role of women in the events from the anti-Rowlatt protest to the Jallianwala Bagh massacre, I have relied on *The Tribune* reports, personal interviews and official records pertaining to Punjab.

The process of psychological transformation, more specifically consciousness-raising among women, was rooted in their experiences during the years of the First World War. Socialized to think in terms of family relationships, the Hindu and Muslim women came to realize that they had sacrificed their sons, grandsons, brothers and husbands for the sake of the empire and yet there was no end to repression.[31] In vain, women of the middle-class families, especially those of limited means, had to cope with the scarcity of essential commodities and their exorbitant prices on account of famine and wartime constraints. Economic distress of the bread-earners of the family, who had been obliged to pay the enhanced taxes and the war contributions,[32] caused privation and hardship to numerous women even in feeding the children and other kith and kin with shrinking incomes, apart from other family expenses. In such a mental state, Punjabi women were vulnerable and sensitive to the rising wave of discontent against the Rowlatt Bills.

The Rowlatt Act agitation, a spontaneous protest against a pernicious measure, had been conducted on constitutional lines. In the Punjab, particularly Amritsar, it was reinforced by other long-standing local grievances and discontents arising out of the Platform Ticket agitation, Rate Payers' Tax, high prices, severe income tax assessment, coupled with the hurt caused by the *khilafat* grievances and frustration with the piecemeal reforms. Numerous public meetings, held in Amritsar, Lahore, Jalandhar and other towns from 31 January to 12 April 1919, reiterated the issues that had already been publicized through the press. After 18 March, when the Rowaltt Bills became an Act, all other issues paled into insignificance. The growing knowledge about the reactionary and insensitive attitude of the British rulers, as reflected in the course of debates over the Rowlatt Bills, had already made the people ready to be galvanized into action over an issue of national importance.

At this psychological moment local leaders in Amritsar undertook the task of mobilizing public opinion. In fact, success of the Rowlatt satyagraha and its nature depended to a great extent on the influence and authority of local leaders among the social groups that took part in the movement. Furthermore, it depended upon the cooperation or provocation offered by the British.[33] It was in proportion to the degree of understanding of Gandhi's teachings by local lieutenants in various parts of India that the satyagraha emerged to be static in Madras, militant in the Punjab and Delhi, and dynamic in Bombay; as for as the local leaders in Bengal, Sind and the Punjab were concerned, they had plunged themselves in the Rowlatt satyagraha without having any close association with Gandhi. In fact, Drs Saif-ud-din Kitchlew and Satyapal had never met Gandhi[34] and their understanding of Gandhi's conception of satyagraha was partial.

In the course of the Rowlatt agitation in Amritsar, Drs Kitchlew and Satyapal emerged to be the primary local leaders.[35] Both of them played a vital role in mobilizing public opinion for the redress of local grievances and the withdrawal of the Rowlatt Act by the Government of India. While Dr. Kitchlew went out to address public meetings at Lahore, Multan and Jalandhar, Dr. Satyapal, as President of the Railway Grievances Committee, concentrated his efforts on launching the Platform Ticket Agitation in Amritsar and concluding it successfully. However, it was their organized propaganda against the Rowlatt Act that added to their influence and authority among the citizens of Amritsar.

The ordinary housewives, too, had been infected by the general awakening and feeling of patriotic excitement that had percolated through their husbands and other male relatives who were either sympathetic witnesses or active participants in the political activities in the various towns of the Punjab. Increasing public receptivity to political propaganda through the press and platform and to the strident criticism of the dictatorial functioning of the Punjab Government had created panic in official circles. It furnished the authorities with an excuse of restricting the participation of Drs Satyapal and Kitchlew in public activities and later to deport them to Dharamsala on 10 April 1919.

The Rowlatt Act against can be divided into four phases.[36] Its first phase lasted from 23 March to 30 March when the leaders could guide the course of the agitation. The second phase from 2 to 6 April reflected the reaction of the local leaders towards the incidents of violence at Delhi during the course of the hartal on 30 march. The third phase extended from 6 to 9 April when the movement had gained such astounding spontaneity and vitality that it took care of itself. Local leaders just watched the course of the agitation and were baffled about its overwhelming success. The fourth phase lasted from 10 to 14 April when the mobs acted according to their own whims or the dictates of their own prudence.

The meeting of 30 March at Amritsar, according to official estimates, is said to have been attended by 30,000 to 40,000 persons.[37] This gathering on the National Day consisted of all grades of society. Dr. Kitchlew was the prime organizer,[38] while Dr. Satyapal was one of its conveners.[39] Pandit Kotu Mal, Dina Nath and Swami Anubhav Nand made speeches while Lala Girdhari Lal presided over the meeting. Swami Anubhav Nand expressed his indignation and protest against the Rowlatt Act and underlined the importance of Home Rule for India. The hartal on 30 March was observed in a thorough manner by the shopkeepers and the trading classes. Participation of the professional classes was automatic since it happened to be a Sunday. The hartal in the city on 6 April was complete. A large number of women, according to Dr. Kitchlew, had also observed a fast on that day and showed great enthusiasm and interest.[40] They held separate protest meetings. One such meeting was held in the Arya Samaj Temple, Ludhiana, on 31 March 1919. Parbati Devi, daughter of Swami Shraddha Nand (earlier known as Munshi Ram), lashed out at the Rowlatt Act.[41] The hartal was again observed on 6 April 1919 with the rest of India according to Gandhi's programme. As a mark of protest and mourning, business was suspended and kitchen hearths remained cold in thousands of households. In Lahore, politically-minded men and women, irrespective of colour, caste and creed, took a holy bath in the river Ravi before sunrise and recited prayers for the repeal of the Rowlatt Act. While walking in processions, cries of 'Rowlatt Act *hai-hai*' were raised.[42]

At other places, too, women and children joined the programme of fasting and prayers in a religious spirit within the four walls of their homes. An unprecedented enthusiasm, interest and earnestness for public activity was evident among the wives, daughters and sisters of Congressmen, who attended public meetings and processions. Prominent among them were Smt. Satyawati, wife of Lala Achint Ram (Lahore), Smt. Bhag Devi, wife of Lala Duni Chand (Ambala), Pushpa Gujral, wife of A.N. Gujral (Jhelum), Smt. Gauran Devi, wife of L.C. Dutt (Sialkot).[43] The village women, too, were infected with the religious spirit of protest. For example, in Sanghoi village, several women observed the fast along with the menfolk and praised Mahatma Gandhi.[44]

In fact, the hartal on both the days showed that the common people, the 'muted groups' including women, had been stirred so deeply that they lent their unstinted support. Their success owed to the ready support of the trading and shopkeeping class.[45] The professional classes like teachers and pleaders had mobilized public opinion to such an extent that a mere suggestion from Mahatma Gandhi to observe 6 April as the National Protest Day by observing the hartal, met with an overwhelming response.[46] There was no pressure or direct organization on the part of local leaders and a complete closure of shops and suspension of traffic to an appreciable extent seemed to be spontaneous. Dr. Kitchlew had not organized the hartal.[47]

Secondary leaders such as Badar-ul-Islam Ali Khan convened a meeting in the evening. The purpose was just to express their appreciation of the unprecedented unity, coordination and self-control exhibited by the people of Amritsar.[48] A resolution was passed requesting the King-Emperor to rescind orders against Drs. Kitchlew and Satyapal, Pandit Kotu Mal, Dina Nath and Swami Anubhava Nand. Public opinion, as *The Tribune* commented, emphatically condemned the action taken by the Punjab Government under the Defence of India Act against Drs. Kitchlew, Satyapal, and others.[49] Obviously, official indifference to public opinion and its failure to appreciate the depth of their emotional attachment for the local leaders unleashed the social anger of the uneducated masses.

Celebration of *Ramnavmi* (a religious festival of Hindus) on 9th April provided a clear demonstration of Hindu–Mohammedan unity. In the larger towns, it was the occasion for scenes of public fraternization between Hindus and Mohammedans. Mohammendans joined in celebrating the festival and the cries of 'Hindu Mussalman ki jai' and 'Gandhi ki jai' were substituted for the names of Hindu deities. At Amritsar, Mohammedans and Hindus set up *chabbils* (stalls for serving water) and *jhankiis* (pageants). Mahasha Rattan Chand also set up a *chabbil* and showed extraordinary enthusiasm in serving water to various communities. The Hindus drank out of the vessels of Mohammedans and vice versa.[50] This had been done on a smaller scale on 6th April.

The participants hailed from all walks of life. The *Ramnavmi* procession presented a cross-section of society, bound by bonds of emotional unity, which was not warped by the considerations of caste or creed or sex. Women, usually not visible in religious processions and other public functions as a matter of prevalent social norm, watched its progress from their housetops and balconies on account of its added significance as an occasion of communal harmony. Spontaneity and mass participation formed the chief features of the *Ramanavmi* celebrations in Amritsar, thus providing a sound basis for the psychological transformation in the Punjab. Michael O'Dwyer found that these spectacular demonstrations of unity, oneness and growing national consciousness were fraught with dangerous potentialities. Bereft of imagination and morose by temperament, O'Dwyer could not but shudder at the possibilities of revolt, and its leaders were none other than Kitchlew and Satyapal.[51] On 10th April, Miles Irving, the Deputy Commissioner, whisked them away to Dharamsala unexpectedly. Their deportation on the pretext of violent speeches, as *The Tribune* wrote, was indefensible and it had exposed the Punjab Government to the severest criticism for its action against independence of thought and strength in expression.[52]

The news of the deportation spread like lightening. As the news travelled from one locality to another, the people closed their shops and joined the crowd, going to plead with the Deputy Commissioner to release Kitchlew and Satyapal.[53] Women, too, were emotionally disturbed by this news. Their resentment and strong disapproval of the sly removal of the beloved leader Dr. Kitchlew was expressed through the recital of songs, composed on the spur of the moment. The refrain of one song ran:

Ratin choran wangr laigaye doctor Kitchlew nun.[54] (The government officials acted like thieves while whisking away Dr. Kitchlew under the cover of darkness).

On 10th April 1919, the British Government had fuelled the public anger to a greater intensity by arresting Gandhi at Palwal railway station in order to prevent his entry into the Punjab.[55] Both these developments caused great excitement and ignited the political atmosphere, which was evident from the spontaneous public gatherings and processions, organized with the intention of securing the release of their popular leaders. But uprovoked firing on mobs at Amritsar, Lahore and other towns in the Punjab led to violence, arson and killing of Europeans. Although Hindu and Mohammedan women had not participated in these demonstrations, they experienced the agony and torture of losing their male family members at the hands of a tactless, vindictive, unimaginative and racist regime. The victims hailed from all sections of society, including those simple-minded people who had gone for a *faryad* to the authorities and not with any rebellious intention.

The Jallianwala Bagh Massacre on 13th April 1919 was yet another act of official high-handedness, which radically changed the attitude of the politically-conscious men and women towards the colonial rule. General Dyer, who had ordered the firing of 1,650 rounds of ammunition without warning at a peaceful crowd, regarded it as a great opportunity to show people the might of British Empire for he imagined that "the Lord hath delivered them into my hands."[56]

By leaving as many as 379 dead and 1,200 wounded,[57] Dyer brimmed with satisfaction over the discharge of his duty but actually he had created a living hell for the surviving women. The imposition of night curfew had obliged a number of women in Amritsar to suffer from mental torture as they could not get any help for locating their husbands, sons and other relatives who lay parched, weltering in their own blood and mangled limbs. The traumatic experience of Rattan Devi, who had ventured into the Bagh despite the curfew order and spent the whole night with her husband's cold head in her lap, was later to be drawn out from the security of her zenana (women's quarters) to public life. Attar Kaur, whose husband Bhagmal Bhatia was a committed local Congress worker, had been forced to spend a number of frightful hours amidst the dead and the wounded (despite the advanced stage of her pregnancy) until she could bring home the dead body of her husband with the help of her family servant and Udham Singh,[58] who had pledged to avenge the dastardly killing of the innocent people of the Punjab.[59] The other women, though not courageous like them, were obliged to shoulder the responsibilities of looking after their children and families and fending for their livelihoods.

Believing that the inhabitants of the Punjab, whom he had earlier lauded for their loyalty, had conspired to wage war against the King-Emperor, Michael O'Dwyer had permitted the proclamation of the Seditious Meetings Act, followed by the imposition of Martial Law in the Punjab from mid-April to June 1919. In fact, the very purpose of O'Dwyer's insistence on the promulgation of Martial Law No. IV showed that his sole intention was that of punishing not only the alleged rioters but also the political agitators. He had always associated political agitation with the educated urban middle classes. Hence, he wanted to spread the net as wide as possible and thus kill the political movement itself and the imagined rebellion. His paranoid mentality led to the institution of a number of cases of conspiracy and rebellion against prominent members of the professional classes and other citizens, including popular leaders under Martial Law.

In Lahore, the popular leaders, namely, Lala Harkishan Lal, Lala Duni Chand, Pandit Ramabhuj Dutt and others, were arrested on 14th April, tried in camera and sentenced to transportation for life (later released under King's Proclamation of Amnesty towards the close of 1919) by special Martial Law Tribunal.[60] Their properties were confiscated and thus exposed their young wives and children to moral and material damage. On the same grounds, Babu Kali Nath Roy, Editor of *The Tribune* and Radha Krishan, Editor of the *Pratap*, were also sentenced to various terms of imprisonment and fined.[61] Similar cases of rebellion and other seditious activities were instituted against Drs. Kitchlew and Satyapal, Chaudhary Bugga Mal and Mahasha Rattan Chand, the primary and secondary leaders, respectively, of the Rowlatt agitation in Amritsar.[62]

Mahatma Gandhi, while severely criticizing the harsh and disproportionate sentences awarded to the accused in the Lahore judgement,[63] also highlighted the hardships of the young wives of other Martial Law victims in the columns of *Young India*.[64] The cases of Mahasha Rattan Chand and Chaudhary Bugga Mal received special notice as the victims' original death sentences were merely changed into transportation for life despite the strong appeals made by Pandit Motilal Nehru, C.R. Das and other leaders.[65]

Besides, the Punjab Government harassed and humiliated lawyers in various ways. By appointing them as Special Constables, they were put to a lot of physical discomfort as they had not only to patrol the city throughout the day but also to report to the authorities twice daily. For example, even a scholarly lawyer like Mr. Manohar Lal, the Vice-President of the High Court Bar Association, was disgraced. His family was harassed and locked up on 18th April 1919. His wife and children took shelter in the servants' quarters and they had to borrow beddings from friends. The search took place on 19th April and thereafter the family could return to their house.[66]

In the other towns of the Punjab, respectable citizens had equally bad experiences. At Wazirabad, the house of Jamiat Singh Bugga was seized in his absence and women and children of his family were turned out without any alternative arrangements being made for them.[67]

The inhabitants of the Punjab, especially the citizens of Amritsar, had to undergo additional suffering and humiliation. For example, the *salaaming* order brought various kinds of punishments to the defaulters in the city of Amritsar, populated by 1,60,000. Women were kept waiting tensely while their husbands, sons and other male relations were marched through the city by the whimsical police officials. While boys and men suffered the torture of being flogged publicly,[68] women watched helplessly. For example, Lachman Kaur articulated the mental agony of many a women when she remarked, "When the people were flogged their cries rent our hearts, we felt helpless. There seemed no remedy against the cruelty and oppression around us".[69] Owing to panic, men stayed in shops and women stayed alone in homes cowering under fear and tension. They had to exist without food or water and the sick could not get medicine. They complained of misbehaviour of the soldiers.[70] Ganga Devi's four-year old daughter died of fright.[71]

During the Martial Law regime even the innocent women of the villages were not spared. They were assaulted by government officials, physically manhandled and even turned out of their houses. The cruelty and barbaric behaviour of Bosworth Smith, Superintendent of Police, is illustrated by the following extract:

> In Manianwali village, on 19th April 1919, some soldiers entered the village and shot a few men without a warrant for shooting. Women fled from their houses on hearing the shoot-outs including those who were about to be mothers. ... Two men, Munshi Nawab Din and Lehna Singh were severely beaten by Mr. Bosworth Smith who assaulted their women, unveiled them and used abusive language. He called them, "Flies, bitches, she-asses!" He said to them, "Your skirts will be examined by the constables. When you were sleeping with your husbands, why did you allow them to get up and go?" He also spat at them.[72]

Gurdevi, the aged widow of Mangal Jat, also recalled a similar experience before Mr. Labh Singh, an ex-Professor and Barrister, who was specially deputed by the Congress Committee to investigate into the shocking incidents which had occurred in the Punjab.[73]

In a village, Chuharkhana, many women were summoned by the police in the absence of their husbands. They were threatened if they did not produce their husbands, their houses would be burnt and land confiscated. It was not an empty threat. A number of residents deposed that their wives had borrowed to pay fines for the release of their husbands.[74]

In Sheikhupura too, houses were locked and women along with their children were turned out.[75] Other forms of harassment were adopted. The male relatives of those women, who were unable to bribe the police, were arrested.[76] In Hafizabad, Hukma Devi's son was locked up in jail because she was unable to find money to bribe the police.[77]

The Government of the Punjab threw a veil of secrecy over the blood-curdling incidents in the province. As the Indian press was completely gagged from 15th April to 9th June 1919,[78] neither the people nor the political leaders in the Punjab and outside could get any news about the sufferings, emotional traumas, deprivation and economic ruin of the beleaguered inhabitants of this region.

IV
NEW SIGNPOSTS IN THE INDIAN CONSCIOUSNESS: FROM AMBIVALENCE TO ALIENATION

The traumatic experience of the Punjab disturbances, from the anti-Rowlatt agitation to the Jallianwala Bagh tragedy and then the Martial Law regime, brought an attitudinal change towards British rule among the politically conscious and the 'muted groups', especially women in the Punjab, as well as in the rest of India. Henceforth, political awakening and disillusionment with the liberal claims of the British rulers grew at a rapid pace. Publication of the *Report of the Commissioners,* which had exposed the inequities of the O'Dwyer regime, tended to erode faith in the British ideals of justice and fairness. It is evident from the statements and reaction of the citizens of Amritsar. For example, Mian Feroz Din, an Honorary Magistrate since 1918 and *rais,* remarked, 'I must say, however, that the pride which I myself, and my countrymen, felt in British justice, has received a rude shock.... So far as the people of Amritsar are concerned, I pray to God that we may not have to see those Martial Law days again'.[79] The people felt enraged owing to the discriminatory treatment towards Indian passengers including women, in spite of holding Martial Law passes.

A comparison between the *Reports* of the Congress Committee and of the Disorders Inquiry Committee further confirmed the fears and suspicions of Indians regarding the latter's laborious attempts to whitewash and gloss over the indiscretions and misuse of power by the Martial Law Administrator in enforcing orders like crawling, flogging and saluting of Europeans in Amritsar, Gujranwala and other towns in the Punjab.[80]

As the sufferings and humiliations of the people of the Punjab came to light, the voice of protest grew louder. The fact that General Dyer, the commanding Officer at the Jallianwala Bagh Massacre, was lionized on his return to England, had provoked anger and resentment; it also undermined the Indian faith in the British sense of justice. Gandhi's denunciation of the British rule as 'Satanic' expressed his changed views about the *Raj*.

Writing to C.F. Andrews from England, Rabindranath Tagore had also underlined his anguish and disillusionment with the British Government:

> The late events have conclusively proved that our true salvation lies in our own hands; that a nation's greatness can never find its foundation in half-hearted concessions of contemptuous niggardliness.[81]

Evidently, branding of the loyal inhabitants of the Punjab as rebels had unwittingly promoted a spirit of defiance and strenghtened the desire to kick off the national bondage. In other words, the suspicious and revengeful attitude of functionaries of the O'Dwyer regime had dispelled the illusions of Indians about retaining their self-respect and national pride as British subjects.

Michael O'Dwyer's determined effort to kill ideas and stifle political consciousness reinvigorated men as well as women. Thus, the virile and action-oriented inhabitants of Punjab were mentally prepared for the resumption of armed struggle. The sacrifices of the Kuka women—Bibi Attri, Bhagwan Kaur (Sailkot), Jai Kaur (Ludhiana), Bholi and Dharmo (Ferozepur), Ratto and Desan (Sirsa)[82]—and of the Ghadrite women, particularly Gulab Kaur, were recalled in this context. It also provided an opportunity for a critical look at the heroes and heroic movements. As a result, a search began for tapping the revolutionary potentialities in local conditions and people; it resulted in a two-pronged experiment with terrorist methods and mass movements. Henceforth, the Punjabi people set forth on a path of self-discovery; new self-images and world-view involving the etching of new psychological contours, articulation of alienation and protest indicated changes in the Indian consciousness.

How was this change in consciousness articulated by men and women? One concrete expression of alienation and protest against the colonial connection was found in the surrender of titles as a part of the Non-cooperation movement, having the rectification of Punjab wrongs as its major plank. Mahatma Gandhi returned the *Kaiser-i-Hind* Gold Medal, Zulu War Medal and Boer War Medal.[83]

The people of the Punjab also followed suit and returned *Kaiser-i-Hind* decorations, certificates, *sanads,* titles of *Rai Sahib*, *Kursinashin*, etc.[84] The women of the Punjab were not in possession of such titles or honorary posts. The lone woman was Sarla Debi Chaudhrani, who returned her war-badge granted for her regiment[85] during the First World War 1914–1918.

An unprecedented increase in the visibility of women in public life was a significant outcome of the Punjab experience. In that moment of personal and national tragedy, the old image of woman such as:

Ander Baithi lakh di
Bahar gayi khakh di.[86]

(The one who stays indoors is worth a lakh, but one who steps out is worth a straw.)

was discarded. The 'new' woman, who had developed a heightened awareness of her vulnerability in the course of Dyer's spree of racist revenge from 13th April to mid-June (wreaked on the plea of protecting the inviolability of the womanhood of the superior Anglo-Saxon breed, personified by Miss Sherwood, from the dirty black hands)'[87], felt emboldened to cross from domestic into public space.

Perceiving Gandhi as a saviour of the bleeding Punjab, especially of womenfolk of one thousand families (who had lost their bread-earners, either as a result of police firing or incarceration in jails),[88] Sarla Debi Chaudhrani invited Mahatma Gandhi to console them and to instil courage and hope into their hearts. The fact, that she acted as hostess to a male leader in the absence of her husband and accompanied him to various towns in the Punjab for organizing public meetings, indicated that Sarla Debi was made of a different metal. Already at an advanced stage of political consciousness and intellectual development, she had mobilized Punjabi women to join her struggle against Dyerism. As a result, a fairly large number of women flocked to attend public meetings when Gandhi visited Lahore, Amritsar, Gujranwala, Kasur, Wazirabad, Akalgarh, Ramanagar, Hafizabad, Sangla Hill, Sheikhupura, Lyallpur and Ludhiana,[89] in October 1919, after the ban on his entry into Punjab was lifted.[90] In order to share the grief of the *purdah* women, Gandhi held special meetings for them at Gujranwala, Lyallpur and Hafizabad.[91] The refrain of his message at all these meetings was that they should cast away fear, become autonomous individuals and promote *swadeshi*.

In the course of his visit, Gandhi came into close contact with the bereaved women of the Punjab. At Gujranwala, he comforted the wife of Diwan Mangal Sen (a Martial Law prisoner) and was impressed by her hospitality despite her sorrow.[92] In Amritsar, he met the wives of Drs. Satyapal and Kitchlew, whose fortitude in the hour of their mental tension and sorrow elicited his admiration.[93] Wherever he went, his heartfelt sympathy helped Punjabi women to abandon their fear and anxiety and devote themselves to constructive work, particularly spinning, and propaganda for *swadeshi*.[94] Many Punjabi women adopted the use of *khadi*. Sarla Debi Chaudhrani became a trendsetter when she attended parties, marriages and purdah club meetings in a khadi sari. Increasing use of khadi by Punjabi women for making dresses for children and male members of their families indicated a change in their self. view. Imbued with a new confidence, those women took an interest in cultivating their minds rather than pandering to male whims as sexual objects. Gandhi had made them conscious of their potentialities as participants in the non-violent movement for the freedom struggle. Henceforth, they were to assert their presence in domestic and national life.

As a result, a large number of Punjabi women was drawn into national politics. Prominent among them were Sarla Debi Chaudhrani, Phul Kaur (wife of the Martial Law prisoner Chaudhry Bugga Mal), Rattan Devi and Attar Kaur (widows of the Jallianwala Bagh martyrs Chajju Ram and Bhag Mal Bhatia respectively), Parbati Devi (daughter of Swami Shraddha Nand), Radha Devi (wife of Lala Lajpat Rai) and a number of ordinary housewives having no political background. Chastened by personal suffering and tragedy, these women had learnt to look beyond domestic roles and later extended their activities to the broad arena of national work which included anti-imperialist demonstrations, processions, picketing, boycott of foreign cloth, *swadeshi*, *Harijan* work and electoral politics.

A concrete evidence of their new perception of the relationship between individual, family and nation was their enthusiastic response to Gandhi's call for donations towards funds for the support of families of Martial Law victims, the Jallianwala Bagh Memorial Fund and Tilak Swaraj Fund. The Punjabi women showed a touching concern for the support of such families as had been left only with womenfolk and children as a result of Martial Law atrocities, killings and imprisonment. For example, women of Amritsar generously gave their jewellery as donation for this cause. Despite their own economic problems, Mrs. Bugga Mal and Mrs. Rattan Chand donated their gold bracelets. For the Jallianwala Bagh Memorial Fund, too, donations came from the relatives of the martyrs primarily. For example, Rattan Devi gave five hundred rupees; a domestic maid servant, who had lost her son in the Jallianwala Bagh holocaust, donated fifty rupees, which amounted to her total annual earnings.[95] Another unidentified woman presented her dead son's clothes and her ornaments towards the Jallianwala Bagh Memorial Fund.[96] These examples showed growing awareness in Punjabi women about the link between their family fortunes and national life.

Even more remarkable was their initiative and involvement in the fund-raising drive. At Ferozepur, women themselves collected funds for the Jallianwala Bagh Memorial during the National Week (6–13 April, 1920). Again, at Amritsar, women actively collected funds for the Tilak Swaraj Fund. At Bhiwani, too, Mrs. Desai and other Gujarati women made house-to-house collections, and a separate women's section for the National Fund was opened.[97]

After taking the first step in public life in the course of the anti-Rowlatt agitation, Punjabi women had learnt to articulate their sufferings as a result of the British oppression, symbolized by the Jallianwala Bagh massacre and Martial Law humiliations and deprivations. During his visit to the Punjab, Gandhi observed that the songs narrating the story of 'Dyerism', reflecting their new spiritedness and resolve to liberate their motherland from the foreign yoke, were on the lips of Punjabi women. One such popular song, sung in the course of the Rowlatt agitation, ran:

Asi nahinaun haarnan,
Bhanve saadi jaan jave,
Taup te bandook kaulon
Khande walli dhar kaulon,
Agg de sholeyan taun,
Asi nahinaun haarnan.[98]

(We shall not accept defeat even if we lose our lives, we are shot dead or cut into pieces by sword and other sharp-edged weapon or burnt alive. We resolve not to surrender.) This song was composed by Sarla Debi Chaudhrani.

In fact, the Rowlatt agitation, which had aroused a spirit of defiance and brought forth women to the streets for the first time, had released their creative potentialities and occasioned the composition of numerous poems and songs in vernacular languages. Kasturi Bai, who was taught the working knowledge of Hindi and Urdu by her nationalist husband Rampat Yadav, was not only active in the Gandhian movements in Rohtak but also a prolific poetess. Published under the title *Rashtriya Geet aur Bhajan 1930–47*, her compositions in Haryanavi-mixed-Urdu reflected her perception of the British Government—ungrateful, oppressive, exploitative and cunning. This is evident from the following extract from her poem 'Angrezi Raj ka Abhishap' ('Curse of the British Raj'):

Pichle vaade saare bhooli Rowlatt bill inaam diya,
Bus tera yehi sanmaan hai, tu nahin bhoolne paave,
Aisa bura masaan hai, bina jaan liye na jaave.
Rowlatt bill se piche bhai 'phauji' laa ke kari jaan,
Jiski rooh se misle saap ke Hindi chale pet ko taan,
Gun ke badle avgun kartaa dekho kaisa baimaan, ji.
Duniya bhar mein aisa koi dekha nahin raaj bhai,
Khaali haath praja par goli jisne ho chalvai,
Amritsar mein Jallianwala Dyer ne laash bichai.
Khud taude yehi kanoon hai, praja par dosh lagave.
Aisa bura masaan hai, bina jaan liye na jaave.[99]

(Addressing unsuspecting and innocent Hindi, i.e. Indians, Kasturi Bai asked them to remain beware of the British *Raj*. It is not a government for the people but a fatal disease which gradually sucks away the life-giving blood. There is no other government

> like the British which had ordered firing on the unarmed crowd. Dyer had covered the ground of Jallianwala Bagh with dead bodies. This is a strange sarkar which violates the law herself but punishes its subjects for law-breaking).

Kasturi Bai also wrote a number of poems glorifying the charkha. Her poems contained a bold criticism of general passivity and lack of courage among Indian men.[100] Like her, Bhag Devi (wife of Lala Duni Chand, a prominent Congress leader of Ambala), was also not formally educated but her anguish over the massacre of innocent men, women and children obliged her to overcome her handicap. Her poems appeared under the caption *Quami Bhajanon Ka Guldasta.* She was also the author of other books, including *Jagriti* and *Gita Sandesh.*[101]

Highly educated women also expressed their reaction against the Jallianwala Bagh tragedy and atrocities committed by the Martial Law administrators. Sarla Debi Chaudhrani wrote in Punjabi, Bengali and English. Her writings, *At the Point of Spindle* and *The Song of Charkha,* which had grown out of her personal experience of the British oppression and cruelty, reflected her strong faith in the efficacy of *charkha* symbolising *sudarshan chakra*. The national-minded men and women read her compositions with great fervour.[102]

Rameshwari Nehru, though not educated through the formal school and college system, emerged as one of the pioneering journalists who expressed her anguish over the Jallianwala Bagh tragedy in her articles and editorials in *Stree Darpan* (founded in 1909). Daughter of the orthodox Raja Narender Nath of Lahore, she became a full-time disciple of Mahatma Gandhi and plunged herself into campaigns for *swadeshi* and *Harijan* upliftment. She also represented the radical change in the self-view and world-view of Indian women. For example, she flouted purdah restrictions and participated in public activities against the wishes of her father. She had also chosen to differ with her mentor Mahatma Gandhi on the issue of economic empowerment, particularly employment of women. In fact, Gandhi and Indian women, in the course of their association from the Rowlatt agitation onwards, helped each other to grow and abandon their prejudices.[103]

The Jallianwala Bagh tragedy had also wounded the hearts of a number of sensitive women not living in the Punjab and it found expression in their writings. Sarojini Naidu's poem, 'Punjab in 1919' expressed her fervent conviction that the blood of martyrs would lead to freedom.[104] Subhadra Kumari Chauhan's long poem 'Jallianwala Bagh Mein Basant' (1929) recaptured the horror of indiscriminate shooting at Jallianwala Bagh which would remain the seat of eternal sorrow, never to be enlivened by the bounties of the spring season.[105]

V
CONCLUSION

The discussion of the entire course of events from the anti-Rowlatt agitation to the Jallianwala Bagh tragedy followed by the imposition of the Martial Law regime, has revealed its indelible and strong impact upon the nationalist psyche. This traumatic experience had proved to be a catalyst of the Indian consciousness especially of the 'muted groups' whose projection and involvement was crucial for the success of the Indian freedom struggle. The colonial state as well as the nationalist leadership competed with each other for conquest over the heart and minds of the Indian people with entirely different purposes, as is evident from the foregoing analysis.

In the present context, protest against the legislation of the Rowlatt Bills had shown that the colonial laws, which sought to give legitimacy to the British rule, were to become the frequent site of contest between the subjects and their rulers from the 1920s to 1940s. It had also indicated the process of psychological leavening among the Indian people and to some extent in their victimizers— the Anglo-Saxon race.

The colonial state's decision to withdraw this 'devilish legislation' (as done earlier in the case of the Punjab Canal Colonization Bills 1907) under the overwhelming pressure of public opinion and to issue Civil and Military Ordinance reflected the shrewd British perception that the perpetuation of the *Raj* depended more upon the co-operation of the subject people rather than upon the frequent military interventions. Gandhi was no less conscious of this compulsion of the hegemonic British–Indian State.

However, it was Gandhi's growing awareness of the crucial role of the Indian people in the national struggle for freedom that had led to his total involvement in the long-term project of psychological and moral revolution among his compatriots in order to wean them away from their addiction to the *angrezi raj ki barketain* (blessings of the *Raj*). Apart from its value as an argument for proving that the Indian freedom struggle was neither 'elitist' nor a camouflage for national leaders' scramble for power and authority, it conveyed a positive message to the semi-literate, poor masses and women who hoped that the transformation of their condition was an integral part of the nationalist agenda.

It may be pointed out that the 'muted groups' did not form a single category. If that is conceded then the problem is how to reconcile and relate it to the broad process of the redefinition of Indian self-hood with the transformation of the consciousness of the 'muted groups', especially women (whose deprivation and subordination varied with race, caste and class) in the course of the national struggle against colonialism and capitalism.

The 'muted groups', particularly women (without underrating the psychological leavening among ordinary peasants, workers and other such social groups), were perforce brought out of their splendid isolation. Chastened by their personal, albeit shared experience of the British repressive laws and brute force of the Martial Law regime, which had assaulted their honour, suppressed the civil rights of their menfolk and affected the well-being and economic security of their kith and kin, they were obliged to extend their nurturing hand from the home to the public arena.

This limited study has shown that the emotional scars left by the Jallianwala Bagh tragedy had led to a positive result in one sense. The general goodwill and ambivalence of Indians towards the 'fair, firm and just' *angrezi Raj* had been replaced by social anger and alienation, thus facilitating Gandhi's almost impossible task of converting each home into a battleground. Once emboldened to articulate their anguish and anger against the public authority in songs and poems, the Punjabi women (who were purdah-clad and educationally backward), were not to be deterred from discovering and harnessing their creative potentialities for social engineering, nation-building and above all for constructing their own autonomous identities. Of course, all this was done within the framework of new patriarchy which accommodated mobility without demanding structural changes.

The Indian National Congress (and later the revolutionary groups and Left party) strengthened its claims as a representative of national aspirations with the induction of women as political workers and leaders. In fact, Gandhi's perceptive act of giving moral and cultural legitimacy to women's role in public life, especially social reconstruction and political struggle, had paved the way for the increasing visibility of women in the non-violent movements from the 1920s to the 1940s. Thus, with the Jallianwala Bagh tragedy, the 'muted groups' recovered their voice, language and dignified presence, as well as their identity.

REFERENCES

1. Edwin Ardener, 'The problem Revisited', in S. Ardener, ed., *Perceiving Women,* (London: Dent, 1975,), pp. 21–23.
2. K.N Panikkar, 'Incomplete Struggle', *Seminar,* 338, October 1987, p. 27.
3. Eric Stokes, *The English Utilitarians in India,* (First published in 1959; reprinted, Delhi: Oxford University Press, 1982),·p. 268.
4. Charles Gough and Arthur D. Innes, *The Sikhs and the Sikh Wars,* (First published 1897; reprinted, Delhi: National Book Shop, 1984), p. 222. Also Foreign Department, Despatch No. 20, 7 April 1849, Governor-General Lord Dalhousie to Secret Committee.
5. Kenneth W. Jones, *Arya Dharma: Hindu Consciousness in the 19th Century Punjab*, (Delhi: Manohar Book Service, 1977), p. 12.
6. Reprinted in N.G. Barrier, 'How to Rule India', *Punjab Past and Present,* 5, 1971, pp. 276–96.
7. *The English Utilitarians*, p. 299.
8. *Ibid.,* p. 269.
9. For an exposition of this point of view see Bipan Chandra, 'Colonialism: Stages of Colonialism and the Colonial State, *Journal of Contemporary Asia,* Vol. 10, No. 3, 1980. Also Sabyasachi Bhattacharya, 'Notes on the Role of Intelligentsia in Colonial Society: India from Mid-Nineteenth Century', *Studies in History,* Vol. 1, 1979.
10. Sudipta Kaviraj, *On the Construction of Colonial Power: Structure, Discourse, Hegemony.* Occasional Papers on History and Society, Second Series, XXXV, (New Delhi: Centre for Contemporary Studies, Nehru Memorial Museum and Library, 1991), p. 19. Also Shashi Joshi and Bhagwan Josh, *Struggle for Hegemony in India 1920-47,* in 2 Vols., (New Delhi: Sage, 1992), Vol. 1, pp. 10–42; Vol. 2, pp. 25–44.
11. For an exposition of the concept of collaboration in terms of patron–client relationship see Anil Seal, *The Emergence of Indian Nationalism,* (London: Cambridge University Press, 1971).
12. Shashi Joshi and Bhagwan Josh, *n.* 10. Vol. 1.
13. Raghavan Iyer, *Utilitarianism and All That: The Political Theory of*

British Imperialism, (London: Concord Grove Press, 1983), pp. 115–23.

14. The policy of establishing hegemonic control was described in various ways such as possessing moral prestige and retaining 'legal authority' by the colonial state itself. For example, Lord Birkenhead characterized the British Government as "government founded so completely as ours is upon prestige". Cited in Simon Epstein, 'District Officers in Decline: The Erosion of British Authority in Bombay Countryside 1919–47', *Modern Asian Studies,* Vol. 16, No. 3, 1982, pp. 483–518.
15. M.K. Gandhi, *Hind Swaraj,* (Ahmedabad: Navjivan Parkashan, 1962, 1982), p. 100.
16. Sudipta Kaviraj, *On the Construction of Colonial Power,* p. 19.
17. K.N. Panikkar, 'The Intellectual History of Colonial India: Some Historiographic and Conceptual Questions', in S. Bhattacharya and Romila Thapar, eds., *Situating Indian History,* (Delhi: Oxford University Press, 1983), p. 421.
18. I have borrowed this argument from Ashish Nandy, *The Intimate Enemy: Loss and Recovery of Self under Colonialism,* (Delhi: Oxford University Press, 1983), p. 7.
19. Kamlesh Mohan, 'The Colonial Ethnography: Imperial Pursuit of Knowledge for Hegemony in the British India (Late 19th to 20th Century) in Roy McLeod and E.L. Ortiz, eds., *New Perspectives on Empires and Science* (forthcoming), p. 14 (typed script).
20. Nandy, *The Intimate Enemy,* pp. 8–9.
21. *Ibid.,* p. 48.
22. *Ibid.,* p. 52.
23. Katherine Mayo, *Mother India,* (London: Howard Baker, 1917), p. 16. Earlier, in his book *History of India* (1840), James Mill had constructed his entire argument for the justification of perpetuating the British rule in India around the issue of the degenerate Indian civilization, abject position of Hindu women and 'effeminacy' of Hindu men who were unfit for self-government.
24. *Collected Works of Mahatma Gandhi,* Vol. XVIII, hereafter referred to as CWMG, (Calcutta: The Annual Register Office, 1916), pp. 13, 443, 454, 496. In the course of his tours around India, he exhorted wives, mothers and sisters to involve their men in military service, because voluntary recruitment will lead to *swaraj.*
25. *The Tribune,* 8 February, 1919.
26. *CWMG,* vol. XX, pp. 15, 189.
27. *The Indian Annual Register,* (Calcutta: The Annual Register Office, 1920), p. 36.
28. *CWMG, n.* 269, pp. 15, 189.
29. *Ibid.,* pp. 290–91.
30. Rameshwari Nehru, *Gandhi is My Star,* (Patna: Pustak Bhandar, 1950),

p. 29. Rameshwari Nehru, daughter of the renowned Hindu leader Raja Narendra Nath, was married to Briji Lal Nehru. Also G. Broker ed., *Selected Speeches and Writings of Raj Kumari Amrit Kaur,* (New Delhi: Archer Publications, 1961), p. 180. Raj Kumari Amrit Kaur, the trusted Secretary and close confidante of Gandhi for the last thirteen years his life, was the daughter of Raja Harnam Singh of Kapurthala. Oral Transcript of Interview with Sucheta Kriplani, (New Delhi: Nehru Memorial Museum and Library). Sucheta belonged to a Brahmo-Samajist family having links with Keshub Chander Sen. Her father was a medical practitioner at Ambala. Gandhi gave his permission for Sucheta's marriage with J.B. Kriplani with great reluctance because he was afraid of losing Kriplani—a devoted constructive worker. Also Bibi Amtus Salaam 'Bapu ke Pas', in Shadi Ram Joshi ed., *Insaniyat ke Pehredar* in Hindi, (New Delhi: Gandhi Pustak Bhandar, 1972), p. 317. Bibi Amtus Salaam belonged to an orthodox aristocratic family of Patiala. Daughter of Mohammed Abdul Majid Khan, she was not sent to school for formal education owing to the observance of *purdah* which she discarded in 1925.

31. *The Tribune,* 7 February 1919.
32. For a detailed discussion of anti-Rowlatt agitation in Punjab, especially Amritsar, see Kamlesh Mohan, *Militant Nationalism in Punjab,* (Delhi: Manohar Book Service, 1985), pp. 13–40. In the case of additional information, relevant sources have been mentioned.
33. H.F. Owen, 'Organising Rowlatt Satyagraha of 1919', in R. Kumar, ed., *Essays in Gandhian Politics,* (Delhi: Oxford University Press, 1971), p. 82.
34. M.K. Gandhi, *The Story of My Experiments with Truth,* (First published 1927; reprinted, Ahmedabad: Navijivan Parkashan, 1958), p. 340.
35. For biographical details of Drs. Satyapal and Kitchlew, see Fauja Singh, *Eminent Freedom Fighters of Punjab,* (Patiala: Punjabi University, 1972), pp. 200–201, 205–206.
36. For the basis of this division see the chronological record of meetings and hartals from 31 January to 13 April 1919 in *Amritsar Conspiracy Case 1919* in microfilm, hereafter referred to as ACC, (New Delhi: National Archives of India), No. 1, in one roll.
37. *Disorders Inquiry Committee Report 1919–20,* hereafter referred to as DICR, (Calcutta: Govt. Printing Press, 1919–20), VI, 80, p. 103 – Evidence of Michael O'Dwyer.
38. *ACC,* p. 72 – Statement of Dr. Satyapal, Accused No. 2.
39. *Ibid.,* pp. 74, 105.
40. *Report of the Commissioners,* II, p. 711 – Evidence of Dr. Kitchlew.
41. DICR, p. 230.
42. *The Tribune,* 8 April 1919.
43. This information is based on my personal interviews with

Smt. Satyawati, Smt. Bhag Devi, Smt. Guaran Devi on 20 June 1989, 10 July 1988, 20 January 1984 respectively.

44. *The Tribune,* 12 April 1919.
45. *Report of the Commissioners,* p. 1, 47.
46. *DICR,* VI, p. 100.
47. *ACC,* p. 721 – Statement of Dr. Kitchlew. For official version see *DICE,* II, p. 19. It was stated that Dr. Kitchlew practically ordered the hartal; also see Hans Raj's statement. According to him Dr. Kitchlew, Chaudhri Bugga Mal, Mahasha Rattan Chand, Badarul-Islam Ali Khan, Gurdial Singh, Narain Dass and Dr. Mohammad Bashir planned on 5 April that a hartal on 6 April should be proclaimed by beat of drum and observed. He further added that the shopkeepers were made to close their shops since they knew that they would be looted. As his statement was uncorroborated, the theory about the hartal being pre-planned and organized, peters out.
48. *The Tribune,* 7 April 1919.
49. *The Tribune,* 8 April 1919. The lead article 'Action against Dr. Kitchlew and Others' argued that the official action was unjust as none of them had acted in a manner prejudicial to public safety.
50. *DICE,* VI, pp. 30, 165.
51. *Report of the Commissioners,* II, pp. 712-20 – Statement of Drs. Satyapal and Kitchlew.
52. *The Tribune,* 11 April 1919. Editorial, 'Blazing Indiscretion'.
53. *Bombay Chronicle,* 12 April 1919.
54. Text of the song obtained through Professor V.N. Datta's courtesy, New Delhi.
55. *The Tribune,* 11 April 1919.
56. Cited in Arthur Swinson, *Six Minutes to Sunset,* (London: Peter Davies, 1964), p. 54.
57. Home Department, Political (Deposit), Proceedings No. 23, September 1919, (New Delhi: National Archives of India, hereafter referred to as NAI).
58. *Ibid.,* pp. 64–65.
59. Sohan Lal Bharati, *Jallianwala Bagh Ki Khooni Dharti aur Mere Mata Pita* in Hindi, (Amritsar: Bharati Prakashan, n.d.), pp. 16–17. Also *The Tribune,* 13 April 1961.
60. K.L. Gauba, *The Rebel Minister: The Story of the Rise and Fall of Lala Harkishan Lal,* (Lahore: Premier Publishing House, 1938), p. 87.
61. For the judgement of various Martial Law Commissions, especially Lahore and Amritsar, see Pearay Mohan, *An Imaginary Rebellion: and How It Was Suppressed* with a foreword by Lal Lajpat Rai, (Lahore: Khosla Brothers, 1920), pp. 82–212.
62. For a detailed account of the Amritsar Conspiracy Case see Kamlesh

Mohan, *Militant Nationalism in the Punjab,* pp. 20–37.

63. CWMG, XVIII, p. 473.
64. M.K. Gandhi, 'A Punjab Victim', in *Young India,* 15 October 1919. It also referred to the case of Behari Lal Sachdeva, sentenced to transportation for life.
65. M.K. Gandhi, 'A Hard Case', in *Young India,* 26 May 1920. Chaudhary Bugga Mal and Mahasha Rattan Chand were released in 1936.
66. *Report of the Commissioners,* I, pp. 83–84 and II, pp. 198–206, Evidence of Mr. Manohar Lal, Bar-at-law.
67. *Ibid.,* pp. 113–14. Also *DICR,* II, p. 210.
68. *DICR,* 1919–20, pp. 208–10.
69. *Report of the Commissioners,* 1919-20, I, pp. 63-64, also, II, Statement No. 125. Also Statement Nos. 127, 133.
70. *Ibid.,* II, Statement Nos. 125 to 132 – Lachman Kaur, Ishwar Kaur (A widow with a sick child), Khem Kaur, Buddhi Devi, Devki and Ganga Devi.
71. *Ibid,* Statement No. 132.
72. *Report of the Commissioners,* I, p. 128.
73. *Ibid.,* pp. 128–129.
74. *Ibid.,* p. 139.
75. *CWMG,* pp. 17, 275.
76. *Ibid.,* p. 27.
77. *Report of the Commissioners,* I, p. 120.
78. *CWMG, n.63,* pp. 15, 334. All issues of *The Tribune,* from 25 April to 31 July 1919, had been confiscated by the Punjab Government in the case of Kali Nath Roy vs. the King Emperor. These are available in Home Department, Proceedings Nos. 228–50. October 1919, pp. 77–92.
79. *Report of the Commissioners,* II, Statement No. 2.
80. *Ibid.,* Statement No. 1 – Girdhari Lal, Deputy Chairman, the Punjab Chambers of Commerce and Managing Director, the Amritsar Flour and General Mills Co. Ltd., Amritsar.
81. *Rabindranath Tagore Papers,* Tagore to Andrews, (Unpublished Private Papers), 22 July 1920.
82. For a detailed account about these women see Home Department Judicial B, Proceedings Nos. 192–93, April 1882, (New Delhi: NAI). Also Proceedings Nos. 186–89, April 1881 and 188–95.
83. *All India Congress Committee Papers* (New Delhi : Nehru Memorial Museum and Library), File No. 5, 1920.
84. *Ibid.* Also *The Tribune,* 28 October and 3, 6, 28 November 1920.
85. *AICC Papers,* File No. 5, 1920. *The Tribune* 4 and 7 August 1920.
86. *District Gazetteer Multan,* 1901, pp. 12, 28.
87. *Command Papers,* No 771 – Statement by General Dyer. Also Ian Colvin, *The Life of General Dyer,* (London: Blackwood, 1929), p. 172.

88. Home Department, Political (Deposit), Proceedings No. 23, September 1919.
89. *CWMG, n.* 26, pp. 16, 286, 316, 324, 348.
90. *Ibid.,* p. 261.
91. *Ibid.,* p. 16, 316, 331, 348.
92. *Ibid.,* p. 316.
93. *Ibid.*
94. *Ibid.,* pp. 329–31.
95. The information given in this paragraph is based on *The Tribune,* 15 and 17 April 1920.
96. Home Department, Political A, Proceedings Nos. 71–72, August 1920.
97. *The Tribune,* 1 May, 16 February and 2 July 1921.
98. For the text of this song see Ramesh Vidrohi, *Jab Roya Punjab* in Hindi, (New Delhi: Bhavna Parkashan, 1977).
99. For the text of Kasturi Bai's songs and *bhajans,* see K.C. Yadav, ed., *Haryana Swatantarta Andolan Mein Kaviyon, Shairon, Bhajan Updeshkon Aur Loknayakon ka Yogdaan* in Hindi, (Delhi: Sadbhavana Parkashan, 1988), pp. 184–206. For the text of 'Angrezi Raj ka Abhishap' see pp. 184–85.
100. *Ibid.,* pp. 203–6.
101. Personal interview with Smt. Bhag Devi on 20 January 1984.
102. The information about Sarla Debi Chaudhrani's role in anti-Rowlatt agitation, popularization of *swadeshi* and organization of women on political basis, has been drawn from *CWMG, n.* 26, pp. 18, 20, and her booklets namely, *The Song of Charkha,* (Madras: Ganesh & Co. n.d.), and *At the Point of Spindle*, (Madras: Ganesh & Co., n.d).
103. Kamlesh Mohan, 'Image of Women in *Stree Darpan* 1909–1928', in *Indian History Congress Proceedings,* 52nd Session, New Delhi.
104. For the text of Sarojini Naidu's poem (Hindi version) see Vidrohi, *Jab Roya Punjab*.
105. For the text of Subhadra Kumari Chauhan's poem see Ramesh Upadhyay, ed., *Jallianwala Bagh,* (New Delhi: Ministry of Information and Broadcasting, Publications Division, 1969, 1985).

Between Democracy and Globalization

5

Jawaharlal Nehru on Democracy and Women

> The future of India cannot consist of dolls and playthings and if you make half the population of country a mere plaything of the other half – an encumbrance on others, how will you ever make progress.[1]

This extract from Jawaharlal Nehru's speech at the Mahila Vidyapeeth, Allahabad on 31 March 1928, had underlined his growing faith in the ideal of an open and egalitarian society which would progress through democracy. His real goal was nothing less than to build a dynamic nation and a new social and economic order[2] through the involvement of all segments of society, irrespective of caste, sex and religion. In his view, the ongoing Indian revolution which had graduated from its struggle against imperialism and fascism to the ultimate task of economic and social reconstruction after India became independent in 1947, would remain incomplete without the whole-hearted participation of women.

In this essay, I propose to analyse Nehru's views on democracy, Indian society and women, especially the latter's crucial role in the Indian democratic experiment subsuming the challenging tasks of economic reconstruction and social engineering. Although my primary concern is to analyse and evaluate Nehru' role in reinforcing Indian women's battle for their own liberation, I have chosen to correlate this theme with the broader theme of national quest for a democratic life under his stewardship. My justification lies in Nehru's integrated view and dynamic philosophy of national life, culture and civilization. The discussion shall be divided into four sections: *(i)* Sources of

Nehru's Ideology and Philosophy, *(ii)* Vision of the Indian Democratic polity and *(iii)* His Views on Indian Society and Nature of Women's Oppression; *(iv)* Nehru's Contribution to the Fight for Women's Rights; *(v)* Conclusion.

I
SOURCES OF NEHRU'S IDEOLOGY AND PHILOSOPHY

An analysis of Nehru's writings and speeches reveals his views regarding the role of philosophy in the life of an individual and of society, the relationship between science and society, the process of the growth of cultures and civilizations of the world and the ethical, spititual and mental considerations. Although Nehru did not usually burden his mind with metaphysical problems,[3] he believed that everybody had more or less a philosophy of life, which reflected the attitudes and values of his generation and the influence of his environment.[4] His philosophical conceptions, which are marked by humanism, nationalism and optimism, and especially his approach to political and socio-economic issues, particularly democratic polity and the nature of women's oppression, had been moulded by varied influences.[5]

In the first instance, Nehru was influenced by the vague concepts of socialism propagated by the Fabians, particularly G.B. Shaw and the Labour Socialists. Broadly speaking, the intellectual ferment caused by these ideas, however gentle and moderate, drew Nehru's attention as of other contemporary intellectuals to the inequities of a social system based on ascriptive status, wealth and exploitation of the weak and the under-privileged human beings including women. Later on, Marxism and Leninism, the second source of his humanism, reinforced his ideas and convictions in an egalitarian world view. The third source of his philosophical views lay in Gandhi. The Indian philosophical and to some extent religious tradition formed the fourth source of influence upon his ideological growth. A process of synthesis between elements of Western liberal ideas and scientific humanism on the one hand and the inner spiritual life—the core of the Indian tradition and culture—on the other hand is visible in the intellectual development of Nehru.[6]

No less important was the impact of his entire span of political activity and the ideological underpinnings of the Indian national movement on his philosophy of social, economic and political change in which men and women were equal and active partners having equal obligations and rights.

It may be pointed out that the degree of the importance of these major sources of his philosophic views and policies as a leader varied with the dominance of individuals or ideological trends in the different phases of his life. Up to the year 1916, the Fabian ideology dominated his thought processes; Gandhi remained his chief source of inspiration during the period between his sojourn in India and his return to Europe in 1926. Between 1926 and 1947, his approach and views on political and socio-economic issues had been strongly influenced by Marxism and Leninism. After 1947, Indian philosophical views, particularly of Gandhi and Radhakrishnan played a crucial role in his choice of the peaceful method for social change and for solving national and international problems[7] and his growing belief in the soundness of the basic components of the Indian tradition.[8] The significant point relevant to the present theme is Nehru's insistence upon the creative interpretation of Indian tradition, re-structuring of social and economic system and recasting human relationships in response to the changing priorities, needs, ideas, values and scientific progress.

II
HIS VISION OF THE DEMOCRATIC POLITY

Nehru's conception of democracy, which was defined, explained and elaborated in his numerous addresses and speeches to students, common people and colleagues, was a broad one. Believing that political democracy was not enough, he spelt out its multi-faceted nature in his speech on 15 December 1952 :

> So, an integrated plan for economic growth of the country, for the growth of the individual, for greater opportunities for every individual and for the greater freedom of the country, has to be drawn up within the frame work of political democracy. If it is to have any meaning, political democracy must gradually, or, if you like rapidly lead to economic democracy. If there is economic inequality in the country, all the political democracy and all the adult suffrage in the world, cannot bring about real democracy.[9]

Nehru had regarded democracy as the best method for the governance of human beings. However, the large-scale participation of a vast mass of human beings (who are not encouraged or do not get an opportunity to think) through the democratic method of adult suffrage made him a little anxious and sceptical. It would affect the quality of the elected representatives whose success might usually be manipulated by the clever management of machinery of propaganda.[10]

Naturally, Nehru, who conceptualized democracy in terms of "....the active and intelligent interest of the people in their national affairs and in the elections that result in formation of governments"[11], was constantly reminding himself and fellow-Indians about the crucial importance of the quality of mind in any such system. To him democracy was, above all, a mental approach to political and economic problems and a scheme of values and moral standards in life.[12]

However, Nehru realized how poorly India was prepared for any kind of democracy after a long spell of enervating political and economic subjugation.[13] He was fully aware of the fact that democracy was the hard way and required a higher quality of human beings. Knowing fully well that people seldom realize their full potential, Nehru could retain unshakable faith in the innate greatness of his countrymen. He had his own reasons. In his address to the Canadian Parliament on 24 October 1949, he observed:

> India is an old nation and yet to-day she has within her something of the spirit and dynamic quality of youth. Some of the vital impulses which gave strength to India in past ages inspire us still, and at the same time, we have learned much from the West in social and political values in science and technology.[14]

Nehru tried to discourage the tendency to glorify human beings and institutions and constantly reminded himself and his countrymen. ".... We have in India a strange habit of making gods of various things and adding them to our vast pantheon".[15] While commenting upon the stiff resistance of a few colleagues to the amendment of the constitution, he further added, "So if you wish to kill this constitution, make it sacred and sacrosanct". That was not the way to grow. The great strength of the democratic system lay in the flexibility of the constitution as the British constitution has proved time and again. But Nehru was aware of the limitations in India when he observed:

> We in this country could not obviously emulate the British in having an unwritten constitution. We cannot do that especially in

> a big country with numerous autonomous provinces and states. Nevertheless, the other extreme of a rigid constitution, too, is a dangerous one.... So if you are flexible in your action and constitution, then you are nearer the living curve of a nation's growth.[16]

Thus, Nehru's vision of a democratic polity demanded from men and women, especially, from the leadership an imaginative and creative approach, as well as a critical temper of a scientific age without losing the moral sensitivity. He advocated industrialization as a means of generating wealth and prosperity for the people, an innovative approach to science and technology and an open-minded, creative multi-religious community actively participating in the material growth and cultural enrichment of India.

It can be said that Nehru's concept of free India's democratic superstructure rested on at least four pillars: *(i)* individual freedom, the freedom of the individual to grow and make the best of his or her capacities and abilities, and tolerance 'not merely of those who agree with us' but also of those who differ; *(ii)* representative government, based on popular sovereignty and elected representatives; *(iii)* economic and social equality, calling for a proper balance between freedom and equality and a socialist pattern of society and *(iv)* social self-discipline.

What was Nehru's view of the people? A close perusal of his speeches and writings reveals a striking fact that he did not look upon people as crowds and masses but as so many individuals each full of potential and worthy of attention and regard in his or her own right.[17] Rejecting the notion of women being a separate class, he saw them as individuals who had suffered from serious disabilities and handicaps.[18] As a humanist, having fervent faith in the democratic polity, Nehru was determined to reinforce Indian women's battle for their personal freedom, dignity and rights by creating a progressive mental environment and a developmental framework of socio-economic life. While speaking about the need to strike a balance between the tendencies of centralization and decentralization, Nehru underlined the central issue of individual growth and freedom. Inspite of his belief that the growth of an individual or group "cannot be imposed" or forced, he did not under-rate the importance of providing favourable conditions.[19]

III
VIEWS ON SOCIETY AND NATURE OF WOMEN'S OPPRESSION

Views on Society

The new image of women, etched by Gandhi and enriched in content by Nehru, was deeply influenced and coloured by the kind of cultural and emotional environment to which each of them had been exposed. Gandhi's use of traditional symbols to convey his socio-political message and to project his ideal of Indian womanhood reflected the influence of Jain-Vaishnavite ideals and *Samskars* on his outlook.[20] Nehru's approach to socio-economic issues particularly the nature of women's oppression was based on more complex and varied sources, largely free from religious sentiments. Without going into the details, it may be pointed that the ideological formulations of Marx and Lenin deepened Nehru's understanding and sensitivity to the process of social development and new meanings in the entire gamut of world history particularly of the Indian civilization and culture.[21]

Any worthwhile exercise in evaluating Nehru's views on the contemporary Indian society, degradation of its arts, culture and institutions and on the ways and means to revitalize it and his own contribution to this process either as a fighter for national liberation or as the Prime Minister of independent India, must take into account his basic approach to life, thought and action. While ruminating on his experiences in life before his imprisonment in Ahmadnagar Fort in 1942, Nehru discussed the rationale of human urge for action and struggle, especially, in the pursuit of social and political freedom in this manner:

> This urge to action, this desire to experience life through action has influenced all my thought and activity. Even sustained thinking, apart from being itself a kind of action, becomes part of the action to come. It is not something entirely abstract, in the void, unrelated to action and life. The past becomes something that leads up to the present, the moment of action, the future something that flows from it; and all three are inextricably intertwined and interrelated.[22]

Having this integrated approach to the process of social development, Nehru tried to search for the progressive deterioration of its social order, institutions, civilization and withering away of its elan vitale. Believing that the Indian civilization and society possessed an innate dynamism, he analysed the long and intricate process how it gradually lost its intense joy of life and nature, creative impulse and flexibility. It was in this context that his views on Indian society had acquired clarity and definiteness. Nehru observed:

> My own conception of Hindu society has been that it is essentially dynamic not static and rigid. Anyhow the coming of the British made the whole conception static, because they codified our law and did that with the help of the most conservative sections of the community they could find ... .[23]

Although he had held the British responsible for the suppression of dynamic element in Hindu society by rendering it unchangeable except by legislation, he was aware of the growing rigidity in social structure, intolerance and orthodoxy in Hindu society with the passage of time. In Nehru's view, the existing inequalities, oppression of women, and of the weaker sections of society including the untouchables, indicated the onset of fossilization in society due to caste divisions and biased interpretation of Hindu Law. It had led to the distortion of human relations, tensions and cracks in the Indian social fabric.[24]

The crucial question is: What was Nehru's conception of a dynamic society? It was composed of individuals not having puritanical attitudes but an advanced, tolerant and generous outlook. Elaborating this point, he observed that "...the test of an individual is how he treats his wife, his sons and his neighbours. How he behaves towards another, how he functions in a social relationship, that is the test of an individual".[25] The position of women in a society and a nation is the reliable indicator of the quality of its life, civilization and culture.[26] A highly cultured and dynamic society, as portrayed in *Mrichkkatika* (a Sanskrit play written in 500 A.D.) was nearest to Nehru's ideal. Composed of self-disciplined, tolerant and generous individuals, the ancient Indian society was marked by tender human relationships. Nehru believed, ''....The more a society grows, the fewer the totems and taboos; because totems and taboos are replaced by self-restraint. That is again a test of society's growth: a self-restraint, not the application of the policeman's rod".[27]

Obviously, the quality of human beings was a crucial component in Nehru's vision of a dynamic society in the Independent India which was not to be circumscribed by conventions, customs, ideas, values and institutions—once adequate for achieving the goals and aspirations of the people of the bygone ages. Hemmed in by the swirling currents of humanism, rationalism, ever expanding scientific knowledge and the ideal of peaceful co-existence, the Indian people in Nehru's view should aspire to establish such a socio-economic order as was highly industrialized, but not without moral sensitivity, creatively multi-religious, secular and egalitarian values.[28]

In this context, it may be pointed out that the main philosophical problem for Nehru was that the moral development of mankind did not correspond to the level of scientific development, man's rapidly growing control over nature and the impending danger of total extinction of mankind through nuclear weapons. In the new world order, mankind must learn to strike a balance between its material and spiritual wants.[29]

The building of such a dynamic society was the goal enshrined in Nehru's social philosophy and democratic vision of free India. As the Prime Minister of India from 1947 to 1964, he was constantly engaged in the formidable but exciting task of fashioning a new and modern India having a unique material, cultural, social and national identity and values. Always eager to share his ideas, dreams and aspirations with his countrymen, he exhorted them on the first Independence Day:

> Each one of us, man or woman, young and old, must, therefore, toil and work. ... We did not win our freedom so that we might rest afterwards but in order to work harder to hold and strengthen then that freedom. ... Our labours as free men and women will lay the foundations for a great future and our labour of love for the cause of India and our people will endure; so will the fact that we are building brick by brick, the great mansion of free India. There is joy in such work.[30]

Views on the Nature of Women's Oppression

As a result, Nehru found that his task as a leader was not merely to transmit 'this sense of adventure and joy' but also to sensitize his countrymen to the tyranny of discriminatory role-models for men and women, the obscurantist modes of thought and social practices and their obstructive role in the process of creating a new society and nation.[31] One such example was the oppression of women which bared three embarrassing aspects of the contemporary Indian tradition: irrationality, inequality and duplicity. Nehru believed that the subjugation of women was not merely an abstract moral condition but a social and historical experience requiring sober appraisal.[32]

With his heightened sensitivity to the various obvious and subtle naunces of human relationships, Nehru tried to analyze the nature of women's oppression. Viewing it in a broad historical perspective, he found that the question of her subjugation was not a purely Indian problem.[33] Women had been denied equal rights, opportunities and privileges all over the world. Nehru's commitment to women's emancipation was inspired by something more than a purely utilitarian motive. Primarily concerned with the problems of the ongoing Indian revolution and acceleration of its pace, Nehru, early in his life, became acutely aware of the need to liberate women from social disabilities and oppression and provide them full opportunities for their mental and physical growth in order to enable them to fight as soldiers of freedom along with men. Addressing a Women Volunteers' Training Camp at Bombay in 1931, he said. "In a national war, there is no question of either sex or community. Whoever is born in this country ought to be a soldier."[34] That was one reason, he gave serious thought to the issue of inequality in social and personal relations. The other important considerations, which inspired his unrelenting crusade for women's rights and education, were rooted in his belief in the principles of rationalism and humanism.

For a proper understanding of Nehru's approach to the issue of women's oppression, it is relevant to scrutinize his observations and reactions to the traditional images of Indian womanhood, marriage laws and customs, divorce, prostitution, women's education and rights.

Unlike Mahatma Gandhi, who frequently invoked the three ideals of Indian womanhood—Sita, Damyanti, and Draupadi[35]— for inspiring the oppressed Indian women, Nehru saw the inadequacy of the ideal of silent and suffering heroines and the relevance of creating their new image as rebels against the tyrannical and unjust social customs.[36] He resented the abuse of these images by obscurantists and reactionaries. While addressing the students of Mahila Vidyapeeth, he expressed his dissatisfaction with the lot of Indian women and said:

> .... We hear a good deal about Sita and Savitri. They are revered names in India and rightly so. But I have a feeling that these echoes from the past are raised chiefly to hide our present deficiencies and to prevent us from attacking the root cause of women's degradation in India today.[37]

While speaking on the Hindu Marriage Bill in the Lok Sabha on 5th May 1955, Nehru again questioned the perpetuation of out-dated social models and conduct for women. He observed:

> ...Sita and Savitri are mentioned as ideals for the women. I do not seem to remember men being reminded in the same manner of Ramchandra and Satyavan and urged to behave like them. It is only the women who have to behave like Sita and Savitri, the men may behave as they like. I do not know whether Indian men are supposed to be perfect, or incapable of any further improvement.[38]

Thus, Nehru had not only lashed at the duplicity of rules of social behaviour but also at the self-righteous postures of Indian men who were unwilling to change from the position of dominance to equality in social life and personal relations.

The code of social conduct ought to be reformed by mutual agreement and respect for each other's personal dignity and freedom to grow. Viewing the process of India's social development in the global context, Nehru urged his countrymen to link social legislation with the major scientific and economic developments. For example, he observed, "The major thing that affects human relationships in the world today is the growth of industrialization. The fact, that because of industrialization vast numbers of people live in huge industrial centres, leads to all kind of neuroses."[39] The new psychological problems of adjustment in context with the changing production relations should be taken into account while forging new role models for men and women, especially in the industrialized cities of Delhi, Calcutta and Madras where female employment was fast increasing.[40]

Nehru argued that the task of giving a fair deal to Indian women should begin by revising or scrapping, if need be, Manu's Commandments and all religious texts, which discriminated against women and enforced different standards of morality on the basis of sex or caste. Nehru's views on identical standards of morality were forcefully expressed in his lengthy note, which he wrote as the President of the Municipal Committee of Allahabad, on the proposal for allotting separate quarters for prostitutes on the outskirts of the city. He observed:

> The segregation of prostitutes, even if possible, would be objectionable precisely as the segregation of criminals would be objectionable. I do not believe in issuing a fiat that prostitutes must not live in any part of the city of Allahabad except a remote corner. If this is done I would think it reasonable to reserve another part of Allahabad for men who exploited women and because of whom prostitution flourishes.[41]

He asserted that solution of social problems lay not in punitive measures but in socio-economic reforms like education, propaganda regarding venereal diseases or providing homes for widows and destitutes. While projecting an unconventional but rational angle on social change, Nehru had indicated the part played by double standards in perpetuating the sexual exploitation of women in various epochs of socio-economic development in India.

As a perceptive student of Indian history and civilization, Nehru pursued his search for the real causes of women's oppression, masked by the glorification of the mythical ideal of Indian womanhood and her image as a mother and goddess in the Indo-Aryan culture. He discovered that the roots of women's degradation lay in her economic and political subjugation.[42] On the basis of his understanding and interpretation of the process of social and political development in India, Nehru observed:

> Even the ancient laws had been unfair to them in regard to inheritance and their position in the household—though even so they were fairer than nineteenth-century English law. Those laws of inheritance derived from the joint family system had sought to protect joint property from transfer to another family. A woman by marriage changed her family. In an economic sense, she was looked upon as a dependent on her father or husband or son, but she could and did hold property in her own right. In many ways she was honoured and respected and had a fair measure of freedom, taking part in social and cultural activities.... This freedom progressively grew less.[43]

Nehru seemed to imply that women, having no access to independent economic resources, were in no position to protect their right of participation in socio-cultural activities. Confined to the four walls of the house, they were gradually denied education and opportunities of distinguishing themselves in artistic and intellectual pursuits. Seclusion, particularly its symbolic form purdah, was increasingly enforced strictly with a difference of degree by Hindus and Muslims. It subjected women to a new social norm, called chastity, leading to the loss of her right to control her own body. Elaborating upon the point, Nehru said:

> .... They were told that their supreme virtue lay in chastity and the supreme sin in a loss of it. Such was the man-made doctrine, but man did not apply it to himself. Tulsidas in his deservedly famous poem, the Hindi Ramayana written during Jahangir's time, is grossly unfair and prejudiced.[44]

Nehru's writings contain no observation on the link between the growth of the institution of property, rigidity of caste-system, increasing emphasis upon ritual purity, and the intensification of women's oppression.

However, Nehru was clear on one point that the legal position of women was definitely bad. Always dependent on somebody, father, husband or the son, they were treated in law almost as 'chattels'.[45] His contention, that the legal position of women in ancient India was far better than in ancient Greece and Rome, in early Christianity, in Canon Law of medieval Europe and even at the beginning of the nineteenth century, is a point of debate and serious enquiry which cannot be taken up here.[46]

Leaving apart the distinctly different modes of socio-economic set up in the tribal and matriarchal cultures, it is difficult to question the logic of Nehru's perception of the crucial link between the economic subjugation of women and their forced withdrawal from public life and denial of any civic rights to influence the political process particularly the organization and running of state machinery. He had viewed the long and complicated process of the deterioration of the Indian women's status and her oppression as a part of the broader question of the decay of Indian civilization and culture.[47] In fact, the segregation of women had suppressed one of the major sources of life-giving and creative force vital for the sustenance of a dynamic society.

The oppression of women had acquired a sinister dimension with the conquest by the foreign invaders—Turkish, Afghan and Mughal. It set in motion a defence mechanism among the Hindus who "retired into their shells, and tried to protect themselves from foreign ways and influences by hardening the caste system".[48] It resulted in the tightening of constraints upon women, who had been regarded as the gateway to pollution. While Nehru expressed his admiration for the synthesis of the Indo–Mughal culture, especially in architecture, he dubbed the growth of purdah or strict seclusion of women as one of the unfortunate developments in the interaction between new elements and the old.[49]

Regarded as a mark of status and prestige amongst the royalty, nobility and other upper classes of Hindus and Muslims during the Mughal period,[50] purdah became the target of vehement criticism by Gandhi and Nehru in the twentieth century. The latter acknowledged the contribution of Gandhi in creating a sympathetic awareness about the victimization of women by the 'vicious and brutal' custom of purdah which led to the infantalization of their mind and loss of independence of thought and moral courage.[51] Nehru opposed it fiercely because, "That it injures women is obvious enough, but the injury to man, to the growing child who had to spend much of its time among women in purdah, and to social life is generally great ...".[52] According to him, segregation of women whether as daughters, sisters and wives or as prostitutes raised major issues concerning India's social and national health, freedom and alround progress—material and spiritual. The following extract from his book, *Glimpses of World History* illustrates the point:

> Whenever I think of the women in purdah, cut off from the outside world, I invariably think of a prison or a zoo! How can a nation go ahead if half of its population is kept hidden away in a kind of prison. Tear the purdah, and let each one of us see the light of day.[53]

Nehru argued that the whole conception underlying the feudal custom of purdah—no work, as the sign of high status—was totally unsuitable to modern times when economic growth and prosperity would depend upon the equal participation of men and women in the production process.[54]

In fact, Nehru strongly disapproved of the irrational and evil social customs such as purdah, child marriage and denial of rights and opportunities to women for physical and intellectual growth on ground of humanism. Believing in the principle of equality and liberty, he lost no opportunity to remind women that "No people, no group, no community, no country has ever got rid of its disabilities by the generosity of the oppressor ...".[55] Freedom and rights have to be snatched and fought for. By advising women to hurl defiance at the man-made customs and laws, Nehru had indicated the need of deconditioning and training them for taking upon new roles, along with men, as soldiers of social and political revolution in India. It may be pointed out that exhortations to women flowed out of his vision of nation-building process in free India.

Crucial to Nehru's passionate commitment to nation building on democratic lines was his concept of education for boys and girls irrespective of their parents' social status. His views are reflected in the covering letter for his daughter Indira's application for admission to Visva-Bharati at Santiniketan. He wrote:

> Her parents would like her to specialise in some subject or subjects which would enable her to do some socially useful work in later life and at the same time enable her to be economically independent. They would not like her merely to possess a literary or other cultural accomplishment which does not help her to fend for herself in the years to come.[56]

In his letter to Indira, apart from expressing his disapproval of a friend's suggestion regarding the separate establishment for his daughter, he underlined the need of intergrating "the real honest work in a factory or in the fields" with the academic programme of education for every boy and girl.[57]

The purpose of education in Nehru's view was to create sensitivity to suffering, discomforts and misery which wrapped up the great majority of people, to understand their viewpoint and to learn in the field the practical means to ameliorate their misery. That was why he wanted the upper class women to come out of their homes and learn to work with their own hands. Dignity of labour was an article of faith for him.

Nehru disapproved of the ideal of women's life and education, set forth by the Mahila Vidyapeeths. Underlying the programme of special instruction to women in these institutions was the mistaken belief in the inequality of sexes in terms of intelligence and ability, thus prescribing different role-models for men and women. Referring to the report of the host institution, Nehru highlighted the basic flaw in such views and their irrelevance for building a new Indian society. He observed, "It was laid down that man was the bread-winner, woman's place was the home and her ideal should be that of a devoted wife and nothing more. Her chief delight should be in skilfully rearing her children and serving her elders." Explaining his stand Nehru further remarked:

> It means that women has one profession and only one, that is the profession of marriage and it is our chief business to train her for this profession. Even in this profession her lot is to be one of secondary importance. She is always to be the devoted helpmate, the follower and the obedient slave of her husband or others. I wonder if any of you has read Ibsen's *Doll's House*, if so, you will perhaps appreciate the word "Doll" when I use it in this connection.[58]

Nehru had urged the Indian women, especially teachers and students as well as the managing authorities of the educational institutions, to reject the stereotyped concept, aims and objects of education. His speeches in the 1950s showed that his views on education had acquired more clarity and definitiveness. An extract from his speech at the foundation ceremony of a women's college in Madras on 22 January 1955 illustrates the point:

> By education I mean education and not merely learning to be lady-like. Learning to be lady-like may be good in itself but it is not education as such. Education has mainly two aspects, the cultural aspect which makes a person grow, and the productive aspect which makes a person do things. Both are essential. Everybody should be a producer as well as a good citizen and not a sponge on another person even though the person may be one's own husband or wife. That is the way we are developing and the persons who do not wake up to this fact and prepare themselves for it will be just left behind.[59]

Undoubtedly, Nehru could foresee that in the future competitive world, wherein science had revolutionized the methods of production on land, in industry, means of communication and had prepared way for subsequent revolutions in techniques, India's material achievements, and economic growth would depend upon the radicalization of its value-system and education.[60] In this way, India would become capable of harnessing the full potential of its human resources, in accordance with the demands of the new world order.

Views on Marriage, Divorce and Women's Rights

A study of Nehru's correspondence and speeches shows that he had also developed rational attitudes towards marriage, divorce and women's rights. As early as 1907, when child marriages were almost an accepted social norm in India, Nehru (an eighteen-year-old student at Cambridge) reacted in an unconventional way to his mother's desire to fix up a nice girl for him. He wrote to his mother, "Why do you want me to get engaged to a small girl of ten? I do not want a child to play with."[61]

In another letter, two years later, he expressed his views in favour of inter-caste and intra-community marriages. He believed that "marriages should be based on a complete understanding, a perfect union of minds"[62] and should take place between two individuals by mutual consent and agreement. Nehru's sisters Vijayalakshmi, Krishna and his cousins had married out of their community and he was not the least perturbed. Even more rational was his reaction to the criticism of the marriage of his daughter Indira to a Parsi young man in 1942. Explaining his viewpoint in his press statement, Nehru observed, "A marriage is a personal and domestic matter, affecting chiefly the two parties concerned and partly their families. ...Though parents may and should advise in the matter, the choice and ultimate decision must be with the two parties concerned."[63]

Even more revealing of his approach to the twin issues of marriage and women's emancipation, was his address to the students of Mahila Vidyapeeth, Allahabad in 1934. He remarked:

> The habit of looking upon marriage as a profession almost, and as the sole economic refuge for women, will have to go before women can have any freedom. Freedom depends on economic conditions even more than political and if woman is not economically free and self-earning, she will have to depend on her husband or someone else, and dependents are never free. The association of man and woman should be of perfect freedom and perfect comradeship with no dependence of one on the other.[64]

No less radical and humanistic was his approach to the issue of divorce which, according to orthodox people, would make the marriage custom fragile. Rejecting their argument, Nehru commented, "If that is so, I say that marriage itself has become a cloak. It is not a real marriage of minds or bodies. If you compel and force people in this way, it will just be an enforced thing which has no value left in ethics or morality."[65] He argued in favour of right of divorce to either of the parties in case all attempts for reconciliation had failed.

Very pertinently, Nehru had opposed discrimination in marriage laws on ground of sex. The logic, underlying his advocacy of equal privileges for husband and wife, was eloquently stated in his speech on Hindu Marriage Bill on 5th May 1955, "You cannot have a democracy if you cut off a large chunk of humanity, fifty percent of the people, and put them in a class apart in regard to social privileges and the like. They are bound to rebel, and rightly...".[66] However, he conceded that law could bring about only a "certain measure of equality" and not real and absolute equality in the social and personal relationships between men and women and thus the process of social change would be affected by many intervening factors such as custom, education and basically the economic position of the individual.[67]

Women should not be denied the right to divorce on the basis of rigid application of religious sanctions and laws, laid down by Manu or Yajnavalkya, which were suitable in social conditions existing two thousand years ago. Giving a creative interpretation of *samsakar* or sacrament, Nehru argued, "I think all human relationships should have an element of the sacrament in them. More so the intimate relationship of husband and wife."[68] In his view, there was no justification for binding two incompatible persons in marriage partnership, if "they begin to hate each other and their life becomes bitter. The whole foundation of their existence becomes bitter. Surely there is no sacrament."[69]

Thus, Nehru challenged the orthodox exposition of religion wherefrom originated the basic disability of women. Having a firm conviction that access and control over economic resources of the family would improve the social status of Indian women, Nehru tried to create awareness about this legal disability. Underlying his serious concern with the question of the grant of fundamental right of property to women, was not merely Nehru's indifference to money but also his liberal instincts, socialist inclination and human concern. Writing to his sister Krishna, after the death of their father Motilal Nehru, when the Hindu Succession Act had not even been contemplated, he showed no desire for inheriting paternal property. Giving his reasons he remarked:

> Technically, in law, I suppose, I am the heir of his property. But my own inclination is against inheriting property or at any rate living on inherited property or unearned increment. ... In any event, however, I can only consider myself as a joint sharer in father's property, the other sharers being mother and you. I am not considering Nan (nickname for Nehru's sister Vijaylakshmi) as she is in no need of money. ... Indeed you and mother are the real sharers. I am trustee for the family property...[70].

These observations are significant in view of the fact that Nehru could not turn to money-making as he was actively involved in the political activities on a whole-time basis.

IV
NEHRU'S CONTRIBUTION TO THE FIGHT FOR WOMEN'S RIGHTS

An evaluation of Nehru's contribution as a crusader for women's right to personal dignity, self-development and her right to choose from a variety of roles has two aspects: *(i)* The first concerns his impact upon women, his image in the mind of women in the Nehru family, his ability to inspire and enthuse them and other men and women to join political struggle, his interaction with his women associates in national freedom struggle, not necessarily belonging to the Congress; *(ii)* The second concerns Nehru's earnest efforts to formulate policies and practical plans to ensure women's representation in the various decision-making bodies of the Congress Party, their induction into positions of power in the central and provincial governments and their appointments in different capacities in foreign countries and world organizations. An even more important part of his contribution relates with his fight for women's economic rights and their economic empowerment at the legislative level.

In the early phases of his political career and of his campaign for the abolition of social evils and women's rights, Nehru's chief task was to reinforce Gandhi's crusade for national freedom, equality and liberation of women from social oppression on moral grounds. Later, he had diversified and enlarged its scope by emphasizing the economic and political content of their rights. Keenly aware of the role of the Congress and social reform movements in mitigating the evil of purdah, Nehru found it sometimes difficult to endorse Gandhi's belief in the simultaneity and coordination of social reform and the struggle for *swaraj*.[71] His reservations were often expressed on two items of Gandhi's constructive programme: Harijan work and khadi.[72] But on the question of women's uplift, he had no disagreement in principle with Gandhi though in content.

Nehru had envisaged himself in the role of a rebel against social conventions and as an advocate of women's rights and education.[73] Influenced by two remarkable women, Annie Besant and Sarojini Naidu, Nehru had become aware of the potentialities of women as political leaders, intellectuals, social reformers and sensitive individuals.[74] Nehru's image in the minds of the womenfolk of his own family and extended family was the direct bye-product of his active involvement in the national freedom struggle and his growing stature as a popular political leader. Vijayalakshmi's observations bear it out. She has remarked:

> .... It was within the framework of the movement of the early twenties that I first came to know him as a person. Before that he was "Bhai,'' the beloved elder brother, but still merely a part of the family. ... The nineteen twenties were dynamic days in India, full of exciting challenge, and one of the most important and significant dramas of the period was enacted in our own home.[75]

Vijayalakshmi never found his attitude towards others as 'self-righteous'. He influenced his immediate family circle "not by argument, not by threats and anger, not by an appeal to emotion but by the force of his own deep conviction that the path he was taking was the right one and the dedication ... with which he sought to fit himself for the great task."[76] Continuing further, she has explained how Nehru had influenced her thinking and the choice of her role in life. Vijayalakshmi Pandit has elucidated this point:

> What I value most of all is the lesson that life is not lived in little compartments—personal life and public life are both guided by the same principles and one is but the projection of the other. His

> actions flow from this belief as does his capacity to 'lead you to the threshold of your own mind'—wisdom of his own.[77]

Vijayalakshmi Pandit's assessment of Nehru's personality and his impact has more or less been endorsed by the other women in the Nehru family.

Nehru's younger sister Krishna revealed another facet of his rationalist and humanist attitude towards women. According to her, Nehru believed in their autonomy and encouraged the women of his extended family to choose from a wide variety of roles and not be confined to the role of a wife, mother and home-maker.[78] That was why he constantly urged them to develop a proper perspective on moral and material values and the capability to handle critical situations in private and public life. Commenting on the issues and problems raised by the ongoing Second World War, Nehru wrote to Krishna from Dehradun jail. "... If we in India as individuals and as a nation have the necessary intelligence, moral fibre and staying power, it [the world] will go with us; otherwise not".[79]

No doubt, the political environment and the Western mode of life in Anand Bhavan was an important factor in preparing women to deviate from responsibilities with fewer constraints. Their interaction with the successful and dynamic women, namely, Sarojini Naidu and Kamla Devi Chattopadhyaya at their home had also diluted their inhibitions about joining public life. But it was Jawaharlal Nehru who had encouraged women of immediate as well as extended family to join Congress movements. Apart from his sisters Vijayalakshmi, Krishna and his wife Kamla, the other women of the Nehru clan who turned to active politics or constructive work, were Uma Nehru and her daughter Shyam Kumari Nehru, Rameshwari Nehru, Lado Rani Zutshi and her daughters Janak and Manmohini Sehgal.[80]

Jawaharlal considered his father Motilal Nehru's attitude to women participation in politics as old-fashioned and paternalistic.[81] Vijayalakshmi had a similar impression about her father.[82] However, evidence of the unflinching courage and organizational capacity of the women in the Congress movements in the 1930s coupled with their increasing involvement in the national struggle aroused his admiration for them. Like his son Jawaharlal, Motilal also began to acknowledge the equality between man and woman. In 1927, he wrote an encouraging letter to his daughter Krishna:

> You seem to have turned into quite a little politician, but do not think that being a girl will be a handicap to you... . There is no bar of sex. ... On the contrary a determined women's influence is much greater than a man can ever sway.[83]

While addressing a Women Volunteers' Training Camp at Bombay, Jawaharlal Nehru had expressed similar views.[84] He was proud of women who had joined politics. He was in Naini Prison when he heard about the arrest of his wife and sister Krishna whom he had earlier drilled as volunteers for the Salt *satyagraha*. Commenting upon this, he wrote in his *Autobiography*:

> We felt proud of our people, and especially of our women-folk, all over the country. I had a special feeling of satisfaction because of the activities of my mother, wife and sister, as well as many girl cousins and friends and though I was separated from them and was in prison, we grew nearer to each other, bound by a sense of comradeship in a great cause. The family seemed to merge in a larger group and yet to retain its old flavour and intimacy. Kamla surprised me, for her energy and enthusiasm overcame her physical ill health.[85]

However, Nehru's joy over Kamla's arrest as a substitute member of the Congress Working Committee on 1 January 1931 did not spring merely from a feeling of pride over his wife's burning patriotic fervour. He was also pleased because, ''And now she had her heart's desire''.[86] Although he accepted Kamla's short message to the press as a normal declaration of an Indian wife's devotion to her husband, he realized that she regarded herself as a champion of women's rights against the tyranny of man.[87]

The close associates of Nehru family also were alive to Kamla's strength of character. In this context, Kamla Devi Chattopadhaya remarked:

> Kamla Nehru could be assertive in her own quiet way. ... She had nurtured a mechanism of her own to preserve her own entity and not be reduced to a shadow by the menfolk in the family especially her husband. ... It was remarkable how she stood out so distinctly beside his overpowering personality. Having to keep up with a demanding life with failing health and feeble body called forth all one's compassion. As she once said, 'It is alright being famous,

but it is very nerve-racking'.[88]

Later, Syed Mehmud,[89] a Congressman and Madhu Limaye,[90] a freedom fighter and intellectual, also recalled Kamla's exceptional will-power and sense of commitment, which enabled her to continue picketing in the hot months of May and June, ignoring her ill health. The former also mentioned Jawaharlal Nehru's acute sense of loneliness after Kamla's death.[91]

It seemed that the principle of healthy assertion of individuality and choices formed the basis of personal relationships and the discordant note was rarely heard over role-conflicts for women in Nehru family. But problems of male ego did crop up in many middle class families wherein women, inspired by the examples of the wives, daughters and sisters of the Congress leaders particularly of the Nehrus, had participated in meetings, processions and went to jail.[92]

However, Nehru's wholehearted preoccupation with the goal of political freedom moulded the personal aspirations of his family members and close associates. In the role of a confidant and guide, he frequently advised his daughter, sister and friends to give priority to their participation in the then ongoing struggle for Indian liberation. In response to his daughter Indira's letter, requesting permission to suspend her studies at Oxford University and return home to join the Congress movements, he advised her to do so because the experience gained in politics was more valuable than university education.[93]

Similar was his reaction to a communication from Bharati Sarabhai who was keen to continue her university education rather than get involved into politics. Writing to her, he observed:

> As you yourself say, how much you learnt last year in the burden of the fray. How you have grown and felt yourself more for a while in a larger unity that is Indian humanity and felt your pulse beat in unison with that of a million others. ... It is no doubt that time will come again when we shall be tested and it will be a more difficult test than ever before. Keep ready for this time.[94]

Jawaharlal Nehru's integrity, patriotic zeal, personal magnetism and intellectual calibre inspired tremendous faith and confidence amongst his contemporaries, particularly, political associates. Sarojini Naidu regarded him as "the other man of destiny", next to Gandhi. In her birthday greetings to Nehru on 14th November 1937, she wished him unflinching faith and unfaltering courage in the pursuit of his mission of national freedom even "if sorrow and pain and loneliness be your portion. Remember that Liberty is the ultimate crown of all your sacrifice ... but you shall not walk alone".[95]

Another remarkable friend was Raj Kumari Amrit Kaur, who had learnt to appreciate Nehru's 'crystal purity' through Gandhiji. In the course of her long association with him primarily as a political activist and later as a cabinet colleague for ten years, Amrit Kaur was drawn to him through the years by his numerous qualities such as:

> his integrity of purpose ... his unfailing devotion to duty, his ability to work for an ideal without counting the cost, his abhorrence of anything that savours of injustice or cruelty, his complete freedom from any racial or religious prejudice, his sensitive nature which appreciates beauty, whether of nature or of arts, his loyalty to friends, his facile and enchanting pen, his love of women and children, his courageous, adventurous and ever youthful spirit, his love of truth, his freedom from malice, and his tender-hearted and very affectionate nature.[96]

This is the most adequate description of elements that composed Nehruvian charisma which had no religious connotation.[97]

In spite of Amrit Kaur's tremendous faith in Nehru's dynamism and progressive outlook and his ability to lead Asia to the haven of peace and prosperity, she was not oblivious to his faults—the greatest being his inability to believe in God. Most of Nehru's friends and women in the Nehru family found him basically a loner, perhaps, by the very nature of his position and also perhaps by reason of circumstances and his own temperament.[98] However, he had not allowed his acute feeling of loneliness to superimpose upon his public image, or interfere with his political work and interaction with his colleagues.

For his political associates, very often, Pandit Nehru performed the role of an interpreter of Gandhi's ideology, decisions and plans to conduct the national fight for freedom against the British imperialism. His political associates confided their reactions, doubts and feelings in him whenever they could not figure out Gandhi's rationale in suspending a particular movement or selecting seemingly insignificant issues as the plank of a new movement. When Kamla Devi Chattopadhay, a prominent Congress Socialist Party leader, apprised

Nehru of her bewilderment over Gandhi's decision to make salt-tax as the central issue of the fresh round of Satyagraha, he gave a knowing nod. Without revealing his own irritation, Nehru told her, "You have yet to learn his ways. We cannot always grasp his ideas in their entirety. But rest assured there is method in what people think is madness".[99] There were many more such occasions when Nehru had to explicate Gandhi's ideas to his comrades.

Another facet of Nehru's appeal as a public leader in the eyes of the educated young women in the 1930s and 1940s, apart from his handsome personality, was his spirit of rebelliousness. As a typical example of the responses he evoked in their hearts in the course of his visit, as President of the historic Congress session at Lahore in December 1929, I shall cite an extract from Bimla Luthra's observations:

> We girls were completely bowled over by him ... he appeared to symbolise the spirit of rebellion against foreign domination and equally important to us at that age—the stifling conservatism which made us feel continually that we were an inferior species, good only for the home and the kitchen. We looked up to him as one who understood the deep urges of youth, and saw justice in women's aspirations to be treated as individuals in their own right.[100]

Such were the impressions of young girls from middle-class families whose self view and world view had changed. But they were neither politicized nor independent-minded enough to exercise their own choices. In Nehru, they saw a kindred spirit on whom they had pinned their hopes for recasting those social values and relationships which had dwarfed the personalities of women through centuries. This idealized view of Nehru's role was a complement to his other image as a comrade, friend, guide and philosopher—projected by the women of the Nehru household, the Congress women and the activists and members of the National Council of Women and All India Women's Conference. The other image left scope for interaction, conflict, a healthy sparring of opposite viewpoints while Nehru was engaged in his crusade for women's rights as autonomous individuals right from the days of the freedom struggle through his tenure as Prime Minister of independent India until his death in May 1964.

Crusade for Women's Rights

The second aspect of Nehru's contribution to the ongoing struggle for women's rights must take into account his efforts for mobilizing the Congressmen to accept the principle of equality as the basis of any constitution for India. At this juncture one crucial question must be raised: How far was Nehru able to influence the Congress policy in the course of the Indian freedom struggle so as to formulate and articulate the national demand for equal political and economic rights for women?

By 1929, the year when Jawaharlal Nehru, as President of the Indian National Congress, had made the historic declaration of *Puran Swaraj* as the goal of the Indian National Congress, his stature as the national leader particularly as the political heir of Gandhi rose tremendously. His image, as the spokesman of the democratic ideals and as an advocate of women's rights, had also acquired prestige and authority in the eyes of educated as well as illiterate masses. As a crusader for women's rights, he functioned in a two-fold capacity.

In the first instance, he understood and articulated the urges and aspirations of the urban-educated young women, belonging to aristocratic or middle-class families, to prove their worth and assert their identity as intelligent and talented individuals in public life. During the Non-cooperation Movement, Gandhi's exhortations to women to contribute to the economic and moral salvation of India by participating in the constructive programme of *swadeshi*, particularly khadi-work, had no doubt harnessed the traditional skills of women, utilized their energies and inherent capacity of non-violent resistance for political work and roused their sense of personal dignity. The khadi-work in the 1920s, which had brought about a feeling of self-fulfilment and a new sense of mission by universalizing their nurturing roles in the family, had lost its novelty and appeal for the new crop of young girls in the 1930s and 1940s.

In the second instance, by virtue of his own position and authority as a Congress leader and a Gandhi's trusted lieutenant, he was expected to help women to graduate from quiet constructive work for social engineering to the exciting arena of political struggle in the capacity of participants and leaders. In Nehru's view, "The call for freedom had always a double meaning for them, and the enthusiasm and energy with which they threw themselves into the struggle had no doubt their springs in the vague and hardly conscious, but nevertheless, intense desire to rid themselves of domestic slavery also".[101]

The most spectacular evidence of this strong combination of the social and political aspirations of women was their large-scale participation in the Civil Disobedience Movement in 1930 about which Nehru came to know as a prisoner in Naini Jail. Recalling those days, Nehru wrote, "Never can I forget the thrill that came to us ... the enormous pride in the women of India that filled us. We could hardly talk about this among overselves, for our hearts were full and our eyes dim with tears."[102]

The massive entry of women into Salt Satyagraha, especially the leading role of Sarojini Naidu and Kamla Devi Chattopadhyay, had brought them a new status and prestige. In spite of their lack of political experience, women *satyagrahis* from diverse social backgrounds showed exceptional fire, dynamism, discipline and organizational ability while conducting raids in salt depots at Dharsana and Wadala and picketing in front of liquor and foreign cloth shops in various towns and cities of India.[103]

So deep was its emotional impact as to compel Motilal Nehru to insist upon recording the nation's appreciation for the memorable role of women in the 'Resolution of Remembrance',[104] passed at thousands of public meetings all over India, on 26th January 1931. By acknowledging the brave and notable contribution of women as soldiers of freedom in the front ranks of national army, this resolution had given social legitimacy to their varied roles in national and public affairs and thus to the long-standing demand for equal voting rights by women's organizations, reiterated since 1917.[105]

Obviously, the temper of the people, their new self-view and world-view and an irrefutable evidence of the prestige and power of women were the major reasons for the incorporation of the principle of political and economic equality of women, irrespective of their status and qualifications, in the Congress Resolution at its Karachi session, 1931.[106] The credit goes to Nehru for introducing the concept of 'equal rights' and 'equal obligations' on the Soviet model in the Fundamental Rights part of the Resolution in respect of adult suffrage, freedom of association, access to public employment, office of power or honour and the exercise of trade and calling. The Economic Policy Part of the resolution, which had been framed by Nehru in consultation with Gandhi,[107] was a concrete expression of his faith that without economic freedom, other aspects of equality would prove superfluous as his speeches in the 1930s showed. Even more significant in context with women's right to employment was its clause regarding "protection of women workers, and adequate provisions for leave during maternity period".

The reaction of a prominent public leader Kamla Devi Chattopadhyay to the entire Resolution—Fundamental Rights and Economic Policy—gave an inkling of the future course of the Congress policy. She wrote:

> The entire Resolution ... injected fresh rudiments into the body politic of the Congress, furnished it with new tools for taking an added measure to meet the age-old cries now risen to a crescendo making compelling demands. To me the clause 'there shall be no discrimination on ground of sex' opened gates to a new world. Vague aspirations, like the right to free speech, assembly, were transformed into meaningful functions.[108]

How far did this proclamation of the principle of equality reflect the readiness of the Congressmen to accept the claims of women for positions of authority in the party and their increasing visibility in public life? No doubt, Gandhi's pervasive moral influence both within the Congress and outside had wiped away vocal antagonism towards women. Jawaharlal Nehru's ceaseless campaign for women's rights and education coupled with his praise for their gallant role in the national struggle for freedom especially in the 1930s had reinforced the climate of sympathetic awareness of their fundamental demands and urges as individuals. As a result, dissident voices—representing feudal views about women—kept silent, though temporarily.

What were the impressions or experiences of the contemporary Congress women? The Congress women did not recall any instance of open ill-feeling or hostility from their colleagues. However, some of them showed awareness of the persistence of old-fashioned views among Congressmen. For example, Hansa Mehta, a prominent social-worker and an elected Parliamentary Secretary 1937–39, revealed that some of the Congressmen had disapproved of the association of women in political life.[109] On the basis of her personal experience, Mridula Sarabhai, a member of the Working Committee in 1946–47, commented upon the hard struggle of those Congress women who wanted to be accepted as independent and responsible colleagues on their own merit. But the ones who complied with the decisions of influential Congressmen, were given important assignments.[110] Vijayalakshmi Pandit, in spite of her political connections, too, sensed the grudging acceptance given to women as members or office-holders in the party.[111]

Nevertheless, women used to attend the annual All India Congress Committee meetings as members and were appointed as delegates. At Gandhi's instance, it became an established practice to elect at least one women member to the Working Committee of the Congress.[112] While Sarojini Naidu served on it for many years, occasionally, other prominent women, namely, Kamla Devi Chattopadhyaya and Mridula Sarabhai were also inducted in 1946–47. But Jawaharlal Nehru, as the Congress President in 1936–37, broke this convention by excluding women from the Working Committee. The All India Women's Conference published a note of protest for ignoring Sarojini Naidu and for not considering the name of Kamla Devi Chattopadhyay as a socialist member.[113] In a letter to Gandhi, Nehru acknowledged having received protests from various organizations. He pleaded that he was forced to accommodate important people and give representation to crucial interests as they carried more weightage as pressure groups than women's lobby.[114] However, Gandhi was not satisfied with his explanation and held him responsible for this omission.[115]

What was Nehru's motive or justification for exclusion of women from the Working Committee? Replying to representations from a large number of Congress women from Gujarat, Nehru explained his position:

> ... it was certainly possible for me to nominate a woman member, but I decided to break the tradition in the hope that this would be ultimately good for women themselves. The representation, I have received, is itself a sign that some good has resulted from my decision.[116]

This press statement as well as his earlier letter to Gandhi had argued that women had "to organize themselves to press for their rights which they were not likely to get if they waited for the goodwill of their menfolk".[117] While urging them to be self-reliant, imaginative and practical, he cautioned them against treating Fundamental Rights Resolution, 1931 as the ultimate victory. In their crusade for social and economic rights, women would have to face far harder obstructions—old customs, men's prejudices and vested interests. In spite of the Congress commitment to equal citizenship and economic rights for women, their male colleagues would seldom grow enthusiastic about such questions. Women, themselves, must bear the major burden of the social struggle.[118] While Nehru often lamented the tendency of women to seek patronage and favours, he failed to urge the Congressmen to modernize their views regarding society and status of women, to redefine their own rights and obligations.[119] For further elucidation of his views on this issue, let us turn to another instance.

Reacting to a suggestion from Gujarat Congress Women to induce the Working Committee to appoint a women's sub-committee to look after women's interests and help to organize their colleagues, he clarified, "The initiative and driving force of a women's movement must come from women themselves".[120]

However, Nehru was aware of the pitfalls of the total separation between women's struggle for their rights and the broader nationalist urge for political and economic freedom. Regarding this as common for men and women, he warned them, "...if you try to function outside these two urges and cut yourself adrift from the living current of national life, your movement will be functioning in the air, and you will be functioning in the little coteries and drawing rooms".[121] Obviously, coordination between various associated movements and the formation of anti-imperialist United Front[122] in the country was an integral part of the strategy of the national struggle against the British *Raj*.

This could be a partial explanation of the increasing involvement of women in Congress activities—whether electoral politics or anti-imperialist movements during the 1930s and 1940s. Despite mental reservations of a number of Congressmen, Nehru had inducted women into electoral politics in 1936. By acceding to the request of All India Women's Conference for sponsoring women candidates—Vijayalakshmi and Lakshmi Ammal along with a few others—the Congress had reinforced women organizations' opposition to the British Government's policy of reservation and nominations to seats for women. Out of the nine women candidates, four won seats from the general constituency, including two from the Upper House, namely, Hansa Mehta and Begum Rasul.[123] The Ministries, formed in

1937, included Vijayalakshmi Pandit as a Cabinet Minister and five women as Deputy Speakers and Parliamentary Secretaries. Sarojini Naidu, Jawaharlal Nehru and a few other national leaders, instead of accepting office, preferred to remain with the Central High Command set up by the Congress.[124]

The Congress experiment in electoral politics came to an end in November 1939 when the Congress Ministers resigned in protest against the Viceroy's Declaration of War and India's forced commitment to it without any reference to Indian representatives.[125] However, no Indian leader could ignore the need of self-defence when exposed to the threat of Japanese invasion in 1942. With a view to training women for the new responsibility of self-defence and self-sufficiency, the women's wing of AICC was created. In his letter to Maulana Azad, dated 5th March 1942, the Congress President Nehru explained the reasons for entrusting women with an altogether new task. He wrote:

> Public morale depends greatly on how women feel and act...I am all against treating women as helpless human beings who cannot look after themselves and who must run away from the danger zone.... So the only way to tackle the problem is to make women realise that they have to and they can face it.[126]

The danger from Japan receded but the tussel between the imperialist forces and the nationalist forces imposed even greater demands upon Indians—men and women alike. Gandhi gave a call for 'open rebellion' when the Quit India Resolution was passed on 8th August 1942 at the Bombay Session of the Congress. Responding to his mantra 'Do or Die', the Congress women along with their male colleagues proved their ability in organizing violent, secret and underground activity as well as non-violent movement. While women who were strict Gandhians such as Sarojini Naidu, Kasturba Gandhi, Sushila Nayyar and Vijayalakshmi Pandit, allowed themselves to be arrested peacefully on 9th August 1942, others like Usha Mehta, Sucheta Kriplani and Aruna Asaf Ali evaded the police and went into hiding.[127]

The simultaneous arrests of the prominent Congress leaders, particularly Gandhi, coupled with the unconventional *modus operandi* of satyagraha called Quit India movement, which depended for its success on the initiative and decision of each individual and not on any specific instructions for guidance,[128] had created a crisis. Believing that initiative and organization could not be provided by each one for himself, a few Congressmen and women, namely, Achyut Patwardhan, Ram Manohar Lohia, Aruna Asaf Ali and Sucheta Kriplani took up the responsibility of organizing and directing the masses. A few years later, explaining the circumstances to Maulana Azad, the then Congress President, Aruna Asaf Ali wrote:

> We all recognized the urgent necessity of providing some guidance to the vast forces that were being unleashed; instructions, directives, appeals and proclamations and the day to day exhortations (broadcast by the Congress Radio) were issued from time to time after our arrest in the name of All India Congress.[129]

Pandit Nehru, lodged in the Ahmadnagar Fort, got piecemeal news about how the rebel Congress men and women had set up the shadow AICC office for providing the much-needed organization, direction and coordination for political groups and individual satyagrahis, monetary help and advice to the families of the imprisoned political workers.[130] By issuing bulletins, reporting the progress of the movement, under the signatures of Achyut Patwardhan and Aruna Asaf Ali, the 'underground' group had sustained the enthusiasm and morale of the satyagrahis.[131] For supplementing the details, the daring task of establishing a secret broadcasting station and purchasing a transmitter, was done by Usha Mehta and her friends.[132]

The leading role played by women in the Quit India movement, especially Aruna Asaf Ali's courage and resourcefulness, attracted a great deal of admiration indicating that women could be effectively assimilated into different political movements and strategies. Mahatma Gandhi, Jawaharlal Nehru and Maulana Azad testified to Aruna Asaf Ali's central role in the 1942 movement, which was full of heroism and romance.[133] She rightly believed that those times of political crisis had provided a unique opportunity for many people to evolve and establish their new identity and to display their capabilities, strength and courage.[134]

As a perceptive observer and a leading participant in Congress movements, Nehru had developed tremendous faith in the capability of women to discharge varied responsibilities with devotion and ability. Once again, women, in spite of their difficult experience of political campaigning in the 1937 elections,[135] showed great enthusiasm to be elected as representatives to the Constituent

Assembly in 1946. Responding to Hansa Mehta's request,[136] the Congress President Maulana Azad persuaded AICC to instruct the Premiers to elect a required number of women to the Constituent Assembly. Jawaharlal Nehru seemed to have played a key role in the preparation of the list of women candidates for favourable consideration by the provincial governments.[137] The Congress Working Committee list leaned heavily in favour of All India Women's Conference. The other women's organizations and even the Women's Department of AICC did not get any representation. This was evident from the letter of Mridula Sarabhai,[138] Secretary of Women's Deptt. AICC, to J.B. Kriplani. When grilled on this issue, Nehru informed Mridula Sarabhai that the list submitted by the Congress Committee to the provinces was neither mandatory nor exclusive.[139]

For Nehru, there was, perhaps, no question of preference of one group to another. The important fact is that he was keen to associate women in the task of constitution-making especially in hammering out its provisions which would ensure an equitable treatment and an honoured place for women in the new Indian nation and society.[140]

The Constituent Assembly, which met in December 1946, included no less than 14 women representatives. These were Ammu Swaminathan, Dakshayani Velayudhan and Durgabai Deshmukh from Madras, Hansa Mehta from Bombay, Malti Chowdhury from Orissa, Sucheta Kriplani, Vijayalakshmi Pandit, Purnima Banerjee, Kamla Chaudhari and Begum Aizaz Rasul from Uttar Pradesh, Sarojini Naidu from Bihar, Begum Jahanara Shah Nawaz from Punjab, and Lila Roy and Begum Ikramullah from Bengal.[141]

One of the remarkable achievements of the Constituent Assembly was the chapter on Fundamental Rights which was based on the Karachi Resolution and recommendations of the National Planning Committee 1939–40.[142] Herein, women were given an equal status with men without any discrimination on the basis of sex. This provision raised neither opposition nor controversy. No less significant was Article 44 of the Directive Principles of State Policy.[143] Concerned with the Uniform Civil Code, it indicated Nehru's commitment to ensure equality in marriage and inheritance laws for Indian women irrespective of their religion. It also dealt with the establishment of a just social, political and economic order for both men and women. Equal pay for equal work as well as just and human conditions of work and maternity relief were stipulated.

The Constitution had aroused great hopes amongst the advocates of women's rights—activists as well as other progressive Indians who looked forward to socio-economic revolution in the country. In actual practice, even the task of reforming the traditional Hindu Law, which regarded women as socially inferior, proved to be extremely difficult. Hence, Nehru, as Prime Minister of free India, had to face stiff opposition while sponsoring legal changes affecting social and economic privileges of men, particularly in the area of marriage and inheritance laws.

Hindu Code Bill

With the exit of the British and establishment of a sovereign democratic republic in India on 15th August 1947, the Congress goal of political revolution had been achieved. The new government under the stewardship of Jawaharlal Nehru hoped to initiate and push forward the process of economic change in the direction of nation building without raising any controversy. But the very first concrete move for social change—resurrection of Draft Hindu Code, originally submitted by the B.N. Rau Committee to the Central Legislative Assembly in April 1947—and its revision by the Ministry of Law in August 1948, opened a seven-year-long period of tussel between the progressive and the orthodox forces.

The proponents and opponents of the Hindu Code Bill, which was debated during 1943-44 in the Central Legislative Assembly and during 1949 and 1951 in the Constituent Assembly (known in 1951 as the Provisional Parliament), justified their positions in terms of three major arguments. These three claims were: *(a)* promoting democracy *(b)* strengthening Hinduism *(c)* serving public interest. Both the lobbies did not put forth any additional arguments to reinforce their case during 1954–56 but Nehru was increasingly more conciliatory to the opponents of the Hindu Code Bill.

Jawaharlal Nehru, as the head of the new government and as the chief spokesman of the Congress, was committed to the broad approach of the Bill as a whole and proclaimed that the Government "will stand or fall on it".[144] Provoked by the delaying tactics of reactionaries and aware of their motives, he had made this observation.

In retrospect, it is clear that Nehru had overestimated his party's commitment to the Hindu Law Reform and underestimated the strength of the opponent camp. Only a few Congressmen extended strong support to the Bill. The other top Congress leaders opposed it vehemently. Amongst the opponents were included Dr. Rajendra Prasad, Congress President (1947–48) and President of India (1950–61), Vallabhabhai Patel, Home Minister (until his death in 1950) and Purshottam Das Tandon (Congress President in 1950). With such dissensions and opposition within the Congress during the first problem-ridden years of the new Government, Nehru wavered in his commitment for the immediate legislation of the Hindu Code Bill. Above all, it was President Rajendra Prasad's threat to cause a constitutional crisis by exercising his right to "examine it on its merits when it is passed by Parliament before giving assent to it",[145] which softened Nehru's commitment to the immediate codification of Hindu Law. In spite of the firm views of the legal luminaries namely, Sir Alladi Krishna Swamy Aiyar[146] and M.C. Setalvad,[147] Attorney General, regarding the limitations of President's power, Nehru dropped the Bill on 6th September, 1951 until its resumption after the General Elections, 1952. The Law Minister B.R. Ambedkar, who had shared Nehru's commitment to the Hindu Code Bill and his eagerness for its early legislation, resigned in protest. In his letter of resignation, he had specified the Hindu Code Bill debacle as a reason for his decision.[148]

Why was Nehru forced to withdraw the Hindu Code Bill even if temporarily? There were several reasons for his decision.[149] Firstly, debates over the issue of Hindu Law reform, particularly marriage and property laws, had reflected the hardening of public attitudes. The public opinion had been influenced by the negative trend in the thinking of orthodox Hindu politicians, who were encouraged to visualize independent India in terms of a Hindu Raj especially after the creation of a Muslim State—Pakistan in 1947.

Secondly, social reformers and the leaders of the women's organizations became complacent, believing that exit of the British from India had removed the primary obstacle in the path of social revolution. They lacked political astuteness which was evident from their assumption that independence and constitutional guarantee of sex equality would ensure the passage of the Hindu Code Bill. The women leaders, perhaps, lacked ability to mobilize public opinion in contrast with their opponents who organized impressive popular demonstrations before the Parliament House whenever the Bill was under discussion. Pandit Nehru noted their adverse psychological impact upon the educated elite as well as the illiterate masses.[150] Moreover, women organizations, upon whom Nehru depended for effective support, lacked political resources for mass politics. The few prominent leaders, having experience of Civil Disobedience campaigns, were busy with other official assignments or programmes other than Hindu Code Bill during 1949–51. Thirdly, the division of opinion among legal experts also obstructed the immediate codification of Hindu Law. In fact, a lengthy note of dissent by D.N. Mitter, a member of Rau Committee, had served as a rallying point for the opponents. Fourthly, the fact, that an untouchable—B.R. Ambedkar—had challenged the traditional social mores and *shastric* wisdom by advocating the legislation of the Hindu Code Bill, provoked even more opposition from the orthodox Hindus.

Four years lapsed before anything was done about the Bill. After his victory in the General Elections 1952, Nehru became the undisputed leader of the popularly elected government and the major political party. Nehru, who had repeatedly declared his support for the principles of the Hindu Code Bill during his election campaign, regarded the Congress victory as the popular mandate for its legislation. His hands were further strengthened when the court cases such as Bombay case in 1952[151] upheld legislation modifying personal law for social reform. The strategy, adopted by Nehru's government to secure the passage of Hindu Code Bill, indicated a more pragmatic approach. Realizing that his thinking was ahead of his party, he learnt to go ahead step by step arousing little hostility and fewer dissensions.

That was why the Hindu Code Bill was divided into five separate Acts and the least controversial one was introduced first. The five Acts were enacted in this chronological order: Special Marriage Act (1954), Hindu Marriage Act (1955), Hindu Succession Act (1955), Hindu Minority and Guardianship Act (1956) and Hindu Adoption and Maintenance Act (1956).[152] The last important measure, enacted during Nehru's lifetime, was the Dowry Restraint Act (1961).

Interestingly, the Hindu Law Reform was given legislative sanction during the tenure of an orthodox Hindu as Law Minister, H.V. Pataskar, who had opposed the Bill in 1951. Perhaps, Nehru Government's spirit of reconciliation, despite its increased authority, and several modifications in the Hindu Code Bill in deference to the wishes of its opponents, dissipated resistance and criticism.

Thus, Nehru was able to fulfil his commitment to secure legal equality for women in the matter of marriage and inheritance. This was a progressive step in the legislation of a Uniform Civil Code for different communities in India. In the absence of a Uniform Civil Code, the Indian democracy is being riddled with such questions: Who is a Hindu? Are women full Indian citizens? How long would their rights depend upon their membership of a particular religious community? What is the fate of those Muslim women who find their marriage and inheritance laws inadequate especially when there is talk of further liberalizing the Hindu Code? However, the impact of changes in the marriage and inheritance laws is much less than anticipated by the stormy debates. As there was no intensive mass education campaign amongst women by the supporters of the Hindu Code Bill, very few women knew about the enactment of the Hindu Code Act and much less about their newly acquired rights to divorce and inheritance of property. Certainly, there was neither chaos nor broken homes as predicted by the opponents of the Hindu Code.[153]

V

Conclusion

How far did Nehru succeed in his crusade for women's emancipation and their rights? It has two aspects. The first concerns the redefinition of the concept of women, and their role in social, economic and political life of the Indian nation. Unlike the nineteenth century social reformers, Gandhi had already raised women from being mere objects or receptacles of reform into active participants in their own upliftment and liberation from the tyranny of male-oriented social customs and conjugal relations. Nehru had added legal, political and economic dimensions to women's moral right to self-development as autonomous individuals. Through his speeches and writings and later on through his policies as the leader of the biggest democracy in Asia, he had endeavoured to carve out the new identity of women as full-blooded human beings. In his view, they should be entitled to full opportunities for self-development, civic rights along with obligations, social and legal equality as Indian citizens rather than as a separate class or category or as adjuncts of men.

The concept of 'equal rights' and 'equal obligations' was Nehru's major contribution to the cause of woman's emancipation. It had stripped the idealized image of women of its halo and brought her down from the pedestal so that she would experience the thrill and excitement of growing up as an intelligent human being. Thus, to some extent, Nehru was reinforcing the struggle for women's rights, carried on simultaneously by a number of enlightened individuals and women's groups particularly National Council of Women and All Indian Women's Conference. His image as an advocate of freedom and revolution provided emotional sustenance, hope and inspiration to the young impressionable minds. Memoirs and reminiscences of the Nehru women, of his political associates, observations of the activists in women's groups and the teenaged girl students during the 1930s and 1940s showed that Nehru had not only understood their urges and aspirations for their personal as well as national freedom but also had articulated them forcefully. That explained his insistence upon the incorporation of equal rights, without discrimination of sex, and protection of the rights of female workers, in the Fundamental Rights and Economic Policy Resolution at the Karachi Session, 1931. That was why Nehru had rejected the conventional ideal of women's education which trained them to regard marriage as their sole destiny and profession.

Nehru's crusade for women's rights, conducted in collaboration with various women's groups on the floor of the Constituent Assembly in 1946, culminated in the grant of constitutional guarantees to women like any other Indian citizen without discrimination on the basis of sex, religion or caste. Conscious of the obstructive role of the long-ingrained social prejudices, inhibitions and the defective socialization process in according social and economic equality to women, framers of Indian Constitution made special provision for them in Articles 14, 15, 16, 39, 42 and 43 in addition to equal privileges and rights.[154] However, it may be pointed out that the principles of protection to women workers and maternity leave benefits, incorporated as Fundamental Rights in the Karachi Resolution, were reduced to the Directive Principles. Similarly, the principle of equal wages for equal work was finally made into a law only in 1976 by his daughter Indira Gandhi as a special gesture in the International Year of Women. Thus, there was a gap between Nehru's thought and action.

Imbued with self-confidence and conscious of their new identity as women, they took advantage of the increased opportunities of education and assumed positions of power and responsibility in political, administrative and professional fields and achieved distinction. The majority of these women had indeed acted as autonomous individuals by exercising their right to choose from a variety of roles—domestic and public. To some extent under the influence of Nehru, some of them even while they campaigned for women's causes—whether from equal rights perspective or uplift of status angle—remained within the framework of the nationalist movement.

However, it may be pointed out that immediately after Independence, pressures of ministerial responsibility or involvement with other issues of socio-economic development, perhaps, diluted their (women leaders') commitment to securing legislation for equal legal rights in respect of marriage and inheritance. That was why Nehru's fight for Hindu Code Bill became almost single-handed without effective support from women's groups or their yester-year leaders. Perhaps, this was the inevitable result of the merging of the social reform movement with the nationalist struggle for freedom especially when the later was the dominating concern and goal for every Indian. Finally, a father's unrestricted right to make a will often made the daughters dependent upon his goodwill for their share in his property. The underlying intention in the inclusion of this clause was to retain family agricultural holdings and urban business in the hands of individual male owners and to prevent their uneconomic fragmentation. Similar was the motive in making the father a natural guardian in preference to a mother under the Hindu Minority and Guardianship Act. Hindu women got a raw deal in the Adoption and Maintenance Act which left the fixation of amount of maintenance to the discretion of the judge. Thus, maintenance provisions were inadequate for girls.

Nehru was certainly aware of the defects in the Hindu Reform Legislation. But he was not inclined to initiate such changes as would require drastic reorganization in the social especially family structure. His major argument in accepting modifications in the Hindu Code Bills, was that the "essential principles underlying them had not been given up".[155] One of these was the linkages between legal advance in the social sector and advances in the political and economic areas. In his view, their integration into one whole would enable the people of India to progress. Second was the principle of women's equality at the conceptual as well practical levels. Nehru had not only accepted these principles but also advocated their limited implementation in the face of stiff opposition.[156] Sometimes, he was forced to make compromises as he did not want to be accused of gagging the opposition.

It is true that the original Hindu Code Bill was practically given up and the Muslim Personal Law was not even touched. It must be pointed out that Nehru's failure to enlarge the scope of his legal initiatives to cover all sections of society rather than being restricted to Hindus only and thereby losing the rare opportunity of formulating the Uniform Civil Code raised doubts regarding his credentials as a secular and modern leader. It has also been argued that he had made no special efforts to involve women either in the task of planning for their development or in the decision-making process. While being engaged in the onerous process of nation-building and governance, Nehru's crusade for women's development as Indian citizens seems to be ebbing away.

Despite the Hindu Reform Legislation of the 1950s, gender inequalities have not been removed. Even a cursory glance at the broad demographic data shows a decline in sex ratio, higher female infant mortality, rising graph of reported cases of dowry deaths and bride-burnings, low level of female literacy and of participation in labour force. Apart from many other factors, the miserable condition of women can be attributed to the loopholes in the Hindu Reform Legislation itself. These Acts were neither adequately publicized nor explained, thus leading to problems of interpretation at the local level. However, those who violated the law couldn't be prosecuted as the offence was not treated as a cognizable offence, for example, under the Child Marriage Restraint Act. Similarly, absence of a clause in the Hindu Marriage Act, questioning the validity of a marriage not registered, diluted the effectiveness of the clause regarding the compulsory registration of marriages. As a result, no effective restraint on child and bigamous marriages could be placed.[157]

Despite Nehru's claim that the Hindu Reform Legislation imparted a ''new dynamism to Hindu society'', it can at best be called a symbolic victory over the orthodox forces. However, it must be conceded that his Government's exercise was worthwhile as it liberalized and updated the marriage and property laws of the majority community, which were the most backward in comparison with the Personal Laws of Muslims, Parsis and Christians. It has paved way for the legislation of the Uniform Civil Code which Nehru had envisioned but could only secure its truncated form. However, it must be conceded that without Nehru's powerful advocay, these social reforms and rights of women would have been postponed for an unlimited time.

REFERENCES

1. *Selected Works of Jawaharlal Nehru*, S. Gopal, ed., (New Delhi: Orient Longman, 1972. Hereafter it shall be referred to as SW), p. 362 – Speech at Mahila Vidyapeeth, Allahabad on 31 March 1928.
2. *Jawaharlal Nehru's* Speeches 1949–53, (New Delhi: Publications Division, 1954), pp. 105–6. For his views on egalitarian society see pp. 105–6, 518–19.
3. Jawaharlal Nehru, *The Discovery of India,* (London: Meridian Books Limited), 1956, p. 7.
4. *Ibid.,* p. 13.
5. For an analytical discussion of the influences on Nehru's ideology see Hiltrud Rustau, 'Some Remarks on the Sources of the Philosophical Views of Jawaharlal Nehru', in *Nehru: His Work and Relevance,* (Prague: Oriental Institute of the Czech Social Sciences Academy, 1981).
6. Jawaharlal Nehru, *The Discovery of India*, pp. 573–74, 576.
7. For example see, *Jawaharlal Nehru's Speeches* 1949–53, pp. 11–12, 72, 434–35. Also O.Novak, 'The Role of Tradition in Nehru's Thought', in M. Krasa, ed., *Jawaharlal Nehru: A Political Leader* (Prague : Oriental Institute of the Czech Social Sciences Academy, 1974), p. 44.
8. 'Reply to Critics', in A. Schillip, *The Philosophy of S. Radhakrishnan,* (New York, 1952).
9. *Speeches* 1949–53, p. 95 – Speech in the Parliament on 15th December 1952.
10. *Ibid.,* p. 387–Address at the UNESCO Symposium, New Delhi on 20th December 1951.
11. *Ibid.,* p. 21–Speech broadcast from All India Radio, Delhi on 22nd November 1951.
12. *Ibid.,* p. 423–Address at the University of Saugor on 30th October 1952.
13. *Jawaharlal Nehru, An Autobiography,* (London: John Lane, The Bodley Head, 1937 edition), p. 445.
14. *Ibid.,* p. 128–Speech delivered at the Canadian Parliament on 24th October 1949.
15. *Ibid.,* p. 525–Resolution for the consideration of the Bill to amend the Constitution on 29th May 1951.
16. *Speeches* 1949–53, p. 526.
17. Jawaharlal Nehru, *The Discovery of India,* p. 45. He said, "I do not

idealize the conception of masses and as far as possible, I try to avoid thinking of them as a theoretical abstraction. The people of India are real to me in their great variety and inspite of their vast numbers. I try to think of them as individuals rather than vague groups".

18. *Ibid.*, p. 27. Referring to his own wife Kamla, he confessed that she had a deep and rich personality. He wrote, ".... We had been married for nearly twenty years, and yet how many times she had surprised me by something new in her mental and spiritual make up". Continuing further, he reminisced how she had enabled him to re-charge the exhausted battery of his mind and body when he was in the thick of the national struggle. Regarding Kamla as a symbol of Indian women, he observed that she wanted to play her own part in the national struggle and not be merely "a hanger-on and a shadow of her husband". Also *Speeches 1953–57,* Vol. III, p. 451–Speech in the Lok Sabha on the Divorce Clause of the Special Marriage Bill on 16th September 1954.
19. *Speeches* 1949–53, p. 72 – Speech at the Silver Jubilee Celebrations of the Central Board of Irrigation and Power, New Delhi, on 17th November 1952.
20. Jawaharlal Nehru, *The Discovery of India,* p. 15.
21. *Ibid.,* pp. 8–9.
22. *Speeches 1953–57,* Vol. III, p. 441 – Speech in Lok Sabha during the debate on the Special Marriage Bill on 22nd May 1954.
23. *Ibid.,* p. 440. – Speech during the debate on the Third Reading of the Hindu Marriage Bill in Lok Sabha on 5th May 1955. Also p. 453.
24. *Ibid.,* p. 443–Speech in Lok Sabha on the Divorce Clause of the Special Marriage Bill on 16th September 1954.
25. *Ibid.,* p. 444. Also SW, Vol. I, p. 362 – Speech at Mahila Vidyapeeth, Allahabad on 31st March 1928. Nehru was fond of quoting a great French idealist Charles Fourier who once said, "One could judge the degree of civilization of a country by the social and political position of its women".
26. *Ibid.*
27. *Ibid.* Nehru used the word 'rod' in the context of any law which oppresses, constrains and punishes. He drew attention to Hindu Laws and customs which fall heavily on the womenfolk especially of the upper strata.
28. *Speeches* 1949–53, pp. 8–9, Speech delivered in the Canadian Parliament, Ottawa on 24th October 1949, pp. 103, 105–6. Also Nehru's broadcast from the Delhi Station of All India Radio on 31st December 1952; pp. 122–24, Address to the East and West Association, Foreign Policy Association, the India League of America and Institute of Pacific Relations, New York on 10th October 1949.
29. Jawaharlal Nehru, *The Discovery of India*. p. 19. While discussing his philosophy of life, Nehru pointed out, "Or again, perhaps the very

progress of science, unconnected with and isolated from moral discipline and ethical considerations, will lead to the concentration of power for the use of the terrible instruments of destruction which it has made, in the hands of evil and selfish men, seeking the domination of others and thus to the destruction of its own great achievements...".

30. *Speeches* 1949–53, p. 7 – Independence Day Speech.
31. *Ibid.,* p. 518–19, Speech while moving the resolution for the consideration of the Bill to amend the Constitution, in the Parliament on 29th May 1951. He observed, "Hence, we must find a middle way between objectives and the existing facts. We must keep our ideal in view and then take steps which will carry us gradually in that direction.
32. *Speeches* 1953–57, Vol. III, p. 443–44, Speech in Lok Sabha on the Divorce Clause of the Special Marriage Bill on 16th September 1954; p. 447–Speech on the Third Reading of the Hindu Marriage Bill in the Lok Sabha on 5th May 1955. Also *SW*, Vol. III, pp. 360–62, Speech at Mahila Vidyapeeth on 31st March 1938.
33. *SW,* Vol. III, p. 480–Speech at Madras, 6th October 1936.
34. *SW,* Vol. V, pp. 236–37.
35. *SW,* Vol. III, p. 362.
36. For Gandhi's interpretation of the meanings of the ideals of Sita, Damyanti and Draupadi and their relevance as models of moral courage, dazzling purity, self-reliance and self-sacrifice see *Collected Works of Mahatma Gandhi,* Vol. XXXI, p. 511; *Young India,* 21st October 1926. Also Vol. XXVI, p. 99–Reply to Women's address in Noakhali on 14th May 1925. Also Vol. XXV, p. 338, *Harijan,* 1st March, 1942.
37. SW, Vol. III, p. 361.
38. *Speeches* 1953–57, Vol. III, p. 451 – Speech on the Third Reading of the Hindu Marriage Bill in Lok Sabha on 5th May 1955.
39. *Ibid.,* p. 449.
40. *Ibid.,* p. 447.
41. *SW,* Vol. II, pp. 15–16.
42. *Ibid.,* vol. III, p. 365, Speech at Madras on 6th October 1936.
43. Jawaharlal Nehru, *The Discovery of India,* p. 264.
44. *Ibid.*
45. *Ibid.,* p. 107.
46. *Ibid.*
47. *Ibid.,* p. 238.
48. Jawaharlal Nehru, *The Discovery of India,* p. 237.
49. *Ibid.,* p. 238.
50. *Ibid.,* Also see Nehru's Speech at the foundation of the Women's College, Madras on 22nd January 1955. Cited in K.T. Narsimha Chari, *The Quintessence of Nehru,* (London: George Allen & Unwin, 1961), pp. 198–99.
51. For Gandhi's views on purdah see M.K. Gandhi, ed., *Young India* 1927–

28, (Madras: S. Ganesan, 1935), especially its issues dated 3rd February 1927, 28th June and 26th July 1928, pp. 72–73, 770–71, 788–90. Also *Collected Works of Mahatma Gandhi,* Vol. XL, pp. 416–17.
52. Jawaharlal Nehru, *The Discovery of India,* pp. 238–39.
53. Jawaharlal Nehru, *Glimpses of World History,* Vol. I, (Allahabad: Kitabistan, 1935), p. 233.
54. Nehru's Speech cited in K.T. Narsimha Chari, *op. cit.*, p. 199.
55. SW, Vol. III, p. 362.
56. *Ibid.,* Vol. VI, pp. 256–57 (emphasis mine).
57. *Ibid.,* (emphasis mine).
58. *Ibid.,* Vol. III, p. 362.
59. K.T. Narsimha Chari, *op. cit.* p. 200.
60. *Jawaharlal Nehru on Science: Speeches Delivered at the Annual Sessions of the Indian Science Congress.* Baldev Singh, ed., (New Delhi : Nehru Memorial Museum and Library. Hereafter it shall be cited as NMML, New Delhi), 1986, p. 69–Inaugural address at the 46th Session of the Indian Science Congress, held at Delhi on 21st January 1956, pp. 95–96; address by Jawaharlal Nehru to the Ceylon Association for the Advancement of Science at the University of Ceylon, Colombo, on 15th October 1962.
61. *Nehru Papers,* Nehru's letter to his mother dated 1st January 1907, (NMML, New Delhi).
62. Nehru's letter to his mother dated 7th May 1909, in *Ibid.*
63. Krishan Bhatia, *Indira: A Biography of Prime Minister Gandhi,* (London: Angus & Robertson, 1974), p. 99.
64. SW, Vol. VI, pp. 235–36, Address to the Women's Meeting, Bombay, on 18th May 1936.
65. *Speeches* 1953–57, Vol. III, p. 444 – Speech in Lok Sabha on the Divorce Clause of the Special Marriage Bill on 16th September 1954.
66. *Ibid.,* p. 451–Speech on the Third Reading on the Hindu Marriage Bill in Lok Sabha on 5th May 1955.
67. *Ibid.,* p. 441.
68. *Speeches* 1953–57, Vol. III, p. 448.
69. *Ibid.*
70. *Nehru's Letters to His Sister,* Krishna Huthee Singh, ed. with an introduction, (London: Faber & Faber Ltd., 1963), pp. 19–20.
71. *Young India* (1927–28), pp. 772–73. In its issue, dated 28th June 1928, Gandhi, while replying to an appeal for the abolition of purdah from a number of influential people including an equal number of women from Bihar, explained the rationale of liberating women from evil customs and conventions that restrict their all-around growth if they were determined to secure their individual and national freedom. Very frequently, Gandhi used to urge Congress men to launch their struggle from their own homes. He observed "To postpone social reform till

after the attainment of *Swaraj* is not to know the meaning of *Swaraj*. Surely we must be incapable of defending ourselves or healthily competing with the other nations, if we allow the better-half of ourselves to become paralysed".

72. Jawaharlal Nehru, *An Autobiography,* pp. 192, 523–26. Many a time, Pandit Nehru felt irritated by Gandhi's preoccupation with non-political issues. Obsessed with the issue of national freedom, he felt unhappy while accompanying Gandhiji in the course of his khadi tours. He had no desire to confine himself to khadi propaganda which seemed to him "a relatively minor activity in view of the developing political situation" in 1929; also p. 184. Similar was his reaction to the Harijan movement. Having no hostility against it, he felt a little irritated by the Harijan movement because it had come in the way of Civil Disobedience.
73. *SW,* Vol. III, pp. 361-63, Speech at Mahila Vidyapeeth, Allahabad on 31st March 1928.
74. Jawaharlal Nehru, *An Autobiography*, pp. 384–85.
75. Vijayalakshmi Pandit, 'The Family Bond,' in Rafiq Zakaria, ed., *A Study of Nehru*, p. 125.
76. *Ibid.*, p. 126.
77. *Ibid.*
78. Krishna Huthee Singh, *With No Regrets,* (Bombay: Oxford University Press, 1952), p. 42.
79. *Nehru's Letters to His Sister,* Krishna Huthee Singh, ed., p. 83.
80. Oral transcript of interview with Manmohini Sehgal, (NMML, New Delhi).
81. Jawaharlal Nehru, *An Autobiography,* pp. 28, 214.
82. Oral transcript of interview with Vijayalakashmi Pandit, (NMML, New Delhi).
83. Krishna Huthee Singh, *With No Regrets,* p. 42.
84. SW, Vol. V, pp. 236–37.
85. Jawaharlal Nehru, *An Autobiography,* p. 224.
86. *Ibid.,* p. 240.
87. *Ibid.*
88. Kamla Devi Chattopadhyay, *Inner Recesses, Outer Spaces: Memoirs,* (New Delhi: Navrang, 1986), p. 118.
89. Syed Mahmud, 'In and Out of Prison' in Rafiq Zakaria, ed., *A Study of Nehru,* p. 161.
90. Madhu Limaye, *Mahatma Gandhi and Jawahar Lal Nehru: A Historic Partnership* 1916–1948, Vol. I, (Delhi: B.R. Publishing Corporation, 1989), p. 214.
91. SW, Vol. VII, p. 164. Also Syed Mahmud, *op. cit.,* p. 161.
92. Oral transcript of interview with Manmohini Sehgal; also personal interview with Pushpa Gujral, a veteran freedom fighter.
93. Cited in Promilla Kalhan, *Kamla Nehru: An Intimate Biography,* (Delhi:

Vikas Publishing House, 1973). pp. 44–45.

94. *Nehru Papers*, Nehru to Bharati Sarabhai, 1931, (NMML, New Delhi).
95. Sarojini Naidu to Jawaharlal Nehru, dated 13th November 1937 in *A Bunch of Old Letters: Letters Mostly Written to Nehru and Some by Him,* (Bombay: Asia Publishing House, 1958), p. 247.
96. Amrit Kaur, 'A Friend Without Friends' in Rafiq Zakaria, *op. cit.,* pp. 153–55.
97. S.P. Aiyer, 'Jawaharlal Nehru and Charismatic Leadership', in A.B. Shah, ed., *Jawahar Lal Nehru: A Critical Tribute,* (Bombay: Manaktala and Sons Pvt. Ltd., 1965), pp. 48–56.
98. Amrit Kaur, 'A Friend Without Friends' and Vijayalakshmi Pandit, 'The Family Bond', in Rafiq Zakaria, *op. cit.,* pp. 127, 155–56.
99. Kamla Devi Chattopadhyay, *Inner Recesses, Outer Spaces,* p. 139. Kamla Devi expressed her doubts to Nehru on a number of other issues such as absorption of Hindustani Seva Dal into Congress, resolution on Bhagat Singh's execution, reluctance of Gandhi to endorse Subhash Chandra Bose's candidature as the Congress President for the second term.
100. Bimla Luthra, 'Nehru and the Place of Women in Indian Society', in B.R. Nanda, *Indian Women: From Purdah to Modermity,* (New Delhi: Vikas Publishing House, 1976), p. 1.
101. Dorothy Norman, *Nehru: The First Sixty Years,* (Bombay: Asia Publishing House, 1965), Vol. I, p. 276.
102. Jawaharlal Nehru, *The Discovery of India,* p. 28.
103. Geoffrey Ashe, *Gandhi: A Study in Revolution,* (Bombay: Asia Publishing House, 1968), pp. 290–92.
104. Jawaharlal Nehru, *The Discovery of India,* p. 28. For the text of the 'Resolution of Remembrance' see Jawaharlal Nehru, *An Autobiography*, Appendix, pp. 606–7.
105. For a first-hand account of women's struggle for franchise rights see Kamla Devi Chattopadhayay, *The Awakening of Indian Women* (Madras: Everyman's Press, 1939). Also Aruna Asaf Ali, 'Women's Suffrage in India', in Shyam Kumari Nehru, ed., *Our Cause,* (Allahabad: Kitabistan, n.d), p. 347ff.
106. For the text of the Resolution on Fundamental Rights and Economic Policy (submitted to the All India Congress Committee, Bombay, August 1931) see Frank Moraes, *Jawahar Lal Nehru, A Biography,* (Bombay: Asia Publishing House, 1956), pp. 493–94. The ensuing references and extracts have been cited from the said source.
107. For contemporary speculation about the authors of the Fundamental Rights and Economic Policy Resolution see *Jawaharlal Nehru: An Autobiography,* p. 267. Also Kamla Devi Chattopadhayay, *op. cit.,* pp. 161–62. According to Kamla Devi, Fundamental Rights Resolution was based on the core draft prepared by Nalinakshi Sanyal, (an active youth

worker of Bengal) who requested the author, a member of the AICC, to pass it on to Nehru, the then General-Secretary. However, the Economic Policy Resolution was Nehru's own.

108. Kamla Devi Chattopadhayay, *op. cit.,* p. 162. Nehru had also regarded the Economic Policy Resolution as an indication of a new outlook in the Congress which had avoided facing economic issues except in so far as it encouraged industries and *swadeshi* generally. In the Karachi resolution, it took a very short step in socialist direction.
109. Oral transcript of interview with Hansa Mehta (NMML, New Delhi).
110. Oral transcript of interview with Mridula Sarabhai (NMML, New Delhi).
111. Oral transcript of interview with Vijayalakashmi Pandit, (NMML, New Delhi).
112. Gandhi to Jawaharlal Nehru dated 29th May 1936. Cited in File No. 12/ADM\71, DIG-CID Office, Bombay.
113. *Stri Dharma,* May, 1936.
114. SW, Vol. VII, (Bombay: Orient Longman Ltd., 1975), pp. 263–64. Nehru to Gandhi, dated 25th May 1936. The full text of this letter is not available. Jawaharlal Nehru informed Gandhi that the members of the Working Committee were not of his choice, though he was technically responsible for them.
115. Gandhi to Jawaharlal Nehru dated 19th May 1936. Cited in File No. 12/ADM\71, DIG-CID Office, Bombay.
116. *SW,* Vol. VII, p. 313, Nehru's statement to the Press on Women's Movement, Allahabad, dated 6th July 1936.
117. *Ibid.,* p. 264, Nehru to Gandhi, dated 26th May 1936.
118. *Ibid.,* p. 313.
119. Unlike Jawaharlal Nehru, Gandhi had set the liberation of women as a fundamental task before Congressmen. He urged them to begin with their own homes by imparting education to their own wives, mothers and daughters. Cited in D.G. Tendulkar, *Mahatma,* Vol. VI, (New Delhi: Publications Division, 1975), p. 24.
120. *SW*, Vol. VII, p. 482–Speech at Madras, 6th October, 1936.
121. *Ibid.,* p. 483.
122. *Ibid.,* p. 222. For Pandit Nehru's views on United Front see *International Press Correspondence,* VIII, 16, February, 1963. It published Nehru's interview under the title 'The National Congress and the Future'.
123. Margaret Cousins, *Indian Womanhood Today,* (Allahabad: Kitabistan, 1947), p. 87.
124. Lakshmi Menon, *Political Rights of Women in India,* (Bombay: Orient Longman Ltd., 1954), p. 28.
125. Francis G. Hutchins, *Spontaneous Revolution: The Quit India Movement,* (New Delhi: Monohar Book Service, 1971), p. 219.
126. *Nehru Papers*–Nehru to Maulana Azad, 5th March 1942, (NMML, New Delhi). Also Jawaharlal Nehru, *The Discovery of India,* pp. 481, 491.

127. Personal interview with Aruna Asaf Ali on 24th June 1988.
128. For a detailed study of Gandhi's plan of action see Amba Prasad, *The Indian Revolt,* (Delhi: S. Chand & Co., 1958), pp 55–58. For example, Gandhi said, "Every man is free to go the fullest length under *Ahimsa* by complete deadlock, strikes and all other non-violent means. A *Satyagrahi* should go out to die and not live. It is only when individuals go out to seek and face death that the nation will survive".
129. Cited in Dhan, *Aruna Asaf Ali,* (Lahore: New India Publications, n.d.), p. 36.
130. Jawaharlal Nehru, *Discovery of India,* p. 495 ff.
131. Francis G. Hutchins, *op. cit,* p. 297.
132. *Ibid.,* pp. 295–96. Also Oral transcript of interview with Usha Mehta, (NMML, New Delhi).
133. Maulana Abul Kalam Azad, *India Wins Freedom,* (Bombay: Orient Longman, 1958), p. 117.
134. Aruna Asaf Ali, *Travel Talk,* (Aundh: Aundh Publishing Trust, 1947), p. 107.
135. Majority of the Hindu women, who had already participated in Satyagraha campaigns, had shed their inhibition regarding purdah. Having a better understanding of political issues, they faced little difficulty in election campaigns. In fact Vijayalakshmi Pandit had relished this experience. Muslim women not only experienced personal hardship and social criticism during campaigning but also difficulty in collecting women voters for seats reserved for Muslim women in the Punjab and Bengal as late as 1952, the year of First General Elections. Experiences of Masuma Begum were not different.
136. *Nehru Papers*, File No. 5, G-64, 1946, Hansa Mehta to Abul Kalam Azad, 25th June 1946.
137. *Ibid.* The Working Committee submitted the following list of women candidates to the provinces:

    Bombay – Shrimati Hansa Mehta, M.L.C., (Bombay) and President, National Council of Women in India (Bombay)

    C.P. – Mrs. Ansuya Bai Kale.

    Madras – Shrimati Kamla Devi, Ex-President AIWC; Smt. Ammu Swaminathan, M.L.A., Central Madras.

    Punjab – Smt. Rameshwari Nehru, M.L.A. (Punjab)

    Following names suggested by AIWC were recommended for Uttar Pradesh.

    1. Smt. Vijayalakshmi Pandit, Minister, Uttar Pradesh.
    2. Smt. Sucheta Kriplani, Uttar Pradesh.
138. *Ibid.,* Mridula Sarabhai to J.B. Kriplani.
139. *SW*, Vol. XV, p. 459, Nehru to Mridula Sarabhai, 8th July 1946.
140. Personal interview with Manmohini Sehgal on 12th June 1988.
141. Frank Moraes, 'In Political Life', in Tara Ali Baig ed., *Women of India,*

(Delhi: Publications Division, 1958) p. 100. For more details see the *Indian Annual Register,* Vol. II, July–December, 1946, pp. 317–25.

142. National Planning Committee, File No. 135 [Pt. IV]. 1939 (NMML, New Delhi). In accordance with the resolutions passed at the conference of Ministers of Industries in October 1938, Subhash Chandra Bose, President of the Congress, set up the National Planning Committee with Jawaharlal Nehru as its Chairman. It resolved that problems of poverty, unemployment, national defence and economic regeneration in general could not be solved without industrialization and as a step towards such industrialization a comprehensive scheme of national planning should be formulated. Twenty-nine subcommittees were appointed and the Planning Committee's work extended until March 1940. One of the sub-committees was charged with examining the role of women in the planned economy of a free and democratic state in India and submitted its report on 31.8.1940. Rani Lakshmi Bai Rajwade was its President and Mridula Sarabhai, its Secretary. Apart from reiterating the declaration of Fundamental Rights, 1931, it made a number of bold recommendations such as legislation on abortion for population control, amendment of the civil marriage law in order to enable the desirous persons to get married without declaration of their religion, right of divorce, identical standards of morality for both sexes, a uniform civil code applicable to all citizens and a few other suggestions. But these reports were never systematically utilized, as the arrests of Congress leaders in 1940 interrupted the project before it was completed.

143. In 1941, the British Government appointed the B.N. Rau Committee to clarify the Deshmukh Act 1937 and another bill concerning the Hindu Women's Right to Separate Residence and Maintenance. The report was issued on 19th June 1941. On 20th January 1944, the British Government reconstituted the Rau Committee for the purpose of preparing a Hindu Code. It published the draft Hindu Code on 5th August 1944 for opinion poll. It submitted a revised draft of the Code to the Central Legislative Assembly in April 1947.

144. India, *Constituent Assembly Debates,* Vol. VII, Part II, December 1949, p. 789.

145. K.M. Munshi, *Indian Constitutional Documents: Pilgrimage to Freedom,* Vol. I, (Bombay: Vidya Bhavan, 1967), Appendix, pp. 578–82, Dr. Rajendra Prasad's note to Jawaharalal Nehru, dated 15th September 1951.

146. *Ibid.,* pp. 586–87, Opinion of Sir Alladi Krishnaswamy Aiyar, dated 20th September 1951.

148. *The Tribune,* 12 October 1951.

149. For an interesting analysis of the reasons underlying Nehru's decision to withdraw the Bill see Gene D. Overstreet, 'The Hindu Code Bill', in James B. Christoph, ed., *Cases in Comparative Politics,* (Boston: Little

Brown & Co., 1965), pp. 413–440.

150. Jawaharlal Nehru, *Letters to Chief Ministers* 1947–64, G. Parthasarthy, ed., (Delhi: Oxford University Press, 1985), Vol. I, p. 499–Fortnightly Letter No. 15, December 1949.
151. *All India Law Reporter* 1952, Bombay, p. 84–Judgement in the Case: State of Bombay V. Narasu Appa.
152. J. Duncan M. Derret, *Hindu Law: Past and Present,* (Calcutta: K.P. Bagachi, 1957), pp. 319–401.
153. *India, Constituent Assembly Debates,* Vol. VIII, p. 253. Ayyangar, a member of the Constituent Assembly predicted that allowing women to inherit property would lead to marriage going out of style and cried, "May God Save us... from having an army of unmarried women".
154. For an account of Aubrey Menon's views see Roloff Beny, *India* (London, 1969), p. 189.
155. Jawaharlal Nehru, *Letters to Chief Ministers 1947-64,* Vol. IV, 1988, 15 June 1956.
156. *Hindustan Times,* 16 May 1956. V. Prasad Rao was a Congress M.P. from Hyderabad.
157. *Towards Equality: Report of the Committee on the Status of Women in India,* (Delhi: Ministry of Education, 1975), p. 144.

6

Globalization and Cultural Invasion
Its Implications for Indian Men and Women

The historical memory of India's forced exposure to the global market forces and its cultural encounter with the West under the banner of the British *Raj* for almost two centuries provides a concrete starting point for hypothesizing about the emerging cultural scenario in the wake of the inexorable communication and commercial revolution throughout the world. Recent developments, particularly the rise of reform movements in the Soviet Union and Eastern Europe, have been described as the 'end of history' by Francis Fukuyama. In his view, we are witnessing the "end-point of mankind's ideological evolution and universalization of Western liberal democracy as the final form of human government".[1] His observation must be contested. I would let it go as it has not a direct bearing on the theme under discussion.

However, we have to concede that the 'end of geography' is a hard reality. The communication revolution has made distance and geographical divisions irrelevant. The lightening speed and ease of information flow through digital bit streams have impinged upon the politico-economic sovereignty and cultural specificities of the Third World countries. In view of the fast-paced globalization of trade and commerce as well as recent trends towards universalization of food habits, modes of dress, patterns of behaviour, there is a widespread anxiety among Indians about saving their cultural heritage and richness of spiritual life.

Globalization has a more comprehensive agenda and a formidable pool of economic resources (underwritten by multinational capital) than the British colonialism whose cultural domination and impact remained confined to the educated elite groups of Indian society owing to the absence of the powerful network of the electronic media. Among its long-term objectives are included the acquisition of a decisive role in the formulation of politico-economic and social policies relating to education, health, water, electricity, etc. and systems, especially, infrastructure for liberalization of the Third World countries through huge but conditional investments in the agricultural and industrial sectors and also through loans by International Monetary Fund (IMF) and World Bank. However, it is a controversial issue.

The major argument in this essay is that the Euro–American project of globalization of open market and free trade through the dissemination of its consumerist culture and its artefacts has serious socio-cultural implications, i.e. preservation of Indian cultural ideals, public perception of sexual relations, gender roles, women's status and empowerment. It may be argued that in the present multi-pronged East–West encounter, Indian women, in the first instance, are likely to become not only the bearers and signifiers of tradition but also the tradition itself. The fear of dilution of patriarchal structures and control over women owing to the full-scale cultural-religious intrusion and anxiety for the defence of religious/communal identies is likely to result in zealous imposition of domestic ideology, the glorification of the cult of 'genteel lady' as it happened during the course of industrial revolution in Britian.[2]

Secondly, it is feared that women may not only be commodified but also used as an agency by the capitalists. The proponents of consumer capitalism regard cultural conquest either through electronic media or through beauty pageants, fashion shows and other pompous extravaganzas as the facilitator of the economic process, i.e. open market and free trade.

For a coherent and meaningful discussion of the problem of 'cultural invasion'. I shall divide this essay into six sections: *(i)* Conceptualizing Culture; *(ii)* Ideals of Indian Culture; *(iii)* Indian Response to the Onslaught of Western Modernity; *(iv)* Ideals of Western Modernity; *(v)* Globalization, Consumerism and Mass Culture: Its Implications for Men and Women; and *(vi)* Conclusion.

I
CONCEPTUALIZING CULTURE

At the outset, it is helpful to refer to the different trajectories of the word 'culture' as it is according to Raymond Williams, "One of the two or three most complicated words in the English language".[3] In the Indian context, its use for entirely contradictory purposes during the colonial rule led to ambiguity. Its early use was made primarily for agricultural operations: 'cultivation', 'tending' and 'growth'.

The career of this word became plural with its gradual shift to the particular and the personal in terms of cultivation of mind and personality and later its application to describe a process or the product of a process in the late eighteenth and early nineteenth century.[4] Its polysemic character and its complex association with modernity (used synonymously with Westernism) is kept in view. A variety of processes and institutions has been grouped under the banner of modernity: industrialization, expansion and consolidation of colonialism, democracy and modern nation-state.

A few common assumptions about culture—its organic wholeness, continuity and growth—were shared by thinkers, literary critics and anthropologists of varied hues in the late nineteenth century in Europe. For example, E.B. Taylor's anthropological conception of culture as 'a complex whole' and its characterization by Mathew Arnold as a domain of highest human values and creations of mankind, which can be crystallized as enduring, traditional and structural values,[5] still dominate the theoretical perspective of social sciences, humanities and even casual discussions. Its organic and transcendent attributes were later elaborated by T.S. Eliot and F.R. Leavis and incorporated in English literature.

However, for understanding the full implications of Euro–American cultural invasion, it is relevant to refer to the complementary use of two other notions of culture—'residual' and 'dominant' (terms coined by Raymond Williams) in the British writings during the late nineteenth century for politico-economic domination of the colonial people. The Orientalist and Utilitarian, particularly, anthropological projects for studying the organization and functioning of 'native' societies and their cultures exemplified pursuit of knowledge for hegemony rather than for pure intellectual or scholarly curiosity and considerations.[6] For example, Edward Said's seminal work

Orientalism has enabled us to understand how construction and projection of 'Orient' as Europe's 'other' in racial and cultural terms was geared to fix the colonial people in a subordinate position in relation to the 'master races' of Europe.[7] The primitive societies were regarded as the museum of mankind where the past of advanced Western societies could be recovered.[8]

Integration of these two senses of culture in the entire project of knowledge about ancient societies, their people and culture was affected skilfully in Orientalist writings. While one set of writers advertised the glories of ancient Vedic–Aryan civilization of India, the other presented its people as irrational, immature, depraved and lazy 'native'.[9] Sharing the negative assumptions of the second group of Orientalist writings, the anthropological studies, which used the paradigm of cultural relativism, utilized ethnography for creating numerous stereotypes about various socio-religious groups and qualified the divisions among them not only in terms of 'inherent' and 'intrinsic' differences but also in terms of their civilized or barbaric attitude and treatment of women.[10]

In fact, indictment of the 'degenerate Indian civilization', 'effeminacy of Indian men' and 'abject' position of women, who required 'protection' and intervention on humanitarian grounds,[11] was ingrained in the colonial ideology and social policy of the *Raj*. The entire argument was crystallized into a rational justification of the British rule in India on grounds of moral superiority.[12] This supercilious approach towards India, appropriated by the Euro–American capitalists, surfaces in their pronouncements and economic policies towards the Third World countries. They continue to condemn, bully and inferiorize, interspersed by occasional pats, the Asian and African nations for their inability to control poverty, population, resolve socio-political problems and protect human rights of terrorists, minorities and women. Regarding these as legitimate grounds for Western intervention, the First World has pressurized the poor nations to mould their economic policies according to their dictates.

The reappearance of the overt Western dominance is regarded as potentially more dangerous to cultural autonomy as there is now more powerful conjunction between the highly sophisticated communication technology, state power and multinational capital. It has facilitated the circulation of particular definitions of national, communal, caste and gender identities suiting the Euro–American agenda of global capitalism. Cultural penetration, increasingly viewed as an adjunct of any sustained system of global exploitation, is an extension of counter-insurgency through non-military means.[13]

In such a situation, culture has become the site of politico-economic battles between the countries of the First World and the Third World. The people regard it as an identity-marker in order to relate themselves with the nation and the world and a guide for individuals to school them into a specific pattern of behaviour. In fact, members of various communities learn to respond to different situations individually or collectively in accordance with their cultural orientation through shared symbols, codes, language and behaviour patterns as well as modes of dress.

Communication, which is not only transmission but also reception and response, plays a central role whether in 'cultural invasion' or 'cultural defence'. The task of cultural defence, through its creative interpretation, requires an in-depth understanding of the nature of Indian tradition and its essential ideals.

II
IDEALS OF INDIAN CULTURE

It is not easy to generalize about Indian culture for three reasons. Firstly, it is an amalgam of diverse traditions (Hindu, Islamic, Buddhist and Jainist), religious symbols, languages and creative products of multiple ethnic imaginations. Secondly, it is constantly in the making, strenuously contested and reconstituted. Being dynamic and open-ended, it is best described by the Persian word *ravayaat,* i.e. flowing or constantly in motion. Indian culture, constantly engaged in the process of experimentation and self-renewal, has been redirecting its social energy throughout its evolution from ancient to modern times. Thirdly, production of knowledge about Indian society and culture by Indians and others has remained burdened by the assumptions of Orientalist scholarship. For example, the dominant ideology of *Hindutva* has appropriated the homogenizing agenda of the Orientalist and thus glossed over the complexity of our cultural and ideological formations. By projecting the Indian culture as monolithic and unchanging, its protagonists have distorted its true nature. The Euro–American academics have also stereotyped understanding of caste and gender inequalities, nationalism or communalism through dominant paradigms such as 'hierarchy' for Indian society, 'filial piety' for China and 'honour and shame' for circum-Mediterranean.[14] Despite these problems, caused by different trajectories of the term 'culture' and the complex nature of Indian tradition, it is possible to identify its essential ideals: *(i)* Communitarian Ideal; *(ii)* Spiritual Ethos; *(iii)* Creativity and Spirit of Accommodation.

(i) Communitarian Ideal

The most striking feature of Indian culture, which survived its encounter with the West, is the location of the individual in the network of powerful communitarian relationships: family, kinship and caste, and their primary use for social cohesiveness,[15] now transformed into a political asset. For example, the patriarchal family as the reproductive unit has continued to be used as a site for the socialization of the girl-child and for the transmission of cultural values, practices and traditions of major religions. The entire complex of community networks was utilized not only for schooling its members for discipline, work culture, social and religious values but also for protecting and reinforcing the structures of land-relations. The major reason underlying the communitarian orientation and practice was the country's agrarian economy. Primarily comprising huge stretches of well-irrigated plains and the advantage of ample sushine for the greater part of the year, India has maintained an agrarian economy over the past five thousand years. The British government exploited and developed this potential with minimum financial investment and technological inputs in order to feed and expand its industrial empire. Such a policy introduced many complexities in the stratification of the peasant society.

A major characteristic of the peasant society is that it values the communitarian ideal and cultivates this orientation. Historically speaking, Indians are known for their deep loyalty to the village, family and *jati*. Another notable feature of this society is its relatively peaceful and closer relationship with rhythm of cyclic seasons. A distinct emphasis upon coexistence, peace and harmony, rather than obsession with overpowering, controlling and exploiting nature, characterizes the attitude of an agricultural community.

(ii) Spiritual Ethos Worldly Concerns

The second important dimension of Indian cultural heritage is its emphasis upon the realization of ultimate spiritual ideal, i.e. unity with cosmos without undermining material achievements. The pervasive presence of spiritual ethos in the Indian life does not imply negation of the other aspects of life. The characterization of Indian outlook (used synonymously for Hindu) as pessimistic and other worldly by Western scholars is exaggerated. In fact, one of the main concepts underlying the ancient Indian civilization was the coordination of spiritual life with worldly life. For example, the Hindu religion has emphasized a balanced albeit gender-biased approach to the four ends of man, viz., *dharma, artha, kama* and *moksha.* It refers to an ideal principle or norm to which man should confirm in the course of his worldly activities. *Dharma* is assigned the first place as it is the regulating factor in the pursuit of material gain and pleasure.[16] Referring to *rajdharma* (king's moral duty), the *Lawbook* of Yajnavalkya states that where there is conflict between the principle and policy, righteousness and material gain or advantage, *dharma* and *artha*, the former should prevail.

For *kama*, i.e. love of pleasure, control by *dharma* is obligatory. The Hindu ideal does not preach abstinence from pleasure for all or at all stages; it rather preaches, universally, the ideal of chastened love or pleasure, regulated by considerations of both morality and well-being. In more than one authoritative text, the householder's life is considered to be the greatest of the four stages of life. Hinduism does not hold up monasticism or hermitism as a common ideal for all. It is because of this consensus that the strains and trials of household management, family life and social obligations discipline man and prepare him for moksha, i.e. liberation from the cycle of death and rebirth. The pursuit of moksha is placed last as the life of retirement and spiritual endeavour is the final and ultimate aspiration of man in the Hindu scheme of values. It is evident that no aspect of life was originally considered unimportant; nothing was denied or repressed. Instead all that appears to be lower could be integrated with the higher according to the Hindu philosophy. There was distinction between the sacred and the profane.

Islam, which had developed a positive interaction with Hinduism from the thirteenth century onwards, was firmly rooted in the material world despite its dominant spiritual ethos.[17] As the 'field of action' and the farming ground for the world to come, the present world is of great importance and value to man. What the Quran emphasizes is that from the relative point of view of man, the world is as real as he himself. The affirmation of life and of physical world is peculiar to Islam.

Contemporaneous with the ongoing cultural ferment throughout India, Guru Nanak launched his crusade for the spiritual purification and moral purification of both Hindus and Muslims. The Sikh tradition, as it evolved from the fifteenth to seventeenth century A.D., aligned religious goals with worldly concerns.[18] In the Sikh, especially Khalsa world view, salvation could be attained by living in the world and pursuing secular objectives such as the acquisition of political power or the accumulation of economic resources in the form of agrarian land. These secular objectives had, however, to be attained within the particular framework of beliefs and religious practices. Paramount among these beliefs was *Khalsa* normative order: *Kirt Karna, Vand Chhakana te Namu Japna* (to labour for one's keep, to share with others and to practise the repetition of the divine name). Obviously, the Sikh religion has remained functional in its approach.

Moral Values

All major religions have concerned themselves with the generation and transmission of not merely moral values for the individual but also with social values. The extent to which they have done this has varied from Islam on the one hand, where a detailed statement of not only social values but even state and social laws is incorporated in the holy Quran itself, to Christianity where Jesus himself separated the two by the statement "Render unto Caesar what is Caesar's and unto God what is God's", on the other. However, it is difficult to compartmentalize these two aspects in practice because of the scope given to interpretation in Islam and the extent of church's involvement in state affairs. The Hindu scriptures also deal with social and individual moral values. However, the position of Hinduism on this issue is as ambiguous as on any other matter owing to the wide variety of these scriptures and the breadth of interpretation accepted by various authorities.

In the present situation created by globalization, it is increasingly difficult to avoid intermeshing of individual and social values and priorities. The efficient functioning of a market economy requires a minimum moral infrastructure just as it requires a physical infrastructure. 'Honesty is the best policy' is not so much a moral dictum as a cost-effective method of organizing inter-human relationships whether for personal concerns or large-scale business purposes. The consequences of all-round deceit prove costly in the long run than the consequences of straight dealing.

(iii) Creativity and Spirit of Accommodation

The great strength of Indian culture is its dynamism, its creativity, its ability to accommodate and synthesize the multiple currents and traditions. A close scrutiny of the process of its evolution shows that the resilience of the inner core has helped it to protect its fundamental values. Its openness has enabled it to respond to new currents of thought and transform them into a source of energy for new patterns of development and growth. Many voices of dissent have enriched its fabric. While Indian culture learnt important lessons from Buddhism and Jainism, it was influenced in a different way by the challenge of Islam.[19] Islam's message of social egalitarianism, democracy, rights for women though within a patriarchal framework, had been incorporated in the social vision of Hinduism in order to make it more responsive to the changing cultural ethos and popular aspirations.

Passing through the initial phase of hostility and ideological conflict, caused by power struggle, interaction between Hinduism and Islam led to several unique cultural innovations in Indian society. Sufism is the best example of this creative fusion. The ongoing cultural movement gained its richness and breadth of vision through the intervention of sufis and saints. For example, Ramanand, Tulsidas, Kabir and Guru Nanak challenged orthodoxies and went beyond the trappings of forms and rituals. Perceiving the fundamental unity of all religions, the sufis had preached the message of unity and devotion to one God whom they liberated from the monopolistic hold of religious priests of all denominations. Most of them conceived and preached divine unity in terms of idealistic monism. Their greatest achievement was to enable the masses to experience spirituality and God's unbounded love without the mediation of external agency and rituals. Representing a revolt against blind conformism, social injustice and suppression of the individual, Sufism functioned as a liberating force for the human mind against the restraints of an imposed system. However, towards the end of the eighteenth century when it came into contact with Western ideas and civilization, it had lost its capacity to imbibe new currents and transform them into potent stimuli for creativity.[20] It may partly be explained in terms of the peculiar nature of the East–West encounter, first in the form of trade, then of armies and administrators.

The accommodative spirit was also evident in the aesthetic consciousness of Hindus and Muslims. Architecture was the main field which afforded the greatest opportunity for the Muslim and Hindu minds to influence each other. What now remains of the first great buildings of the Delhi Sultans, such as the Jama Masjid of Ajmer and the Quwatul-Islam mosque near Delhi, shows that from the very begining Islamic conceptions of architecture had to be adapted to the genius of the Indian environment, Hindu architects and artisans. Fergusson has pointed out that the design of the Jama Masjid in Ajmer has been taken from the Jain temple of Mount Abu. The creative impulse and the spirit of mutual give and take percolated to the popular speech in the thirteenth century; the mixture of Persian with a dialect of western Hindi gave rise to a new language called Urdu. In due course of time, Urdu became the vehicle of a rich literary tradition, evolved by Hindu and Muslim writers and poets. It travelled to Deccan as the lingua franca in which the Hindu and Muslim advisers and companions from the north conversed with one another. It was in the Deccan that this language increasingly became not only a popular medium of communication but also the vehicle of expression for creative minds.

It may be said that these three ideals of Indian culture ought to be regarded as the ideals to be aspired for. I would not argue that Indians were always community-oriented, peaceful, spiritual and tolerant. India also passed through phases of violence, hatred and war; nor was there in India any lack of people with materialistic and individualist ambitions. However, in times of cultural upheaval caused by the British conquest, primacy of the cultural ideals bound the people together, irrespective of differences in religious faith and practice.

III
INDIAN RESPONSE TO THE ONSLAUGHT OF WESTERNISM/MODERNITY

With the coming of the West through the British colonialism in India, radical departures occurred in the manner of redefinition of society, polity, family and gender, rendering the eighteenth-century praxis irrelevant. A drastic change in the balance of politico-economic power against Indians and blockade of channels of socio-cultural communication made them insular and robbed them of creative thinking for more than a century.

Confronted with the colonial state's systematic programme of cultural hegemonization as a part of its strategy for political control, the Indian people responded in a variety of ways. Their response ranged from grateful acceptance of Westernism as an agency for rejuvenating the Indian tradition to Gandhi's protest against its attitude of arrogant superiority because of its material achievements, mindless mechanization and irreligiosity.

I wish to focus briefly on the predicament of the nineteenth-century reformers, whose development as an intellectual community had been facilitated by the objective conditions created by the colonial rule but their bonding matured in the course of their social struggles.[21] It is likely to give us a clue about responses to the present cultural crisis, caused by the onrush of Westernism/modernity on the heels of liberalization.

In the nineteenth century, the British highlighted the weaknesses of India's traditional social order, inferiorizing its culture, epistemology and the people as a race; and this obliged the Indians to launch cultural-ideological struggles on two planes: against the traditional social order on the one hand and against cultural hegemonization by the colonial state on the other. While the reformers had found traditional culture inadequate to meet the challenge of Western modernity, they were not inclined to adopt the bourgeois liberal model in toto as the cultural and intellectual engineering had caused anxiety among many of them about the survival of tradition itself. Thus, ambivalence and contradiction in their attitude towards tradition and modernity, which is characteristic of colonial consciousness, surfaces repeatedly in their ideological formulations throughout the nineteenth and early twentieth century.

It is not surprising that the reformers of all hues—a 'liberal' Ram Mohan Roy or a 'rationalist' Akshay Kumar Dutt or 'revivalists' like Dayanand and Swami Vivekanand—had based their political, economic and social thought on the premises of Western liberal discourse such as constitutionalism, rationalism, individualism and capitalism. Their utter dependence upon the West for social and moral regeneration is illustrated by their version of India's idealized past and its bourgeois future. Its impact was also reflected in their image of 'new' woman who combined the bourgeois virtues of orderliness, thrift, personal hygiene, cleanliness, sense of responsibility, literacy and accounting with the traditional feminine virtues of chastity, self-sacrifice, service, submissiveness, devotion, patience, etc.[22] The reformers' ideal of *sahadharmini* or companion in a monogamous marriage also suited the work culture of a capitalistic economy, envisaged in the liberal framework. Obviously, the creation of a new social ethos was to complement the emerging bourgeois order.

The current debates between the liberals and the revivalists about the multiple consequences, particularly cultural, of globalization of economy tend to reproduce the past arguments, sense of urgency and perceptions of contemporary situation. One such example is the adoption of language of socio-cultural reform in the late nineteenth and early twentieth century, which was inscribed with the discourse of 'crisis' having frequent allusions to 'continuity and change', 'new times' and 'tradition and modernity'. The second example is the vigorous defence of the bourgeois ideology which reflects a perpetual fascination for Western (non-Euro–American) practice of consumer capitalism, its tantalizing visions of prosperity and modernity.

However, critical temper has not been completely lacking. Nearer our own times, Gandhi's insightful and creative reading of Indian and Western tradition in the context of hegemonic British rule in India had urged him to reject social reformers' alternative. Thus, he launched a 'trans-cultural' protest against the materialist and hyper-masculine world view of colonialism.[23] I shall return to his critique of Western civilization and its claim to modernity a little later. At this juncture, let me discuss briefly the ideals of Western modernity whose renewed onslaught in the wake of economic liberalization has aroused fears of cultural invasion.

IV
IDEALS OF WESTERN MODERNITY

The present-day connotation of Western modernity, which signified something new in life experiences rather than social totality and emphasized its transitory nature, its arbitrariness and its sense of opposition to unilinear time in the nineteenth century, regards it as 'fixed end-state' of progress or development.[24] As advocates of this view, the Euro–American nations like Britain not only equate modernity with Westernization but also claim monopoly of transformatory role. It is from this angle that the West continues to define the ideals of modernity, which are strikingly different from the ideals of Indian culture. Though an integral part of the Enlightenment project, modernity subsumes many currents—democratic liberalism, Marxian socialism, rationalism, expansionism, industrialism, post-colonialism, urbanism, etc. Despite its complex nature, it is possible to define the salient features of this world view as under:

(i) It is conceived as a closed monolith incapable of being shaped or changed by modern men. Berman pointed out that "open visions of modern life have been supplanted by closed ones".[25]

(ii) In this world view, modernity as a "fixed end-state of progress" or development divides societies or social entities into either traditional or modern. In the case of non-Western societies, modernization has become synonymous with Westernization. This theory offers no alternative for understanding change in any other way than Westernization and moving to that state in the universal history of secularism and differentiation.[26]

(iii) According to the exponents of modernity, history advances in a linear direction. Everything being dynamic, human beings are always engaged in improving the world they live in. Thus, it is future oriented and evaluates achievement in material terms.

(iv) Being modern implies the acceptance of value—neutral scientific, universalistic rationality and rejection of emotional and affective relationships and religious beliefs. It is secular as it regards psychic and mystic explanations irrelevant for understanding the phenomenal world.

(v) Modernity has become gender-biased by not only continuing the gender-division of labour but also the monopoly of men in public affairs, e.g. administration, politics, science and art. Its dominant feature being the rationalization of economy, politics, culture and knowledge, it was perfectly logical to justify exclusion of women from the public sphere on the ground of the 'genderification' of rational and emotional capacities of people. "Values such as rationality, objectivity, logical thinking and matter of factedness", in Tijssen's view "came to be considered as primarily masculine".[27] This

mindset was integrated into the ideology that legitimated the role of middle-class women as wives and mothers. In all European countries, the presupposition of this ideology was that these nurturing capacities have been instilled into women's nature[28] equating biological function with mental capacity. Thus, the need of bourgeois businessmen for a secure retreat from the harsh and competitive world[29] became central to the project of domesticity in the Victorian Britain. A similar concern or compulsion is likely to assume a great value for the entrepreneurs of the Third World, pitted against the multinational consumer capitalism on their own home-ground.

(vi) According to the modern world view, scientific progress should be measured in terms of man's capability to master the secrets of nature, control and exploit its resources. Harmonious relationship with nature has been regarded as a sign of primitive rather than advanced societies until recently.

Obviously, such a world view is based on the notion of hierarchical relationship between West as the teacher and East as the taught. The West (and now Euro–American nations) with all its Enlightenment experience, regards itself as superior in all respects —cognitively, materially and culturally—to the non-West. In order to become modern, a nation and its people must learn the knowledge system of the West, its lifestyle and its behaviour patterns. In short, the East must become the mirror-image of the West. Undoubtedly, India's first encounter with modernity under the British rule had already exposed her to the bitter experience of a hierarchical relationship, having its terms defined, elaborated and fixed in the course of two centuries of colonial domination. Indian people have yet to forget how hyper-masculine values of Westernism had been used as a criteria to denigrate their eugenical fitness for self-rule and dub their epistemology, technology and culture as static and primitive in the scale of world civilization. Britain also claimed to use it as an agency to modernize its people in the role of a self-appointed teacher.

However, the colonial state was not particularly keen on modernizing Indian economy, culture and society as it never wanted another dynamic rival. It is evident from its policy of limited application of technology for agricultural development[30] and its alliance with feudal and traditional elements against the weaker sections of society, particularly women. Its social policy, particularly the codification of customary law which deprived women of the right to agricultural property and access to economic resources in general, showed its feudal orientation.[31] In addition to its political manoeuvring, systematic dissemination of Western ideals was instrumental in the colonization of Indian consciousness which was a knotted combination of ambivalence and resentment against the cultural invasion in the garb of modernization.

Indian attitude towards modernity had acquired more criticality, clarity and sharpness when Gandhi pulled the intellectual community out of the orbit of bourgeois values through his powerful critique of Western civilization. In his pamphlet, *Hind Swaraj* (1909)[32], he indicted the West for its stance of arrogant superiority over its material achievements, mindless mechanization, barbarity and irreligiosity. His cultural agenda was based on such principles as seldom coincide with the ideals of Western modernity. For example, Gandhian action for recasting gender relations was far more original and comprehensive in scope than the social reform movements we have already discussed. The strength of his project for social and moral regeneration of India lay in three areas. Firstly, it did not compartmentalize social and political. Secondly, his understanding of the dynamics of social change and power-equations as they affect gender relations was far more perceptive and realistic than was true of the earlier movements in any part of the world. Thirdly, it was neither limited by scriptural injections, nor by considerations of class, community or religion, while rectifying inequity in gender relations.[33] It may be pointed out that Gandhi had tried to reach out to each section of Indian society as is evident from the response of women, scheduled castes and tribal communities to his movements. Above all, his sensitivity to the untapped potential of India's rich cultural, particularly folk resources and relevant elements of modernity has been conceded not only by the advocates of Western modernity, particularly feminists, but also by the traditionalists.

However, the decolonization process initiated by Gandhi has lost much of its force as his thought and practice could neither capture fully India's urge for 'relevant' modernity in terms of the multiple needs of its fast-growing population and its national aspirations. The changing parameters of global economy and inability of India to resist multinational pressures for liberalization have once again made people vulnerable to the tantalizing visions of Western modernity.

Obviously, 'inevitability of modernity' is posing a real threat to the three great ideals of Indian culture, which have already been spoken of. Firstly, the ethos of an ultra urban and industrial orientation militates against the ethos of an agricultural society— its close identification with local communities and family-kinship ties. The mindset for a future-oriented and achievement-based view of life disrupts the relatively peaceful character of a non-modern community living.

Secondly, the externalization of modernity, its secularity, its logic of technological manipulation of nature for man's continual, material well-being goes against the spiritual ethos and ideals of Indian culture. The process of objectification of nature—the most fundamental feature of modern scientific and technological enterprise—has not been integrated into Indian outlook and way of life. Even a casual reading of the *Vedas* and *Upanishads* shows that the Indian sages approached nature with a spirit of humility and self-surrender. In short, our cultural tradition viewed nature as an expression of cosmic order and not something to be objectified, controlled and exploited. As it had put a premium on being environment-friendly, its relevance for modernity cannot be doubted.

Thirdly, the ethos of Western modernity—its cognitive arrogance, scientism and universality—is not comfortable with heterogeneity, plurality and differences. Thus, there is an inherent clash between the homogenizing impulses of modernity and accommodative spirit of Indian cultural ideals. The practice of theological disputation, which formed an integral part of Indian intellectual quest, showed that Indian society favoured fair play and freedom in propagation of the principles of various religions and thereby encouraged coexistence of plurality of faiths. This was why activities of Christian missionaries had continued for centuries without attracting any serious opposition. However, an open-ended approach to religion was gradually replaced by construction of rigid polarities, sealed boundaries and organized and enumerated religious communities with the establishment of a nexus between government officials and missionaries.

It can be said that the powerful current of Western modernity, which accompanied colonization, Christianization and anglicization, is now hitting us with full force. Thus, the spectre of cultural invasion is no longer imaginary but real.

V
GOLBALIZATION, CONSUMERISM AND MASS CULTURE: ITS IMPLICATIONS FOR MEN AND WOMEN

In the present discussion of globalization and cultural invasion, the project of Western modernity, which seeks to standardize cultural patterns, perceptions, expectations and responses in the Third World, has remained central as it underpins the philosophy of consumer capitalism. In other words, modernity as a grand system relies upon the efficient interconnections between worldwide dissemination of 'global culture', telecommunication and deregulated markets and free trade in the Third World for the success of globalization. Thus, globalization, despite its obvious economic agenda, poses a serious threat to cultural autonomy as conditioning and fixation of human choice and value is a facilitator of economic process. The era of liberalization has forced an overhauling of the existing value system with a view to uplinking of the tastes of the average Indian, particularly, the young and the adolescents in middle classes with those of their counterparts in the West. The underlying logic is that global market economy shall create interlinkages between 'forward' and 'backward' societies.[34]

The Western argument has special significance in view of the fact that India's burgeoning middle class, according to a recent survey by International Bank for Reconstruction and Development, forms about one-third of the country's population. This chunk of population is more than what entire Europe has, leaving out erstwhile Soviet Union. Its thrustful purchasing power makes India a country with a rich marketing potential. Such a possibility prompts the West to clamour for the Indian domestic market which they believe is largely untapped. The process of capturing it progresses only when there is a corresponding change in the value pattern of the targeted society. The target groups of people have to be attuned to the ethos of global culture. Even more tactical is to capture hearts and minds of the adolescents and the young for mounting a full-scale cultural invasion.

A study of the cultural invasion obliges us to discuss various aspects of global culture and its universalistic mission that seeks to deny all cultural differences and specificities. With their tremendous techno-economic power, the Euro–American nations are privileged to define and dictate the contents of global culture, popularly known as consumerist culture. Claiming to be based on the ideals of modernity and Western rationality, it seeks to bridge the gap between all cultures and generate a set of uniform responses and expectations. Using the latest communication technologies as an instrument, the Euro–American industry in collaboration with multinational business managers is transmitting words, images and symbols of a consumerist culture into our world.

What is the consumerist culture? Consumerism assumes the form of a culture when its function is stretched beyond the fulfilment of basic needs of each member of society, arising from biological demands. Its salient features may be specified as follows:[35]

(a) Consumer needs are artificially generated. Limits on them are determined by intellectual and cultural motivations which education can help to generate and foster. Since our education system does not train and build refined tastes and desires, the electronic and print media would manipulate our choices and preferences to serve commercial interests. Obviously, the seductive and colourful advertisements of consumerist products or items, promising more sexual thrill, fun and pleasure, play a vital role in moulding their tastes in this direction. Hence, each new need reflects that craving.

(b) Consumerism means multiplication of possessions for material comforts, luxuries and possessions which signify a way of living. One may buy a new model of a car not to satisfy need for transportation but as a status symbol. Hence, consumerism is not just the consumption of things and commodities.

(c) Consumerism, which is the culture of late capitalism, depends for its success on the numerical strength of the middle class having more than ample leisure time and extra purchasing capacity.

(d) The ethos of consumerism thrives on the perversion of the acquisitive instinct of men and women. As a successful life is equated with having everything, not having something implies failure and loss of status. Obviously, the people, living in the ethos of a consumerist culture, perpetually suffer from a sense of insecurity, anxiety, nervous tension and an incessant craving for latest models, fashions and fads. In the long run

they get addicted to the excitement of instant achievement and success and are alienated from their history, culture, particularly folk memories.

(e) The target of consumerism is the creation of mass culture[36] which requires standardization of perceptions about fun, lifestyles, behaviour patterns and choices of products for daily use on the basis of opinion polls. The mass culture, while moulding and catering to average taste, de-individualizes as do techniques required for mass production and marketing. In fact, it is the product of an industrial society which has more equally distributed income, mobility, education and leisure.

(f) In mass culture, gregariousness is internalized owing to the high psychological costs of individuality and privacy. People fear solitude and unpopularity; thus popular approval becomes the only moral and aesthetic standard. Love for art and learning gradually becomes restricted to a small number of people. To put it succinctly, the growing lure of mass markets for both producers and consumers diverts potential talent from the creation of works of art and literature.

(g) As mass culture creates addiction to pre-fabricated experience of emotions, majority of the people are deprived of the "remaining possibilities of autonomous growth and enrichment and their lives become ever more boring and unfulfilled", as pointed out by Earnest van Dan Haag.[37]

At this juncture in our discussion, it may be useful to review briefly the changing perspective on massification of culture since the end of Second World War as we are hypothesizing about the attendant ill-effects of such a phenomenon with the adoption of 'open door' economic policy in India. With increased impetus to industrialization, urbanization and the development of mass media, especially television, regarded as major factors for the development of mass culture in America during the 1930s,[38] some people are getting anxious about the destruction of cultural diversity and deterioration of taste levels to the lowest denominator. For example, in the late 1950s, Rosenberg, while reiterating the shrill warning of American research studies regarding the misuse of tools of mass persuasion for social control, underlined the dangerous possibilities of use of culture by totalitarian regimes.[39]

Actually, this approach had become the intellectual base for motivation research in the advertising industry by the 1950s and 1960s; these developed techniques were applied to the American political process.[40] At present, these tools of mass persuasion are being used by the multinational capitalists in collusion with the Euro–American governments and the Indian ruling elite not only to capture untapped markets but also to reorient economic, social, science and technology policies to facilitate their penetration and hegemony. From this perspective, the mass audience is a huge, inchoate, socio-cultural compost in which everything is mixed up together.[41]

This concept of massification had been challenged by Edward Shils at the Taminent Institute Seminar on Mass Culture in 1961. He asserted that mass culture actually enhanced individuality owing to the availability of increasing number of consumer choices.[42] Bypassing the interpretations of the other advocates of this approach,[43] I shall focus on a more relevant hypothesis for visualizing the Indian situation. Peterson and Maggio have broken the mass culture argument into two parts:[44] (i) that the forces of modernization significantly reduce cultural diversity, and (ii) an increasingly homogeneous mass culture has emerged. While it is true that much cultural diversity of ethnic, regional and folk type has been destroyed in post-industrial American society, in India, a different course of development may be chartered as it is far from being an industrial society and may skip various stages in search of 'relevant' modernity. As Indian society is not a monolith, existence of several 'taste cultures'[45] is likely to resist the total massification of culture. The selectivity of choice, which has been empirically documented in the American case, shows that development of a homogeneous culture may be uneven in such a vast country as India is.

However, it may be conceded that consumerism has gradually tightened its grip over Indians, especially middle classes, during the past one decade. What are the long-term implications of consumerism for Indian society and culture? For a realistic assessment, three specificities of Indian situation must be kept in view. Firstly, the presence of one hundred million illiterates in the age group of 15 to 35 years makes India an ideal ground for testing the power of tele-advertising in moulding the mental ethos of such a huge chunk of population whose sense of discrimination may gradually be blunted owing to its narcotic effect over time. Secondly, an equal number of

Indian middle class people, especially the impressionable adolescents and young women, are seen by the commercial interests as the potential purchasing agents whose systematic conditioning would ensure long-term market control. Thirdly, new communication technologies in the hands of ruthless and avaricious multinational capitalists are no longer amenable to check or control either by the developed or developing countries, especially when illiteracy rules out the intervention by books.

The power of books and the power of television may be differentiated in three different ways. Firstly, entry into the world of books requires a certain level of intellectual and literary skill. For watching television, no such mental training is required. Anyone can watch and enjoy visuals whether at home or in the market-place and also play electronic games. Unlike printed words, visual images are much more effective in spreading values of the global culture. Secondly, watching television is a relaxed, passive and, to some extent, an uncritical exercise. Reading a book requires response in the form of thinking and argument with its author. Obviously, constant viewing of television does not develop the critical faculty. Thirdly, colourful and glamorous images while talking and smiling are intensely seductive but unreal. These images make the viewers mad and blind. Thus, penetration of visual media into the humblest home has made the possibility of cultural intrusion real and serious.

It may be pointed out that the foreign television, with its attractive cultural package, is not the only threat to the ideals of Indian culture. It has an ally within the country itself in the form of Doordarshan, Zee and ABCL. In its eagerness to survive in the competitive market, the Indian television is beaming a diluted version of Euro-trash such as late night sex games in clubs, musical extravaganza, beauty contests, fashion shows, soap serials, etc. Thus, the spread of consumerist culture is being aided by the commercial market managers in India.

Anyone familiar with the media scene knows how easy it is to captivate the hearts and minds of uncritical viewers and persuade them to regard the consumerist culture as their own. Constantly exposed to the values and outlook of a dominant culture, the illiterate and impressionable adolescents as well as the young tend to copy sexual behaviour and life-styles of glamorous men and women. By watching images and advertisements of expensive clothes, cars, gadgets and luxurious houses on television, members of middle classes with limited means and the poor people get frustrated as this 'hyper-real' world, to use Baudrillard's phrase,[46] is beyond their reach. Free circulation of visions of affluence in the absence of democratization of economic resources breeds imitative tendencies, violence, sexual crimes and all sorts of pathological complexes among the economically weaker sections who happen to be illiterate also.

With their growing consumerist orientation, the viewers tend to shun the basic simplicity of life and ethos which used to be the major feature of an agricultural society. Their blunted sensibilities fail to find joy and meaning in harmonious relationship with nature's rhythm and beauty. Their growing dependence upon artefacts and external agents for entertainment and enjoyment weakens the will-power of the majority of the people to mobilize their inner resources for enrichment of life such as introspection, reflection and contemplation.

Despite the potential importance of electronic media for promoting social communication and bonds, i.e. improvement in the depth and breadth of harmonious interpersonal and intergroup communication, it seems to have become instrumental in the dissemination of consumerist culture. People in the developed societies have got so addicted to mass media that they have very largely withdrawn themselves from community life. The programmed life dished out by television has weakened social bonds and alienated people from their neighbours, friends and even family members. The proliferation of video-culture has led to the development of a new brand of narcissism in the Indian middle classes.

Obviously, this narcissist ethos of consumerist culture militates against the communitarian orientation of Indian culture which values fulfilment of individuality within familial and kinship network. It does not imply that a positive grounding in culture has helped the Indian people to become models for the quality of family values and interactions, social solidarity, public order and safety. But so far it has kept in check the number of divorces, desertions and separation cases, parent-child clashes, vagrancy, delinquency, indulgence in crazy thrills and mindless addiction to video games, crime and violence and scale of social anomie and alienation. However, increasing exposure to Euro–American modes of behaviour, glamorous lifestyles, materialist values extolling consumption-linked pleasure, have brought about a noticeable change in public perceptions. Repeated bombardment of messages through commercials and tele-shopping regarding products and artefacts ranging from home appliances, designer clothes and jewellery to computers does block other inputs and the task of decision-making is gradually taken over by media, jointly controlled by innovative advertisers, industrialists and capitalists.

The proliferation of consumerism-generated mass culture leads to the regular establishment of a 'culture industry'. It manufactures culture like any consumable item. Like any other industry, it uses every new form of technology to improve its product. Technology touches almost every aspect of mass culture. Music, film and industry, sports and everything else get reduced into a great technological spectacle. People are seen talking more and more about techniques but not about life. Their tastes and evalution of performing and plastic arts are guided by attractive packing. They buy cultural artefacts like any other commodity—food, soft drinks or cosmetics.

The process of commodification of art and culture in a consumerist society affects attitude to human, especially gender relations and public perception of women. The woman of the consumerist era is not idealized either as an enlightened mother or as a self-fulfilled working person, or as the equal partner and companion of man, deriving fulfilment from creativity—both physical and spiritual. A consumerist society (representing the essentialist view of Euro–American sponsored culture) projects woman as the glamorized sex object and as a source of pleasure. The major purpose of her existence is providing titillation to the over-stimulated sensuality of the male-dominated world. Software producers in such a society are motivated to innovate infinite variety of forms and methods of voluptuous entertainment for men whose over-stimulated and over-strained orgasm seeks lower forms of thrill, excitement and relaxation for their life. This indicates a powerful, though invisible alliance between managers of communication systems and the kings of vast industrial empires. The former stimulate the appetite and greed for infinite variety of goods and services towards which the later channelize the economic resources and technical skills.[47]

Indian women are increasingly being seen as purchasing agents for their family by the multinational commercial interests who seem to utilize their American experience in the course of globalization of consumerist culture as a part of the Euro–American project of carving out politico-economic empires. The domestic division of labour has long positioned women as the primary consumer in Western and

Eastern societies. The consumption of products and services by unpaid housewives and single women in their homes is indeed critical to recreating and maintaining a production style and pattern that functions to support the capitalist economy. In this respect, consumption activity would promote both gender and economic stratified forms of exploitation.

Studies on Euro–American television and women yield enough evidence to show that consumer capitalism has substantial stake in reinforcing domestic ideology. Several programming genres such as quiz shows, talk-shows and cooking slots recognize women as the target viewers as well as the target consumers. Each programme is divided into slots for sponsoring advertisers of various products to whom audience is sold in return. Take, for example, soap-opera, the melodramatic serial which is usually considered to be almost exclusively a women's genre though many boys and men watch this as well. While commenting upon the contradictions built into the enjoyment of television soaps by women, Michel Mattelart has insightfully pointed out that for the politically aware viewers, the soap-operas can be seen as a tool of capitalism. Its social function is to colonize women as consumers by preying upon their loneliness and desperation over being excluded from the production process. Ironically, such pleasures are trivialized both by the feminists and the popular press.[48] However, the videos of American soap-opera, films and Euro-trash beamed by Doordarshan in late-night slots and by the cable operators and Zee and Star TV, generously interspersed with advertisements of multinational products, have now been using Indian housewives and teenaged girls as their target guinea-pigs.

Globalization of consumer capitalism has long-term negative implications for cultural, especially religious practice. These implications are likely to be two-fold. Firstly, the plea of cultural defence shall increasingly result in the manipulation of religion for electoral gains and competitive fundamentalism for preserving religious patriarchies. Secondly, the colonization of religion by the money power of big multinationals and the powerful Indian commercial houses, which has already converted it into an object of glamorization, shall lead to the negation of spirituality and the dominance of material over spiritual goals.

Turning to the argument of cultural defence, it may be said that the proponents of Hindutva have unwittingly projected the role of religion as divisive. Taking their cue from colonial ethnographers, they have reinforced the conceptualization of religion as enumerated community which may be used for electoral politics. Unlike Gandhi, who utilized his creative interpretation of various religious traditions for forging tools of political protest, e.g. *Ahimsa* and *Satyagraha*, they have manipulated the notion of cultural diversity, religious precepts and idioms for homogenizing Hindus, engineering communal riots and activating hatred and intolerance. Instead of promoting egalitarian values, movements against gender and caste injustice and oppression, the religious leadership of Hindus and Muslims has encouraged the growth of exclusivist identities and hierarchical relationships instead of an ethos of tolerance, spirituality and fairplay. Their greed for power has exacerbated social tensions, intra-religious conflicts and egoistical drives rather than the spread of sanity and spirit of mutual accommodation. Take, for illustration, the violence and bloodshed caused by flamboyant *rath yatras*, the so-called liberation movement of Ram Janambhoomi of Ayodhya.

Let me refer briefly to the implications of globalization of capitalism and its nexus with state and religion for gender justice. The new policy of economic liberalization has prompted the minority and majority community leaders to protect male privilege with the help of state, which has been called upon to legislate new laws regarding labour, wages, property rights and active involvement of women in the economic and political processes in order to appear just and progressive in Western eyes.

For the success of new economic policy, the Asian values of family cohesiveness, discipline and education are likely to assume new importance. Instead of recasting gender equations in the family, the minority communities are advocating the preservation of personal laws and the majority is clamouring for the legislation of uniform civil code. Neither of them is interested in conceding real conjugal, guardianship, custodial and property rights to women. Indian state is, obviously, acting in collusion with these religious leaders and capitalists for politico-economic reasons as is evident from its withdrawal from its welfarist functions whose maintenance could have mitigated patriarchies operating in family, community and workplace. For all of them restriction of women to domestic roles is crucial.

Secondly, colonization of religion by money-power has diluted its positive role in socio-cultural life of the Indian people. The growing reliance of religious leadership on their wealthy constituency for displaying their organizational strength has reduced spirituality to gorgeous rituals. It is evident from the competitive sponsorship of religious festivals by big multinationals and the Indian industrial and commercial concerns. Anyone who has witnessed the gorgeous spectacle of Durga Puja in Delhi and Calcutta would feel disgusted by the quantification of religion in terms of money-power. Thus, the fast-growing trend of measuring success in proportion with its external trappings has led to despiritualization and erosion of the noblest cultural ideals and their strengths. Naturally, it is affecting daily behaviour and religious practice of the people in a negative manner.

V
CONCLUSION

The growing awareness of cultural intrusion as well as penetration and acute sensitivity to the threat to Indian culture implies neither insulation from fresh ideas and resistance to interaction with other cultures nor defence of regressive values, outdated social customs and resistance to change. It means critical exploration into our past and contemporary history and retrieve those components of our knowledge and culture as well as institutions which can serve as a nucleus for constructing a framework of 'relevant' modernity for India.

The first question to be asked is whether India's earlier experience of politico-economic and cultural domination has equipped the present political leadership and intellectual community with foresight and historical imagination to differentiate between the purely rapacious motive of Euro–American nations and their professed fraternal concern for economic, scientific and social development of the Third World countries, also known as the South. The ruling party's (Congress/ United Front) commitment to implement the new economic policy—privatization, marketization and free trade—and the opposition party's (BJP) advocacy of 'swadeshi' and 'protectionism' seems to rest on the considerations of electoral politics because the new economic policy orientation is geared towards the generation of wealth without clarifying the social purpose for which wealth may be used. Their policies do not seem to be based on a realistic assessment of the strengths and weaknesses of existing infrastructure, social institutions and cultural resources, requisite for formulating a long-term strategy for revitalizing the country's economy. No serious exercise has been undertaken to devise ways and means for the utilization of foreign capital or investment and expertise as a catalytic agent.

The intellectuals, who at best form a dispersed intellectual community at present, have fortunately seen through the underlying linkages between the Euro–American lobbying for global culture and its relentless pressure on the Third World to give them access to their resources and markets. While commenting upon MIA (Multilateral Investment Agreement)—the latest instrument on the anvil for economic domination—Martin Khor (Director, Third World Network, Malaysia) has rightly dubbed it as "a return to a colonial era situation". The European Community has already introduced other instruments or concepts for controlling rivals and decreasing their competitiveness such as TRIMS (Trade Related Investment Measures) and others but MIA has the most serious cultural implications. The proposed treaty would not allow exclusion on cultural or moral grounds or for the media, communication and information sectors. Foreign companies in these sensitive areas would be allowed to enter and be treated at par with local firms. Thus, cultural imperialism is inbuilt in the long-term strategy of globalization of capitalism. Obviously, the target group is the country's nearly 400 million lower and upper middle-class population whose crass consumerism is the best bet for the neo-imperialists.

The present situation is particularly piquant for the young (whether hailing from poor and illiterate sections or from the educated and well-to-do middle classes) who are forced to live in a transitional world because new cultural sensibilities, social values and reference points have not yet been created even after more than five decades of Independence. With the removal of literacy and geographical barriers through the ever-widening reach of television including cable network, it is a challenging task for the impressionable viewers to resist cultural conditioning by soap operas, visual images of opulence, coupled with glowing descriptions of Western superiority in epistemological, social, political and material advancement. Thus, democratization of images without democratization of resources has caused bewilderment, resentment and anger against the social institutions and political system which are unable to satisfy its people's needs and craving for quality consumer goods and cultural artefacts. In the absence of an education system, which can inculcate a deep understanding, appreciation and sense of pride in the Indian culture, imitative tendencies in dress, food habits, behaviour, lifestyles, values and perceptions are increasingly visible among boys and girls. Such a situation has been used as a tangible evidence by sociologists like Ernest Gellner and political scientists like Fukuyama to argue that no culture can remain indifferent to the 'superior Western industrial culture' and bourgeois ideology.

However, this argument about the inevitability of Western modernity must be contested. It is not surrender to it but a critical reflection and voice of dissent against pathologies of modernity which is desirable. We need to focus our creative energies on formulating a new cultural agenda which ought to retain its criticality in order to have a meaningful dialogue with the West. In this agenda, an investigation into all aspects of 'relevant' modernity and dialogue with the West must be given top priority. The relevant modernity for our country neither advocates the rejection of a rich cultural heritage nor withdrawal from community-based social life which draws its sustenance from constant interaction with the folk culture. In our pursuit of modernity, we must fully realize the emancipatory potentials of the cultural ideals discussed in this essay. For example, the peaceful communitarian ideal that our culture emphasizes, can rescue the world from devitalizing competitive mentality, its aggressive individualism and the resultant social alienation. Similarly, the accommodative spirit of our culture can serve as an antidote against the ruthless drive for universalization of tastes, behaviour patterns and homogenization of culture.

The paradigm of modernity for India does not ignore material aspect of human existence. It acknowledges the need to multiply generation of wealth from industry as well as agriculture through the sophisticated but labour intensive technologies of production. As India can never hope to attain either the targets of production or consumption in the Western societies, its pursuit of modernity has to set its sight at 'sustainable development' which avoids five distortions identified by *Human Development Report, 1996*: jobless growth, ruthless growth, rootless growth, futureless growth and voiceless growth. It may be possible to avoid these distortions if the economic policy adopts the bifocal strategy of accelerated economic growth and a broad focus on the social sectors—health, women's welfare, education, credit to low—income groups and small-scale entrepreneurs, as has been done in the Far East and South-East Asian countries.

To follow the economic ideals of global capitalism is not beneficial for India because it equates development with consumerism and application of advanced technology to every sphere of life with progress. It is urgent to prevent the market forces from colonizing our mind and life once again. Cultural recovery is impossible without formulating an alternative agenda for politico-economic development which should give priority to the development of human resource capital and the construction of a civil society—gender-sensitive, communitarian, ecologically friendly, morally mature and cultured. It is apt to end this discussion of globalization and cultural invasion with Gandhi's sensitive observation:

> I don't want my house to be walled in on all sides and my windows to be stuffed. I want the cultures of all lands to be blown about my house as freely as possible. But I refuse to be blown off my feet by any.

Thus, neither traditionalism nor Westernism but a third alternative can save us from cultural takeover by the West leading to its economic and political hegemony which is the ultimate target of globalization as it functions at present.

REFERENCES

1. Francis Fukuyama, 'End of History Debate', *American History Review,* 34, 3, 1990, p. 8.
2. Catherine Hall, 'The Early Formation of Victorian Domestic Ideology', in Sandra Burman, ed., *Fit Work For Women* (London: Australian National University Press, 1979), p. 23.
3. Raymond Williams, *Keywords : A Vocabulary of Culture and Society* (New York : Oxford University Press, 1979, 1983), p. 87.
4. For a review of the career of 'culture' particularly from the angle of literature, see Raymond Williams, *The Long Revolution* (London: Oxford University Press, 1961), pp. 41–71. Also see his *Culture and Sбciety,* 1780–1950, (London : Chatto & Windus, 1959, 1996), pp. 295–338.
5. James Clifford, *The President of Culture* (Cambridge : Cambridge University Press, 1988), p. 87.
6. For a discussion of anthropology's relation to colonialism, see Talal Asad, ed., *Anthropology and the Colonial Encounter* (London, 1973); James E. Marcus, *Writing Culture: The Poetics and Politics of Ethnography* (Berkeley, 1986); Johnnes Fabian, *Time and Other: How Anthropology Makes its Object* (New York, 1983).

7. Edward Said, *Orientalism* (London: Penguin Books, 1978, 1995), p. 87. Although Said's argument and illustrations are based on the Middle East (now known as West Asia), his conclusions are also applicable to other colonial societies, particularly India.
8. Bernard Cohn, 'The Command of Language and the Language of Command', in Ranajit Guha ed., *Sabaltern Studies*, iv (London: Oxford University Press, 1961), p. 325.
9. Edward Said, *n.* 7.
10. E.A. Gait, *Census of India 1991*, Report, i. pt. I, p. 120: Robert Burn, *Census of India 1901*, North-West Provinces and Oudh, Report, iv, pp. 75–76.
11. James Mill, *The History of British India* with notes by H.H. Wilson (London : Madden, 1858), pp. 312–13.
12. Kamlesh Mohan, 'Clamping Shutters and Valorizing Women: Tensions in Sculpting Gender Identities in the Colonial Punjab,' in Pritam Singh and Shinder Thandi, eds. *Globalisation and the Region: Explorations in Punjabi Identity* (London, 1990; reprinted, New Delhi: Oxford University Press, 1996), pp. 175–76.
13. Samit Kar, 'Miss World '96: Cultural Invasion of the Worst Kind', in *Mainstream*, 23 November 1996, p. 8.
14. Arjun Appadurai, 'Theory in Anthropology: Centre and Periphery', *Comparative Studies in Society and History*, 28:2 April, 1986, p. 157.
15. My discussion of the communitarian ideal is based on David G. Mandelbaum, *Society in India* (First printed 1972; reprinted Bombay: Popular Prakashan, 1984), pp. 33–180.
16. For a sympathetic angle on this issue see Theodre de Bary, ed., *Sources of Indian Tradition* (First printed in 1958; reprinted Delhi : Motilal Banarsidass, 1988), pp. 211–366.
17. S. Abid Hussain, *The National Culture of India* (First printed, 1978; reprinted, Delhi, 1992), p. 66. Mohammed Sahib's sayings, compiled in *Hadith*, repeatedly emphasize that the present world is a preparation for the next world.
18. For a detailed discussion of this aspect of Sikhism, see Upinder Jit Kaur, *Sikh Religion and Economic Development* (Delhi: National Book Organisation, 1990), pp. 70–159.
19. For information on Islam's influence upon Indian society, especially its cultural implications, see M. Mujib, *Indian Muslims* (London: George Allen and Unwin, 1967); S.A.H. Abid, *Sufism in India* (Delhi: Oxford University Press, 1992), pp. 81–121.
20. M. Mujeeb, *Islamic Influence on Indian Society* (Delhi, Meerut : Meenakshi Prakashan, 1972), p. 65.
21. For a discussion of the process of the formation of the intellectual

community in the nineteenth century, see K.N. Panikkar, 'Culture and Ideology: Contradictions in Intellectual Transformation of Colonial Society in India', in *Economic and Political Weekly,* 5 December 1989, pp. 2115–20.

22. Kamlesh Mohan, *n.* 12, p. 194.
23. Ashish Nandy, *The Intimate Enemy: Loss and Recovery of Self under Colonialism* (Delhi : Oxford University Press, 1983), p. 48.
24. David Frisby, *Fragments of Modernity, Theories of Modernity in the Works of Simmel, Kracauar and Benjamin* (Cambridge : Polity Press, 1985, 1986), p. 13. For a detailed discussion of difference of approaches to modernity between nineteenth and twentieth-century sociological thinking, see M. Berman, *All That is Solid Melts into Air* (London: Verso, 1983).
25. M. Berman, *n.* 24, p. 24.
26. Aysegul Baykun, 'Women between Fundamentalism and Modernity', in Bryan S. Turner, ed., *Theories of Modernity and Post Modernity* (New Delhi, London: Sage Publications, 1990, 1991), p. 138.
27. Cited in Lieteke van Vucht Tijessen, 'Women between Modernity and Post-modernity', in Bryan S. Turner, ed., *n.* 26.
28. E. Wilson, *Women and Welfare State* (London : Tavistock, 1977), p. 22.
29. Tijessen, *n.* 26. She has based her argument of 'genderification' on L. Braun's exposition (1901: 190) whose writings are not available in English.
30. For illustration see Rai Bahadur Ganga Ram's failure to experiment with tube-well technology owing to Punjab Government's uncompromising stand on the limited modernization of agricultural and irrigation technology. It has been discussed in Imran Ali, *The Punjab under Imperialism 1885–1947* (First printed in 1988; reprinted Delhi : Oxford, University Press, 1989), pp. 219–22 and 231–36.
31. David Gilmartin, 'Women, Kinship, and Politics in Twentieth Century Punjab' in Gail Minault, ed., *The Extended Family: Women and Political Participation in India and Pakistan* (New Delhi: Chanakya Publishers, 1981).
32. *Hind Swaraj,* originally published in Gujarati in the *Indian Opinion* of 11 and 18 December 1909, was issued as a booklet in January 1910. Its proscription by the Government of Bombay in March 1910 hastened Gandhiji's decision to publish its English translation (with his foreword written on 20 March 1910), which was issued by the International Printing Press, Phoenix.
33. I have borrowed these ideas from Ravinder Kumar, 'On Gender Theory, the Social Sciences and "Relevant" Modernity' in *Manushi,* No. 68, p. 26.

34. For an insightful sociological perspective on the cultural dimensions of contemporary global capitalism, see Max Weber, *The Protestant Ethic and the Spirit of Capitalism* (First printed in 1958; reprinted, London: George Allen and Unwin, 1965), Samit Kar, *n.* 13.
35. My discussion of the features of consumerist culture is based on Jean Baudrillard, Trans. George Ritzer, *Consumer Society: Myths and Structures* (London : Sage Publications, 1983, 1998). His ideas regarding the making of consumer culture and its features, are scattered throughout his book, see pp. 49–87.
36. For a critical view of Edward Shil's theory of three-tier classification of culture, see Earnest van dan Haag, 'A Dissent from the Consensual Society', in Bernard Rosenberg and David Manning White, eds., *Mass Culture Revisited* (New York,1971), pp. 85–92.
37. *Ibid.*, p. 92.
38. For an understanding of the theory of the development of 'mass culture' in America, see Y. Gasset, *Revolt of the Masses* (New York, 1932); D.MacDonald, 'A Theory of Mass Culture' in Rosenberg and D.M. White, eds., *n.* 36.
39. B. Rosenberg, 'Introduction', in B. Rosenberg and D.M. White, *n.* 36.
40. Mc Ginnis, *The Selling of the President* (New York : Trident Press, 1968, 1969).
41. R. Clauss, 'The Mass Public at Gripps with Mass Communications', *International Social Sciences Journal,* 20, p. 624.
42. Edward Shils, 'Mass Society and its Culture', in N. Jacobs ed., *Culture for the Millions?* (Boston, 1961).
43. For example, see T. Parsons and W. White, 'The Mass Media and the Structure of American Society', in *Journal of the Social Issues,* 16, pp. 67–77; Harold Wilensky, 'Mass Society and Mass Culture : Interdependence or Independence?' in *American Sociological Review,* 29, pp. 173–97.
44. R.A. Peterson and P.D. Maggio, 'From Region to Class : The Changing Focus of Country Music', in *Social Forces,* 53, pp. 497–560.
45. I have borrowed this term from Tom Wolfe, *The Kandy Colored Tangerine Flake: Streamline Baby* (New York: Knopf, 1965), p. xv.
46. J. Baudrillard, *Simulations :* Trans M. Foss (New York: Semiotext (c) Foreign Agent Press 1983a), *In the Shadow of the Silent Majorities,* Trans M. Foss (New York: Semiotext (c) Foreign Agent Press 1983 b), p.27.
47. The ideas expressed in the foregoing three paragraphs are borrowed from Lisa A. Lewis, 'Consumer Girl Culture : How Music Video Appeals to Girls', in Mary Ellen Brown ed., *Television and Women's Culture : The Politics of the Popular,* (London : Sage Publications, 1990), pp. 89–101.
48. Mary Ellen Brown, 'Consumption and Resistance', in *Ibid.,* pp. 203–4.

Bibliography

Agarwal, Bina, *A Field of One's Own: Gender and Land Rights in South Asia* (Cambridge: Cambridge University Press, 1994).

Alexander, Joan, *Voices and Echoes: Tales from Colonial Women* (London: Quartet, 1983).

Altekar, A.S., *The Position of Women in Hindu Civilization: From Prehistoric Times to the Present Day* (Delhi: Motilal Banarsidass, 1991).

Appadurai, Arjun, Frank J. Korom and Margaret A. Mills., eds., *Gender, Genre and Power in South Asian Expressive Traditions* (Delhi: Motilal Banarsidass, 1994).

Baig, Tara Ali, *India's Women Power* (New Delhi: S. Chand, 1976).

Ball Hatchet, Kenneth, *Race, Sex and Class Under the Raj: Imperial Attitudes and Policies and their Critics, 1793–1905* (London: Weidenfeld and Nicolson, 1980).

Barrett, Michele and Anne Philips, eds., *Destabilizing Theory: Contemporary Feminist Debates* (Cambridge: Polity Press, 1992).

Basu, Amrita, ed. *The Challenge of Local Feminists: Women's Movement in Global Perspective* (Colorado: Westview Press, 1995).

____*She Comes to Take Her Rights: Indian Women, Property and Propriety* (New York: State University of New York Press, 1999 and New Delhi: Kali for Women, 2000).

Beteille, Andre, *Caste, Class and Power* (Berkeley: University of California, 1965).

Blunt, Alison, *Travel, Gender and Imperialism: Mary Kingsley and West Africa* (New York: Guildford, 1994).

Boserup, Ester, *Women's Role in Economic Development* (New York: St. Martin's Press, 1970).

Butler, Judith and Joan W. Scott, eds., *Feminists Theorise the Political* (London: Routledge, 1992).

Capran, Patricia, *Class and Gender in India* (London: Tavistock Publications, 1985).

Chakraborty, Renu, *Communists in Indian Women's Movement, 1940–50* (New Delhi: People's Publishing House, 1980).

Chakravarty, Uma, *Rewriting History: The Life and Times of Pandita Ramabai* (New Delhi: Kali for Women, 1998).

Chanana, Karuna, ed., *Socialization, Education and Women: Explorations in Gender Identity* (New Delhi: Orient Longman, 1988).

Chandra, Sudhir, *Enslaved Daughters: Colonialism, Law and Women's Rights* (New Delhi: Oxford University Press, 1998).

Chattopadhyay, Kamladevi, *Indian Women's Battle for Freedom* (New Delhi: Abhinav Publications, 1983).

Chaudhari, Maitreyee, *Indian Women's Movement: Reform and Revival* (New Delhi: Radiant Publishers, 1992).

Chaudhary, Prem, *The Veiled Woman: Shifting Gender Equations in Rural Haryana, 1880–1990* (New Delhi: Oxford University Press, 1994).

Chen, Martha A., *Widows in India: Social Neglect and Public Action* (New Delhi: Sage Publications, 1998).

Cornwall, Andrea and Nancy Lindisforne., *Dislocating Masculinity: Comparative Ethnographies* (London: Routledge, 1994).

Davis, Nira Yuval, *Gender and Nation* (New Delhi and London: Sage Publications: 1997, 1998).

Davis, Nira Yuval and Hoya Anthicas, eds., *Women-Nation-State* (London: Macmillan, 1989).

Desai, Neera, ed., *A Decade of Women's Movement in India* (Bombay: Himalaya Publishing House, 1988).

____, *Women in Modern India* (Bombay : Vora & Co., 1957).

DeSouza, Alfred, *Women in Contemporary India: Traditional Images and Changing Roles* (New Delhi: Manohar Book Service, 1975).

Diver, Maud, *The English Women in India* (Edinburgh: Blackwood, 1909).

Donaldson, Laura E., *Decolonizing Feminisms: Race, Gender and Empire Building* (London: Routledge, 1992).

Dyson, K.K., *A Various Universe: A Study of the Journals and Memoirs of British Men and Women in the Indian Subcontinent, 1765–1856* (New Delhi: Oxford University Press, 1978).

Everett, J.M., *Women and Social Change in India* (New Delhi: Heritage, 1981).

Farukhi, Sarah, Celia Lury and Jackie Stacey, eds., *Off Centre: Feminism and Cultural Studies* (London: Harper Collins, 1991).

Forbes, Geraldine, *Women in Modern India, New Cambridge History of India* (Cambridge: Cambridge University Press, 1996).

Gandhi, Nandita and Nandita Shah, *The Issues at Stake: Theory and Practice in the Contemporary Women's Movement in India* (New Delhi: Kali for Women, 1991).

Good, Anthony, *The Female Bridegroom* (Oxford: Clarendon Press, 1991).

Harris–White, Barbara, 'Gender-Cleansing, The Paradox of Development and

Deteriorating Female Life Chances in Tamilnadu', in Rajeshwari Sunder Rajan, ed., *Signposts: Gender Issues in Post-Independence India* (New Delhi: Kali for Women, 1999).

Jackson, C., 'Rescuing Gender from the Poverty Trap', in Jackson, C. and R. Pearson, eds., *Feminist Visions of Development: Gender Analysis and Policy* (London: Routledge, 1998).

Jain, Devaki, *Indian Women* (New Delhi: Publications Division, Ministry of Information and Broadcasting, Government of India, 1975).

Kapadia, Kavin, *Siva and Her Sisters*: *Gender, Caste and Class in Rural South India* (Colorado: Westview Press, 1995).

Kaur, Manmohan., *Role of Women in the Freedom Movement, 1857–1947* (New Delhi: Sterling, 1968).

Krishna Raj, Maithreyi, ed., *Remaking Society for Women: Visions, Past and Present* (Delhi: IAWS, 1995).

Krishnamurthy, J., ed. *Women in Colonial India: Essays on Survival, Work and the State* (New Delhi: Oxford University Press, 1989).

Kumar, Nita, ed., *Women as Subjects* (Charlotteeville: University Press of Virginia, 1994).

Lewis, Reina, *Gendering Orientalism: Race Femininity and Representation* (London : Routledge, 1996).

Levy, Anita, *Other Women: The Writing of Class, Race and Gender, 1832–1998* (Princeton: Princeton University Press, 1991).

Liddle, Joana and Rama Joshi, *Daughters of Independence: Gender, Caste and Class in India* (London: Zed Books and New Delhi: Kali for Women, 1986).

MacCormack, Carol P. and Marilyn Strathern, eds., *Nature, Culture and Gender* (Cambridge: Cambridge University Press, 1980).

Malhotra, Anshu, *Gender, Caste and Religious Identities: Restructuring Class in Colonial Punjab* (New Delhi: Oxford University Press, 2002).

Mehra, Rekha and K. Saradamoni, *Women and Rural Transformation* (New Delhi: I.C.S.S.R. and Centre for Women's Development Studies, 1983).

Mills, Sara, *Discourses of Difference: An Analysis of Women's Travel Writing and Colonisation* (London: Routledge, 1991).

Muir, Edward and Guido Ruggiero, eds., *Sex and Gender in Historical Perspective* (Baltimore: John Hopkins University Press, 1990).

Nanda, B.R., ed., *Indian Women: From Purdah to Modernity* (New Delhi: Vikas Publishing House, 1976).

Pawar, Kiran, ed., *Women in Indian History: Social, Economic, Political and Cultural Perspectives* (Patiala: Vision and Venture, 1996).

Poonacha, Veena, *Women's Rights as Human Rights* (Mumbai: RCWS, 1997).

Rajput, Pam and Hemlata Swarup, eds., *Women and Globalization* (New Delhi: Ashish Publishing House, 1994).

Ray, Bharati, ed., *Women and Science* (Calcutta: Women's Studies Research Centre, 1990).

____ed., *From the Seams of History: Essays on Indian Women* (New Delhi: Oxford University Press, 1995).

Scott, James, *Weapons of the Weak* (New Haven: Yale University Press, 1985).

Scott, Joan Wallach, *Gender and the Politics of History* (New York: Columbia University Press, 1987).

Sen, Illina, *A Space Within the Struggle* (New Delhi: Kali for Women, 1990).

Sen Gupta, Padmini, *The Story of Women in India* (New Delhi: Indian Book Company, 1974).

Sharma, Radha Krishna, *Nationalism, Social Reform and Indian Women* (New Delhi: Janaki Prakashan, 1981).

Tharu, S. and Lalitha, eds., *Women Writing in India: 600 BC to the Present Day, Vol I.*, (New York: The Feminist Press, 1991).

Van, Baal J., *Reciprocity and the Position of Women: Anthropological Papers* (Amsterdam: Van Gorcum, 1975).

Ware, Vron, *Beyond the Pale: White Women, Racism and History* (London: Verso, 1992).

Williams, Patrick and Lama Chrisman, eds., *Colonial Discourse and Post Colonial Theory: A Reader* (Harvester: Hemel Hampstead., 1993).

Yana Gisako, Sylvia and Carol Delaney, eds., *Nationalizing Power: Essays in Feminist Cultural Analysis* (New York: Routledge, 1995).

Yegenoglu, Meyda, *Colonial Fantasies: Towards a Feminist Reading of Orientalism* (Cambridge: Cambridge University Press, 1998).

Young, Robert J.C., *Colonial Desire: Hybridity in Theory, Culture and Race* (London: Routledge, 1995).

Index